PRAISING
GOD

Also by Ruth C. Duck
from Westminster John Knox Press

Finding Words for Worship:
A Guide for Leaders

PRAISING
GOD

The Trinity in Christian Worship

Ruth C. Duck
Patricia Wilson-Kastner

Westminster John Knox Press
Louisville, Kentucky

Book design by Sharon Adams
Cover design by Kevin Darst

First edition
Published by Westminster John Knox Press
Louisville, Kentucky

This book is printed on acid-free paper that meets the American National Standards Institute Z39.48 standard. ∞

PRINTED IN THE UNITED STATES OF AMERICA
99 00 01 02 03 04 05 06 07 08 — 10 9 8 7 6 5 4 3 2 1

Library of Congress Cataloging-in-Publication Data

Duck, Ruth C.
    Praising God : the Trinity in Christian worship / Ruth C. Duck and
Patricia Wilson-Kastner.
        p.   cm.
    Includes bibliographical references.
    ISBN 0-664-25777-1 (alk. paper)
    1. Public worship.   2. Trinity.   I. Wilson-Kastner, Patricia.
II. Title.
BV15.D83   1999   99-22981
264′.001 — dc21

In loving memory of
Patricia Wilson-Kastner

CONTENTS

PREFACE

Long before we met, we recognized in each other kindred spirits, in our desire to integrate feminist emancipatory practice with vital Christian faith. We were familiar with each other's work—*Faith, Feminism, and the Christ*[1] and *Imagery for Preaching*[2] by Pat Wilson-Kastner, and *Gender and the Name of God,* hymns, and worship resources by Ruth Duck.[3] Given the consistency of our theological and pastoral concerns, Pat proposed writing a book together only five minutes into our first conversation (while she was visiting Garrett-Evangelical Theological Seminary as the Episcopal representative on the United Methodist Commission on Christian Unity and Interreligious Concerns). This idea remained a matter of conversation for several years.

Ruth Duck: Pat was not aware that I had already been exploring the idea of a book, an idea that grew out of a visit to Memphis Theological Seminary at the invitation of systematic theologian Ronald Cole-Turner and homiletician Mary Lin Hudson. I had lectured, preached, and led conversations with faculty and students about the Trinity and inclusiveness in theology and worship. Ron, Mary Lin, and I also exchanged work-in-progress about trinitarian theology, preaching, and worship. Although other commitments did not permit Ron (now at Pittsburgh Theological Seminary) or Mary Lin to contribute to this book, without their initial invitation and our dialogue, it would probably not exist. It was also personally meaningful to me to hold these conversations in the city of Memphis, where I lived from 1964 to 1969, a formative time in the shaping of my faith and theology.

Patricia Wilson-Kastner: In the fall of 1996, I spent a quarter as Georgia Harkness scholar and professor of Church History at Garrett-Evangelical Theological Seminary, where Ruth is on the faculty. During that time, we were able to move this joint project from a dream to a committed plan. We built a working relationship, discussed logistical issues such as finding a publisher and organizing material, and explored the issues of the book over tea, breakfast, and lunch.

On one level, this book comes from a number of conversations that included both of us and others. On another level, it emerges in both of us from living trinitarian Christian spirituality, from the experience of knowing God-as-Trinity.

Duck: I began my journey of faith as an evangelical Christian; my faith first focused on personal relationship with Jesus Christ. Then, through the witness of charismatic Christians, I learned of the power of the Spirit to transform my life through the direct experience of God's amazing love at work within me. But my years in Memphis, where I attended a small Presbyterian college (now called Rhodes College), propelled me beyond the individualistic faith I had known before. Through encounter with liberal Christianity, and through the ministry of Martin Luther King Jr., I learned that the God from whom all life comes is bigger than any creed or social group, and so God known as Father of all became a reality to me. Thus, my own journey toward trinitarian faith has grown out of living experience of God powerfully present in my own life and the life of the world. Though the church may use many metaphors to speak of God, I perceive in my own faith experience the trinitarian reality of God.

Teachers, mentors, and colleagues who have challenged me to make my trinitarian faith more articulate include Horace Allen, Elizabeth Bettenhausen, Ronald Cole-Turner, Constance Collora Groh, Mary Lin Hudson, Marjorie Scott, Dwight Vogel, and Patricia Wilson-Kastner. Catherine Mowry LaCugna, with whom I studied in the summer of 1986, and whose books and articles I have read voraciously, contributed immeasurably to my thinking, not least by inspiring my interest in the Cappadocian theologians and the relational trinitarian theology they expressed. A consummate trinitarian theologian and inspiring teacher, LaCugna died of cancer in 1997.

I am grateful that the seminary administration (president Neal Fisher and former dean Rosemary Keller) supported this project by providing me with a sabbatical in winter term of 1996 to work on my chapters and by making Pat's visit possible. Thanks also to Constance Collora Groh, Robin Knowles Wallace, and Carole Hoke for their work in researching and preparing the manuscript, as well as to Linda Koops for typing various drafts of the manuscript over the six years it has been in process. We also thank Stephanie Egnotovich of Westminster John Knox Press for believing in and supporting this project as it has unfolded.

Wilson-Kastner: When I was in parochial school, the Trinity fascinated me. God was Trinity: Father, Son, and Holy Ghost. How could three persons be one God? Much to my surprise, instead of telling me that when we grew up we would understand, Sister John Marie told me that it was a mystery. A mystery, we were assured, is something so great that no one can fully understand it, no matter how hard one tries. All the pictures and the words would help us know God a little better, but we would never fully understand such a mystery.

I carried with me through my college and graduate school days this root sense of God as mystery, knowable to us only through glimpses and signs. However, even in my younger days, I was irritated and a bit embarrassed by pictures of God as an old man with a beard, Jesus nailed on the cross, and a dove in flight somewhere between them. In college, I was introduced to serious biblical study and to real theology, especially the Cappadocians. I began to understand a bit better (O paradox!) what mystery was and to learn something more about relationships, perichoresis, and the varied nuances of personhood in the Trinity.

During this time I was also introduced to the liturgical prayer of the church in a more serious way, as well as to different sorts of personal prayer. Knowing God through prayer was even more mysterious than theology but certainly had its own rewards and pitfalls. And there was always the mysterious and ever-present Trinity!

The two great experiences that have shaped my own ongoing search for a way to speak about the trinitarian God are my ordination to the priesthood, with responsibilities for preaching and presiding at worship, and my feminism, with new visions of the human community and the divine presence in our world. Each, from different perspectives, has continued to prod and provoke me in my search to know and express the Trinity with faithfulness to new insights and a radical commitment to God and the Christian community.

Special thanks to my teachers in long past but treasured years, especially David Balas, S. O. Cist., Gilbert Hardy, S. O. Cist., and Rochus Koretszy, S. O. Cist. The late Rev. Sister Rachel Hosmer, O.S.H., is now face to face with the mystery we so happily discussed not so long ago. I am also most grateful to Rosemary Skinner Keller, then dean of Garrett-Evangelical Theological Seminary, who helped me to obtain a Georgia Harkness Fellowship in the fall of 1996. This opportunity, with the use of the library at Garrett-Evangelical and Seabury-Western Theological Seminary, allowed me to work with Ruth Duck, my friend and colleague, to bring this book toward its birth. Of course, thanks beyond measure to Ron, my spouse, whose unflagging support and knowledgeable conversations have brought me and the book to its launching.

My pilgrimage, made with a host of other seekers today and in ages past, leads me to utterly practical expressions of trinitarian life in social reform and transformation, and to less tangible but equally real expressions of divine mystery in worship together, complemented by quiet and solitude. On this journey, which reaches both inward to my depths and outward to the whole wide world, my guide and goal is the three times Holy One, ever changing and ever constant.

Together we affirm that the ultimate source of this book is in the love of the triune God seeking us through all the pathways of our lives and calling us to make our own small contribution to the church's life of worship and praise.

EPILOGUE

Ruth Duck: The above words were written in early December 1997, when Pat and I completed drafts of our chapters and sent them to our publisher. Six weeks later, on January 18, 1998, Patricia Wilson-Kastner joined the saints in God's presence after an illness of one week.

In the days in which I have been completing the final draft of the manuscript, my faith communities have been celebrating All Saints' Day. It has been a time to remember Pat with grief and with thanksgiving. She was a warm friend and an extremely capable collaborator; students who studied with her at Garrett-Evangelical Theological Seminary remember her fondly because of her encouraging presence and encyclopedic knowledge. I dedicate this volume to Patricia Wilson-Kastner, one of God's saints, deep in faith, expansive in knowledge, cordial in friendship, impish in humor, generous in spirit.

It is of course customary to acknowledge one's editor, but a special word of thanks goes to Stephanie Egnotovich for the pastoral manner in which she has responded to the completion of the manuscript following Pat's death. She has never failed to be sensitive to my experience and to the challenges of completing a book without one's collaborator.

David Cunningham of Seabury-Western Theological Seminary graciously assisted me in lightly editing chapter 1 so that it would communicate as clearly as possible, while respecting Pat's original intentions. Cunningham is a trinitarian theologian whose scholarly and creative book *These Three Are One: The Practice of Trinitarian Theology*[4] furthers the Christian feminist project of expanding theological and liturgical language for the Trinity.

Thanks are also due to Ron Kastner, Pat's loving spouse, for his willingness to answer questions, copy computer files, and otherwise support the completion of this project.

To the triune God, loving Source of all things, incarnate Word among us, and vibrant Spirit of new creation, who surrounds all the saints in our joys and griefs and in all our endeavors, be all glory.

November 7, 1998

ACKNOWLEDGMENTS

Grateful acknowledgement is given to the publishers of the following works:

A New Creed, used by permission of The United Church of Canada; General Council 1968; alt.

"Alternative Blessings," p. 545; and Trinitarian invocation, p. 464, from *A New Zealand Prayer Book: He Karakia Mihinare O Aotearoa*, © 1989, 1997 The Anglican Church in Aotearoa, New Zealand and Polynesia.

The Book of Common Prayer, © 1979 Church Publishing Incorporated.

Bread of Tomorrow: Prayers for the Church Year edited by Janet Morley, © 1992 Orbis Books. Used by permission of Orbis Books, Maryknoll, NY, and SPCK, London.

"Child of Blessing, Child of Promise," © 1981 Ronald S. Cole-Turner.

"Come, Great God of All the Ages" by Mary Jackson Cathey, © 1990 Hope Publishing Company, 380 South Main Place, Carol Stream, IL 60188.

"Creating God, Your Fingers Trace" by Jeffrey Rowthorn, © 1979, Hymn Society of America, administered by Hope Publishing Company, 380 South Main Place, Carol Stream, IL 60188.

"Creator God, Creating Still," © 1980 Jane Parker Huber, from A SINGING FAITH. Used by permission of Westminster John Knox Press.

"Doxology," p. 39; "Gloria in Excelsis," pp. 39–40; and "Excerpts from Word and Sacrament II," pp. 69–71, from *Book of Worship United Church of Christ*, © 1986 United Church of Christ.

Doxology from *The New Companion to the Breviary with Seasonal Supplement*, © 1998 Carmelites of Indianapolis.

English translation of Gloria in Excelsis prepared by the English Language Liturgical Consultation (ELLC), 1998.

"Eternal Light, Shine in My Heart," Alcuin, para. Christopher Idle, © 1982 Hope Publishing Company, 380 South Main Place, Carol Stream, IL 60188.

Gender and the Name of God by Ruth Duck, © 1991 The Pilgrim Press.

"God Is One, Unique and Holy" by Brian Wren, © 1983, 1985 Hope Publishing Company, 380 South Main Place, Carol Stream, IL 60188.

"God of Eve and God of Mary" by Fred Kaan, © 1989 Hope Publishing Company, 380 South Main Place, Carol Stream, IL 60188.

"God of Many Names" by Brian Wren, © 1986 Hope Publishing Company, 380 South Main Place, Carol Stream, IL 60188.

"God Who Made the Stars of Heaven" by Ruth Duck, © 1996 The Pilgrim Press.

"Mothering God, You Gave Me Birth" and "O Holy Spirit, Root of Life," © 1991 Jean Janzen.

New words to the Doxology, © 1990 Neil Weatherhogg.

"O God, Almighty Father," translation © 1959, 1977 Order of St. Benedict. Administered by The Liturgical Press.

"O God, Great Womb of Wondrous Love," © 1983 Harris J. Loewen

"O Mighty God" by Erik Routley, © 1985 Hope Publishing Company, 380 South Main Place, Carol Stream, IL 60188.

"Praise the Lover of Creation" by Brian Wren, © 1989 Hope Publishing Company, 380 South Main Place, Carol Stream, IL 60188.

"A Prayer for Christmas Eve," p. 48; and prayer for ordinary use, pp. 46–47, from *All Desires Known* by Janet Morley, © 1988 Morehouse Publishing. Used by permission of Morehouse Publishing, Wilton, CT, and SPCK, London.

The prayer over the oil, p. 76 in *The Book of Offices and Services* by Timothy Crouch, © 1988 Order of Saint Luke.

Supplemental Liturgical Texts: Prayer Book Studies 30, © 1989 Church Hymnal Corporation.

The Text of the Alternative Opening Prayer from the English translation of *The Roman Missal* © 1973, International Committee on English in the Liturgy, Inc. All rights reserved.

Introduction

Christian worship is, by nature, trinitarian. Reflection on the sacraments reveals that they are actions of the triune God. Baptism, which marks the very beginning of Christian life, is not trinitarian solely because of a particular formula or phrase, but more fundamentally because it is immersion into the life of God in union with Christ through the power of the Spirit.[1] Similarly, in the eucharistic meal, the church gives thanks to God, the source of bread, cup, and life itself, as Jesus did in his earthly ministry before and after his death and resurrection. Jesus the risen Christ is host at the meal through the working of the Spirit.

Other aspects of worship are trinitarian as well. Preaching in the Christian context is trinitarian. The gospel of Jesus Christ is the content of Christian preaching. As pastor and homiletician James Forbes has argued in his book *The Holy Spirit and Preaching*, faithful preaching relies on the anointing and guidance of the Holy Spirit; it has as its goal the mission of God to bring resurrection to places where there is death.[2] The hymns of the church praise and pray to God as Father / Mother, as Christ, as Spirit, even more boldly than do sermons and prayers. Though human tongue or pen knows no language adequate to praise and pray to the Holy One, the Spirit gives utterance (Acts 2:4; Rom. 8:26–27).

Christian worship is trinitarian because it grows out of and renews the church's relationship with the God made known in Jesus Christ through the Spirit. This relationship is primary, providing the inspiration for texts that may, in turn, nurture the church's relationship with the triune God. As theologian Ted Peters has written, "the primary Christian experience is . . . trinitarian in form."[3] This statement applies to the revelation to which the New Testament witnesses and also to the continuing experience of Christian life and worship. Though in this volume we advocate the search for ever more adequate language for the Trinity, with a greater diversity of metaphors, we believe the Trinity is basic to Christian faith.

This book grows out of two convictions: first, that the Trinity is central to Christian faith and worship; second, that language used in worship to speak about the Trinity should be gender-inclusive. Though we are not identical in either the theological positions we espouse or the liturgical strategies we propose, both of us seek to renew a sense of the trinitarian reality in the church in ways that reflect the just and egalitarian nature of the gospel. This sets us apart from many of our contemporaries, for many liberal Christians view the concern for the Trinity as irrelevant, while some conservatives reject the concern for inclusive trinitarian language as heretical or at least dangerous. Yet we are concerned not only about the academic debate but even more with the life of the church. For we believe that, when used to the exclusion of other metaphors, the language of Father, Son, and Spirit is too limited and stereotyped to encourage trinitarian faith. And, with many trinitarian theologians in recent decades, we sense that Christian worship in North America is rarely fully trinitarian.

Concern for gender-inclusive language may seem at first to lead away from more fully trinitarian praise, given the claims of some traditionalists that "Father, Son, and Holy Spirit" cannot be augmented and the charges of some feminists that the doctrine of the Trinity, with its Father-Son metaphors, is intrinsically patriarchal. Both Geoffrey Wainwright (who is quite reserved about change in trinitarian language) and Gail Ramshaw (who advocates change) note that churches concerned about inclusive language sometimes avoid speaking of the Trinity altogether instead of seeking alternative language.[4] We recognize the great challenge of finding adequate language to talk about the Trinity, and know our answers will be incomplete, yet we are not content to let the matter rest there. For we testify to our own experience of the grace of the triune God, not as patriarch, but as loving, relational presence known in the Christian story. Indeed, as this book unfolds, it will become apparent that the concern for inclusive language has generated much creative liturgical and theological work on the Trinity that may serve to revitalize trinitarian faith.

THE TRINITY: PERIPHERAL
TO FAITH AND WORSHIP?

Trinitarian theologians, in all their diversity, appear to agree on one point: These days the doctrine of the Trinity is generally peripheral to everyday Christian faith, life, and worship. Many Christians, lay and clergy, consider the Trinity to be an abstract doctrine describing the inner life of God, of interest only to academic theologians. Whether they consider the Trinity a late doctrine unsupported by scripture, or they accept the teaching as true but beyond the average person's understanding, such people do not consider the Trinity essential to Christian life or even worthy of thoughtful reflection.

The fact that Christian tradition so often speaks about the Trinity in the language of formal academic theology, and not the language of praise, faith, and piety, may contribute to the perception that the Trinity is peripheral to Christian life and worship. Roman Catholic liberation theologian Leonardo Boff describes the situation poignantly:

> The rigidity of trinitarian formulas and the exactness of theological expression serve the purposes of those who are learned in the Christian faith. They do not, it must be said, make for ease of praying, nor do they exactly kindle the hearts of the faithful.[5]

According to Boff, the church has erred in treating the Trinity as a logical puzzle rather than the mystery of salvation. Such terms as "person," "procession," "mode," and "substance," together with the focus on the inner relationship of the trinitarian persons as abstracted from the story of salvation, often mystify the Christian believer.[6]

The main liturgical alternative to academic explanations of the Trinity has been the formula "Father, Son, and Holy Spirit," which, without further elaboration, may become a matter of rote recitation without room for wonder and growth in devotion and praise. Before the theological disputes of the fourth and fifth centuries, liturgical language was the primary theology, and secondary theology grew out of reflection on the liturgy. The formula *lex orandi, lex credendi* (the law of praying is the law of believing) characterized the connection between worship and theology in the first four centuries of the church. In later centuries, concern for correct theological formulation in the church's liturgy came to overshadow the search for vital praise.

The Trinity may be peripheral in the worship and life of some congregations because the members or leaders are actually unitarian, though part of a Christian denomination. The doctrine of the Trinity grew out of reflection on the church's pattern of praise that implicitly assumed the participation of the Christ and Spirit in the divine life. Churches and church leaders who do not accept Jesus Christ as the incarnation of God and who do not see the Spirit as a personal, divine reality, often speak and live as if they were simple monotheists. For example, I have experienced more than one United Church of Christ congregation that expressed some discomfort when a newly called clergyperson preached too much about Jesus. The former pastor of one such congregation confessed to me privately that, rather than the Bible, the sacred writings of a New Age cult were his personal inspiration. No wonder the congregation was surprised, after he left, to hear preaching focused on scripture passages about the life, ministry, and person of Jesus Christ. Their previous pastor had promoted a form of unitarianism that presented Jesus as a good teacher, but not as the incarnation of the living God.

More often, churches are trinitarian in their stated beliefs but present only a partial picture of the triune God in their worship. For example, some evangelical Christians emphasize Jesus Christ so much that their hymns sometimes speak only of "he" or "him"; the worshiper must guess from the context that Jesus is the subject of the hymn. Charismatic Christians who emphasize "baptism in the Holy Spirit" and speaking in tongues but not evangelical witness to the gospel of Jesus Christ also present a partial picture of God. Liberal churches tend to be unitarians of the first person: Witness the social slogan promoting the "fatherhood of God and the brotherhood of man" as the hope for world peace and justice. Emphasis on only one person of the Trinity in worship may result from a lack of intentionality in expressing faith, rather than a considered theological position. Since, however, worship shapes the faith of Christians, over time inadequate language of praise will distort a church's understanding and experience of faith.

The liturgical language of Anglican, Roman Catholic, Lutheran, and Orthodox churches tends to be more fully trinitarian than that of Protestant churches just described. Yet theologians from these communions such as Karl Rahner, Catherine LaCugna, Ted Peters, and Gail Ramshaw have also expressed the concern that the Trinity is not central to Christian faith and life.

When Christian preaching and worship do not point to the possibility of new life in Christ, when the church does not witness to the power of the

Holy Spirit, when Christians do not express their dependence on the holy Source of life, the faith experience of congregations is impoverished. Our participation in the life of God is a work of the Holy Spirit, yet holistic witness can nurture human openness and desire to be in relationship with God. The triune God, fount of all blessing, comes to us with gifts of abundant life, joy, and "courage in the struggle for justice and peace."[7] Fully trinitarian worship lays out before the congregation the gifts of God and invites Christians to new life.

Recent ecumenical trends indicate a deepening trinitarian experience within Christian worship. The widespread use of lectionaries derived from the Roman Lectionary of 1970, such as the *Revised Common Lectionary*, has helped many churches recover the centrality of Jesus Christ in their worship. Charismatic renewal movements and growing ministries of healing in Roman Catholic, Anglican, and Protestant worship have led to a deepened sense of the reality of the Spirit in worship. The work of churches—separately and together—on the sacraments of Baptism and Eucharist have also led to an enhanced sense of the working of the Spirit in Christian worship. Western churches, for example, have learned from the East the importance of invocation of the Spirit during the Great Thanksgiving and of anointing as a sign of the Spirit's work in Christian initiation. As the church more fully encounters the living Christ and the empowering Spirit in its worship and life, the Trinity once more becomes a living doctrine, and the church recovers its true identity.

Our vocation as Christians is to give glory to God through our words, our work, and our life together. Though all human words are inadequate to the glory of God, worship calls forth the best we have to give, whether as modest as the widow's mite or as priceless as the prophet's jar of nard. One aspect of doing our best to glorify God is to consider how adequately the words of our worship express our faith. The words of intentionally trinitarian Christian worship witness to the way God has been revealed in time, from the beginning of creation, to the coming of Jesus Christ and the outpouring of the Spirit, to the very moment we gather for worship. Though God's labor of love toward creation transcends all we do or fail to do, Christian worship can nurture the congregation's growth in love toward God, one another, and the whole creation.

Our intent in this book is to contribute to more fully trinitarian praise, both by challenging churches to be intentional in their liturgical language and by suggesting practical and inspiring ways to enrich the church's praise of the triune God.

THE PROBLEM OF EXCLUSIVELY MALE LANGUAGE FOR GOD

"Father, Son, and Holy Spirit": these contemporary English words epitomize the way the church has affirmed trinitarian faith in worship since the councils of the fourth and fifth centuries. Yet despite long-standing traditions and concerns about sacramental validity, Christians who wish to nurture trinitarian faith and to promote justice between the sexes must consider how problematic it is to use only masculine language when describing the divine reality.[8]

When masculine language is used for God without corresponding feminine language, some find it more difficult to receive the gospel of Jesus Christ. Many women and men are discovering today that including feminine as well as masculine images for God in worship helps them comprehend God's love and justice with new depth and clarity. Churches are learning that expanding the imagery they use to speak of God's reality leads to fuller and deeper praise.

Masculine language for God that predominates over feminine language is also ethically problematic. The use of predominantly masculine language is one significant way in which patriarchal culture is passed from one generation to another. Using many masculine images and no feminine images for God sends the message that women are not made in the image of God and thus are less valuable than men. This message in turn lends credence to values that condone the violation of females by males — from rape to battering to sexual abuse to economic discrimination.

"Father," in particular, is a term laden with possibility and problematics. It is rich with possibility because a good relationship between father and child is one of the greatest gifts anyone can receive in life, in any historical or cultural context. Few would dispute that Jesus called God "Father" (if among other names); that alone gives it a convincing claim in Christian worship. On the other hand, the father-child relationship may be one of abuse or neglect as well as one of encouragement and nurture. Our words in worship — while grounded in God's self-revelation to us — cannot avoid evoking embodied responses based on individual human experience.

Thus, it is helpful to provide alternative images, along with the familiar image of God as Father, since the possibility of fatherhood is not always fulfilled in real human experience. We do not believe that Jesus' words, "When you pray, say, "Our Father . . . ,"" preclude other ways of imaging God, any more than we believe that the Lord's Prayer is the only acceptable prayer for Christian worship.[9]

Our goal in this book is to suggest ways of faithful witness to the triune God, in a constellation of metaphors that includes yet goes beyond the language of "Father" and "Son." In so doing, we hope to encourage trinitarian faith, worship, and life and their expressions in just and loving human relationships.

THE ORGANIZATION OF THIS BOOK

As a foundation for all that follows, chapter 1 (by Patricia Wilson-Kastner) elucidates our perspective that in liturgical language the church speaks through metaphor and analogy of a God who is not simply a projection or creation of humanity, but a reality with whom we are in relationship. Chapters 2 and 3 (by Ruth Duck) uncover how in worship we can and do give witness to the triune God: chapter 2 explores varied language for the Trinity, and chapter 3 examines the trinitarian dimensions of particular aspects of worship, such as the sacraments and the celebration of the church year. Chapter 4 (by Wilson-Kastner) explores preaching as trinitarian proclamation, and chapter 5 (by Duck) mines the riches of Christian hymnody as a means of praising and testifying to the Trinity. Chapter 6 (by Duck) tackles the use of Wisdom imagery in worship, a contemporary issue that has aroused much discussion, from the perspective of trinitarian faith. In chapter 7, Wilson-Kastner points to the connection between the Trinity, its representation in art and liturgy, and human life and behavior in the world. In the concluding section of the book, both of us provide worship resources for use in local churches that demonstrate possibilities for expanded trinitarian language.

It is in the local church and its worshiping life that this conversation must continue, if praying is to shape our believing. Worship, like Christian life, must proceed on an action-reflection model: We examine our praise, consider how it might be found wanting, and then in all humility seek more faithful alternatives, which inspire another round of reflection and testing.

Any who are concerned about expanding our liturgical language about the Trinity long for greater clarity and more widely accepted solutions to the thorny issues we engage here. It would be foolhardy to think issues of such magnitude could be resolved in a generation, yet the task is ours to address. We can find confidence as we proceed by remembering that the doctrine of the Trinity centers on divine love poured out into the life of the world, drawing us into relationship with God and one another. The mystery of divine love, which goes beyond any words we can imagine, undergirds and moves through our search for words and our worship. To the triune God be glory!

Where Do We Start?

Where do we begin the discussion of inclusive language about God in worship?[1] By that question I do not mean to ask where we begin chronologically, or with which image or metaphor, or with which worship service, but rather: what is the theological starting point for our language about God? What, if anything, suggests or determines the parameters for inclusive language about God?

I believe that there are identifiable theological origins for the language chosen by any writer about the divine and that the sorts of verbal expression one uses emerge from these roots. These apprehensions shape and offer directions and norms, broad or narrow, for God-language, including images, metaphors, and analogies. If we ourselves are unclear about our assumptions, beliefs, and understandings about the divine, our language and our expressions may be murky, inadequate, or misleading.

Ruth Duck has described the contemporary search for language that "pictures humanity and the divine in such a way as to include, honor, and do justice to diverse human experiences." In the United States the interest in inclusive language was encouraged in the 1970s, with the reemergence of feminism and its concern for the language of scripture and worship.[2] Our current concern about inclusive language can thus be linked to the changing role of women, the renewed value of women's experience and perspectives, and critical reassessments of various religious traditions. Language about God, and especially about the Trinity, the specifically Christian understanding of God, inevitably became the focus of exploration, discussion, and various opinions and interpretations.

If we are constructively to explore the issue of inclusive language about the Trinity, we must first be clear about the underpinnings of the discussion. Our assumptions are rooted, I believe, in distinctions that are radically important in determining the language that we believe we may or may not use, particularly in the context of public worship.

The great distinction is so elementary that it is often overlooked or not clearly articulated. Nonetheless, it is where our theological discussion about language concerning God must begin. It is certainly where consideration of the language of worship begins. Put in the most elementary manner possible: Are we addressing a divine reality, no matter how frail, feeble, or uncertain our perceptions of this divinity may be? Or are we talking to ourselves, trying to stir up our best feelings and values in order to personify the greatest human ideals with which we want to identify ourselves?

Our response to this question will determine how we continue the inquiry central to this book: how can we speak of the divine trinitarian reality whom we worship in our churches? If we respond to the first question that we are not addressing a divine reality that is distinguishable, independent, or interdependent and distinct from us, then we can speak about God or Goddess in any way that is pleasing, interesting, and beneficial to us. Language about the Trinity will be acceptable or not, depending on the norm we ourselves choose, for our own stated reasons, to use or employ. As feminists, our norm(s) will relate most frequently, in practice, to women's self-realization or betterment.

But if we believe that worship is an encounter with divine reality that is not identical (completely or partially) with us, and that the term "Trinity" refers to divine reality, then the parameters of discourse are different. We might affirm that only traditional biblical words and images found in the scriptures should be used about the Trinity. We might decide that only certain words or images from scripture are suitable to refer to the Trinity. We might assert that we can use a variety of scriptural words, images, and metaphors about the Trinity, as well as language that is congruent with scripture, even though not actually in the scriptures. Each of these decisions will depend on our understanding of the relationship between ourselves and divine reality.

How then will we speak of God, the Trinity? In this chapter I address three topics that encompass the questions I have raised, and I suggest directions for further development. First, I look at the distinction between the divine as an expression of human ideals and the divine as a distinct living reality. Second, I suggest why language about the Trinity is necessarily metaphorical or analogical. Third, I suggest why our liturgical language about the Trinity must change in order to be faithful to the essential role of liturgy in the church.

My intention is not to be comprehensive, or to be critical of those with whom I may not agree. Instead, I hope to offer a coherent perspective on liturgical language for the Trinity that is both faithful to the scriptures and tradition and also open to new ways of speaking about God. I wish to provide clarity and perspective as the church wrestles with the feminist critique of God-language, which will not be silenced in the church and which can contribute to renewal and revival of the church's life.

THE PRIMARY DISTINCTION

Distinctions can be harmful. They can cause conflicts, alienate people from each other, and set up false separations based on prejudice and deceit. Distinctions can also provide helpful tools for fuller and deeper understanding by offering a clear vision that opens us to the truth and the healing that nurtures real love. The distinction I will explore now in more detail is that between those feminist thinkers who use language about the divine as a vehicle to express human ideals in words intended to promote women's liberation and self-realization, and those who use language about the divine to express human liberating experience of an active divine reality that they have encountered in the context of the Christian tradition.[3]

The Divine as Expressive of Our Deepest Ideals

Many contemporary secular feminist women are increasingly aware that by "the divine," they mean the expression of their highest human values and ideals; for other feminists, the divine is the sacred energy of life itself. Some worshipers of the Goddess, such as theologian and novelist Starhawk, regard her as the force of life in the world, a life force in which all humans share; who or what she is remains in the poetic and nondefined realm. Thus, "the divine" designates the whole of reality or the life power within the universe, or it is a figure of speech personifying an impersonal cosmic life force. Many of those who identify with Wicca or New Age movements find this pantheistic approach congenial.[4]

Jewish feminist Naomi Goldenberg's *Changing of the Gods* gave words to a straightforward Freudian psychological interpretation of religion. Goldenberg understands God to be a projection of psychological needs, wants, and desires. Males have controlled the religious systems, and the images used for God have expressed their human experiences and needs. She argues that when women change religion so that images of the divine that affirm women become commonplace, we will be radically trans-formed. Goldenberg praises feminist witchcraft because in turning religion into psychology, it "place[s] divinity or supernatural power within the person."[5] Consequently, image making and discourse about the divine are directed by the principle of what is most beneficial to the empowerment and self-realization of women.

Enacting God/dess: Feminist Relational Views of the Divine

There is another approach that is, from my perspective, somewhere between those who understand the divine as an expression of human ideals in words that promote women's liberation and self-realization, and those who use language about the divine to express human experience of an active divine reality that they have encountered in the context of the Christian tradition. Its adherents have been influenced for the most part either by process philosophy or by New Age Wiccan feminism, and they regard the divine as a reality that we are making.

In philosopher Alfred North Whitehead's process schema, God's nature is both primordial and consequent. God's primordial life and energy express themselves in the world, in which God exists, inchoately and potentially, in created reality. Through our actions and conscious relatedness to the divine, we evoke and shape the good and true in the world. We are creating God's consequent nature; the reality of the world, including ourselves, continues, refined and reconfigured, in God's primordial nature.[6] Thus God is a reality, distinguishable but not distinct from ourselves, which both produces us and is also in part our creation.

Richard Grigg, associate professor of religion at Sacred Heart University in Bridgeport, Connecticut, identifies a strand of feminist theology that conceives of "God as a relation that is enacted by human beings, in conjunction with nature and the power of being."[7] The divine (God/Goddess) is understood as a relationship that we participate in making; Grigg sees this underlying notion of the divine in certain feminist thinkers to whom "the divine is a relation that human beings decide to enact."[8] According to Grigg, theologians such as Rosemary Radford Ruether, Mary Daly, Elizabeth Schüssler Fiorenza, Carol Christ, and Rebecca Chopp start with the pragmatic principle that the concept of God must promote the empowerment of women and hold that the divine reality is totally immanent and necessarily dependent on humanity.[9] Although their view is a radical reformulation beyond traditional theism, these theologians differ from others for whom the divine is only a projection of human needs and desires; they acknowledge a truly existing Goddess whom humans take part in enacting. Their views result in language that portrays the divine in process of becoming, in the essential relationship with creation without which there is no deity.

Inclusive language growing out of such a conception of the deity is affected both by what we understand the divine now to be and by what we intend the divine to become. Because our language can shape and motivate our actions, which contribute to creating the consequent nature of God, language is important. Our prayer evokes action from us to create the deity who empowers women, but also addresses the deity who is being formed in this interaction.

The language of worship, in such a perspective, is not bound by any belief that God or Goddess is in any way trinitarian in nature. Language helps the worshipers in the creation of God. God is not a gracious gift, but the central and worthy project of our lives. The norms of discourse derive from the feminist concern for the empowerment and self-actualization of women and from the theological concern for the divine. This divinity is, in part, created through human effort and through relationships among humans, the world, and the divine—as much as those are distinguishable.

The Divine as Active Subject

Several different understandings of the divine regard the deity not as a simply human construct, nor as a reality that we are making, but as an active subject, personal or supra-personal. The divine reality is understood to be a living, self-revealing reality. This is the perspective that is most relevant to our discussion about the Trinity and inclusive liturgical language. For only if the divine is a reality with which we are in relationship can the language of worship be an act of communication between humanity and the biblical deity of Christian life and tradition.

In this context, the language we use to express our experience of the divine is not simply free for our choosing. Rather, it endeavors to articulate our encounter with a divine reality distinct from ourselves and our world. Feminism properly critiques the language in which Christian faith tradition has spoken about the divine, but it does so affirming that the task of religious language is to describe the human encounter with a divine reality who is distinct and distinguishable from ourselves and our projections, as well as intimately interconnected with us. Any discussion of trinitarian language in worship takes place in this perspective. In this context, I suggest two major perspectives for ways of speaking about God: God-language as literal or God-language as metaphor and analogy.

GOD-LANGUAGE AS LITERAL

The assumption here is that the God of the Bible is a transcendent being who has revealed God's self to us. Therefore, in addressing God or discussing God, we must use only those words which are contained in the scriptures, in the ways translated and interpreted by the tradition, interpreted by its authentic and informed spokespersons.[10] While it is not entirely accurate to refer to adherents to this approach as biblical or doctrinal literalists, it is broadly adequate.

William Oddie (a British theologian who is a religion correspondent for the *London Daily Telegraph*) is a representative of this approach. He sounded a clarion call against feminist theology in the early 1980s on the grounds that Christian feminism is rooted in secular humanist feminism, which is genuinely revolutionary and aimed at destroying and dismantling traditional biblical Christianity.[11] He argued that because of its roots in secular feminism and its intention to attack the hierarchical and male symbol system, Christian feminism cannot ultimately be reformist. The Father-Son relationship of Christ and God illumines not only God's nature but also that of humanity and the church. That language, with its attendant symbols and intellectual and ecclesial structures, cannot be changed or modified because it is the true expression of revelation.[12]

Episcopal priest and theologian Alvin F. Kimel, in *Speaking the Christian God*, gathered the contributions of scholars, many of whose opinions coincide with Oddie's perceptions. This volume, the touchstone of most contemporary opposition to inclusive language about God, presents various perspectives defending the traditional male-dominated language. Feminists who move from asserting the "absolute equality and dignity of man and woman" to attempting to critique and rethink "God, Trinity, Christ" are understood to be opposed to and destructive of the "creedal fundamentals of Christian belief."[13]

Kimel and linguist Donald Hook have articulated the fundamental issue about trinitarian language. They assert that English translations of the biblical stories of God use masculine nouns and pronouns that are "essential, necessary, and definitive."[14] Therefore, God must always be referred to as male: Father, Son, and Holy Spirit are to be spoken of in grammatical terms. Hook and Kimel purport to refute all Christian feminist proposals about referring to God in gender-neutral language or to the Holy Spirit as female. They also find no feminine language or images used as direct predication or address for God in scripture; the only feminine language used in reference to God uses simile and comparison.

They reject all feminist alternatives in the light of this assertion: "The basis of the language of the Judeo-Christian tradition is a language of a specific and unique revelation which all believers in the tradition share."[15] In other words, the language of Judeo-Christian revelation can only be accepted as stated and given (that is, as Hook and Kimel state and give it); no discussion is possible. There is only one possible language of worship and theology, and in it God-language is masculine; any other approach must be inferred to be outside authentic or faithful Christianity. This perspective must be taken as utterly true on its own assumptions, impervious to reason or discussion. It proponents are unwilling to recognize the conditioned character of any human language, especially the inspired language of scripture.

GOD-LANGUAGE AS METAPHOR AND ANALOGY

Unlike Kimel and Hook, many Christian feminists value scriptural language about God as referring to divine self-revelation, while recognizing that biblical imagery for God (like all human language about the divine) is metaphorical or analogical and is based on conditioned human experience. (The nature of metaphor and analogy will be explored in the section that follows.) This perspective suggests that to employ only a male-dominated, literalistically interpreted biblical language about the trinitarian God is neither faithful to the biblical image of God nor appropriate in the context of the feminist critique of theological language. Liturgical language about God must first incorporate a full range of biblically rooted masculine and feminine comparisons, words, and imagery for God and, second, be understandable today in the context of a Christian feminist critique.

The theological tradition itself suggests how such an enterprise may be undertaken. In the fourth century, Athanasius was struggling against the Arians, who were in many ways much more biblically literal than he, to express the doctrines of the nature of Jesus Christ and the life of the Trinity. He argued that one sometimes has to use nonbiblical language to explain and express what is not explicitly said in the scriptures. But what is necessary, he believed, is that the new theological and even creedal language be rooted in biblical language and express God's saving life and work in creation. One may even find in Athanasius "novel phrases," new language, being spoken about God to express scriptural truth.[16]

Athanasius was certainly not contemplating inclusive language about the Trinity. Most Christian feminists would not begin their work with a reference to Athanasius, and many might not even be aware of or care about his thoughts and their relevance to their situation. However, Athanasius, along with other early trinitarian theologians (as well as contemporary feminists), struggled with the perceived inadequacy of many of the words and concepts used to speak of God and God's relation to the world.

Most Christian feminists would explicitly claim that their words are either scriptural or congruent with scripture, and that they clarify the Trinity's life in relationship with the world. They also believe that the perception of and language about God's relationship with the world needs to be reassessed and transformed, with attention to the way language affects and is affected by the liberation and empowerment of women. On this road, Athanasius is not a bad traveling companion.

In the twentieth century, Christian feminist theologians have struggled both to be faithful to the biblical tradition of God's creative, redeeming, and sanctifying life and work in the universe and to respond to the feminist critique of language and our conceptualizations of God and humanity. Such a critical relationship always exists in a creative and healthy tension. For many Christian feminists, this tension is felt most severely in the contrast between the undeniably patriarchal language of the Trinity as "Father, Son, and Holy Spirit" and divine holiness, which frees us from all idolatry and servitude to any human power.

Although many different approaches are taken by Christian feminists, the encompassing criterion of their theological work is that the biblical revelation of God as the trinitarian deity most commonly called Father, Son, and Holy Spirit is the central divine self-disclosure to us. As feminist theologians, their role is—in the context of women's experience and search for full humanity in the image of God—to critique and to re-envision, reform, and reconfigure Christian worship and doctrine in faithfulness to the divine self-revealing in scripture.[17] Because they have eschewed literalism, they regard language about God as metaphorical or analogical.

Some theologians such as Catherine Mowry LaCugna, Elizabeth A. Johnson, Anne Carr, Pamela Dickey Young, and Marjorie Hewitt Suchocki have grounded their theological presentations in particular and articulated philosophical perspectives.[18] Others, Ruth Duck and Gail Ramshaw, for example, focus on the implications of this theological discussion for liturgy as encounter with God, as they seek an authentic Christian feminist vocabulary of worship.[19]

I do not intend to explore any of these positions in detail. I merely wish to indicate that there are many Christian feminist theological positions among those who take seriously the reality of God's self-revelation in human experience and thus work with the assumption that God-language expresses an encounter with a deity that is not merely a projection of our own desires. The criteria for their God-language grow from a determination to be faithful to the encounter between God and the world to which the scriptures testify and also to this encounter in contemporary language that is given birth, and shaped, by a feminist perspective. I regard myself as belonging to such a group of Christian feminist theologians and will now turn my attention to their understanding of inclusive language about the Trinity.

MODELS AND METAPHORS

How will our language express the divine-human encounter of the Christian faith? In the theological ways I have identified[20] for speaking about God, two things are clear. First, our language cannot be a projection about a deity that is the same reality as we are. Second, we do not believe the deity to be totally removed from us and unlike us. Those of us who speak of a divine reality not comprehended in this world, but in some way present in and to this world, must speak in metaphor and analogy. Careful theological work undergirds and strengthens this assumption.

Theologian Sallie McFague identified the role of models, with their accompanying images, metaphors, and analogies: "The central role of models in theology is to provide grids or screens for interpreting the relationship between the divine and the human."[21] The term "model" has become popular in theological circles and is adapted from the work of Ian Barbour, a philosopher of science who popularized the term in scientific theory. A model is an aid to understanding, in which the greater reality is explained in terms of a smaller, known reality. Philosophical theologian Ian Ramsey suggests models for God's disclosure to us: economy (administration) and presence.[22] His models are not pictures, as he insists repeatedly, nor do they attempt to reflect the life of the Trinity. Rather his concern is for the moment of God's self-disclosure to us.

In the view of John Habgood, Anglican church leader and theologian, both analogy and metaphor are used in theology in ways similar to the contemporary theological language of models.[23] I think that he is essentially right, and that the primary concern of such language is to express how God relates to us, assuming some relationship between the one who creates and the world that is created.

Metaphor compares two realities—one of which is directly accessible to us and one of which is not—in order to illumine and help us apprehend the reality that is not directly accessible. The use of metaphor does not assume an intrinsic relationship between the realities compared, although such a relationship may be present. Sallie McFague, for instance, proposes using the metaphor "friend" to express our relationship with God, instead of "Father."[24]

Analogy, however, does assume such a relationship, and on this basis makes its comparison.[25] An analogy for God might be the parental imagery of Father or Mother. In the fourth century, Basil of Caesarea used for the Trinity the analogy of four men: Peter, Andrew, James, and John, who are distinct persons but are of one human species.[26] And Augustine of Hippo wrote of the interconnection of the mind, its knowledge, and its love as a human analogy for the Trinity.[27]

Images or illustrations, which do no more than illumine an aspect of the divine, can carry some of the burden of the metaphor in religious discourse. For instance, in Irish usage, the shamrock became a popular image of the Trinity because it was one plant with three distinct leaves.[28]

Metaphor, analogy, symbol, and imagery are interrelated in classical and modern theologies.[29] They assume a relatedness of the divine and the created order; they reject a useful adequacy of literal discourse to express the interrelationship of the divine and human realities; they also allow that one can and must speak about and to the deity.

This brings us to the key issue of this book: How do we speak to and about the trinitarian God in worship?

METAPHORICAL AND ANALOGICAL
LANGUAGE ABOUT THE TRINITY

Christians do not worship "the deity" or an undifferentiated "God." The distinctively Christian deity was invoked by the apostle Paul: "The grace of the Lord Jesus Christ, the love of God, and the communion of the Holy Spirit be with all of you" (2 Cor. 13:13). We worship a trinitarian God, who created us in love, who redeems us through the unmerited power of the resurrection of Jesus, and in whose Spirit we are joined together in the holy and eternal life of God.

How can we speak of this trinitarian God? Obviously, only through models—by analogy, imagery, and metaphor. Literal language is nonsensical. One can, in trying to explain literally how One God is a Trinity, find oneself trying to nourish faith from the dry bones of such doctrinal safeguards as the Athanasian Creed or complaining with the young girl writing an essay, "The Holy Trinity are a grammatical problem."

The trinitarian God is not a product of theology or philosophy, but is the God experienced and spoken about by the Christian community. Theology is at best a witness and teacher. As Christians, we root our understanding of the Trinity in the words and teachings of Jesus. In recent years, we have seen a revival of interest in the theology of the Trinity, under the influence of several movements: our renewed connections with the Orthodox churches, the twentieth-century revival of study of the early church, and the later twentieth century's reassessment of its theology of God. We are increasingly conscious as a Christian community that the Trinity is a practical doctrine, with explicit effects on our Christian life, and that the church's renewal and our lives as contemporary Christians must be interwoven with a reconsidered and explored trinitarian theology.[30]

Rather than to attempt here to recapitulate the whole doctrine of the Trinity, I want to focus on two concepts that are crucial for feminist theology and its liturgical language: (1) the nature of the trinitarian God is communion;

that is, God is relational; and (2) the language for expressing God's nature and relationship with us must be metaphorical and analogical.[31] The doctrine of the Trinity is an effort to express the relationship of Jesus Christ with God, who is to him Abba, or Father, and with the Spirit of God. This trinitarian reality is both a relation of Jesus, God, and Spirit, one with the other, and of this divine reality with us. How is it possible to speak of such a reality?

Elizabeth Johnson, C.S.J., a Roman Catholic feminist theologian, suggests that we might call the Trinity itself an analogy. The doctrine of the Trinity is an attempt to express the relationship of God/Abba, Jesus, and the Spirit as being like a threeness, a threefold relationship. The relationship expressed to us, and the internal life of God that we infer from this self-revealing, is not literally a triunity, whatever that in fact might mean. Our God is both like a Trinity, and at the same time not, in the sense that the divine reality cannot be captured adequately in the analogy of Trinity.[32]

That the primary Christian analogy for God is relational and personal unquestionably sets out our essential understanding of God as communion, a personal interrelationship of an intimacy we can only imagine, an equality expressing infinite sharing and self-giving. Thus our language must express this Trinity as we have experienced glimpses of such infinite communion, and as we have been invited by Jesus to be in communion with this Trinity in the new creation.[33]

This perspective of relationship and communion naturally provides certain expectations of the language used to express the Trinity. To be adequate and faithful to the Christian tradition, the words that express the Trinity must articulate relationship, both with us in creation and among the persons of the Trinity, and must also indicate communion. Of course the appellation of Father and Son became very popular in the early church in expressing the Trinity because it focused on Jesus' relationship to God (Abba) and God's acknowledgment of Jesus as the beloved Son. Spirit is breath of life, and expresses both a divine action in creation, and also the life shared between Father and Son, offered in communion to creation.[34]

However, as feminist theologians have long observed, today the traditional patriarchal and male-dominated language is inadequate, and by itself, unacceptable. We need an expanded language about God that encompasses the experience of women in their God-given humanity and strengthens and empowers their liberation and their growth in the "image and likeness of God" in which, as Genesis assures us, God created us all. Thus we come to the nub of this book: How do we articulate for worship a metaphorical and analogical language about the Trinity that is both rooted in scripture and also responsive to feminist insight and criticism of destructive and noncommunicative religious words? To illustrate some of the issues involved, let us take as an example the Gloria Patri.

The traditional wording is: "Glory be to the Father, and to the Son, and to the Holy Spirit; as it was in the beginning, is now, and ever shall be, world without end." This doxology, especially its invocation of the Trinity, appears throughout the eucharistic liturgy, as well as in the hours of the Daily Office, and is usually prayed several times in the course of most Protestant Sunday Services of the Word. Like the invocation "In the name of the Father, and of the Son, and of the Holy Spirit. Amen," it is extraordinarily influential on Christian piety because of its constant repetition.

This trinitarian formula implies relationship and communion among the persons of the Trinity, but it also suggests a patriarchal, familial, and subordinate relationship between at least the Father and the Son. Further, this formula hints at the Father's relationship to us through our redemption by Jesus but does not directly speak of God's relationship to us.

Let us look at some other doxologies for comparison:

> Honor and glory to the holy and undivided Trinity
>   God who creates, redeems and inspires:
> One in Three and Three in One,
>   For ever and ever. Amen.[35]

The Carmelites of Indianapolis have developed another alternative to the traditional doxology:

> Glory to you, Source of all being,
>   Eternal Word and Holy Spirit:
> As it was in the beginning, is now,
>   And shall be forever. Amen.[36]

The United Church of Christ in the United States offers this doxology for liturgical usage:

> Glory to God the Creator
> And to the Christ,
> And to the Holy Spirit:
> As it was in the beginning,
> Is now,
> And will be forever.
> Amen.[37]

Each of these doxologies is actively used in worshiping communities, and each tries to avoid sexist language, using terms for the Trinity that are not linked to the Father-Son expression of Jesus' relation to God. The words are rooted in biblical terms or venerable liturgical language. They avoid the shallow, if recently popular, gender-free formula, "In the name of God, Creator, Redeemer, and Sanctifier."

These examples also point up the complexity of composing or reanimating a trinitarian formula that expresses relationship of the persons to creation and to each other and at the same time avoids language of sexism and patriarchal domination. The doxologies are inclusive, liturgically usable, theologically responsible, and faithful to the tradition, but it appears that the issue of relationship, that of each of the persons to each other and that of the Trinity to us, is the most difficult to express, at least in short liturgical formulas. Perhaps it always has been: the terms "Father," "Son," and "Holy Spirit" have their own intrinsic difficulties expressing analogically or metaphorically the fullness of communion which the Trinity is and offers to us.

This volume explores trinitarian liturgical language that will feed and deepen our faith and will also be faithful to the Christian tradition and feminist critique. We will propose change and challenge. The suggestions will be of varying value in various traditions and in particular worshiping communities. But careful consideration of all of them can only be of benefit in stretching the theological imagination, as well as constantly connecting us to two thousand years of Christian worship.

CHANGING OUR LITURGY

Liturgy plays a vital role in forming our identity as human beings and as Christians.[38] That, of course, is why the issue of the language of liturgy, especially its sexism or inclusivity, is so disputed and conflicted in contemporary Christianity. Patriarchal God-language identifies the male with the divine and, by excluding the female, intimates that the male is more worthwhile, more in the divine image, than the female. We began this chapter with this insight; now, we confront the practical and pastoral activity that we must undertake. That task is the work of this book.

With the faith and feminism affirmed here, we are ready to explore how our liturgical language of sacraments, preaching, and prayers to the Trinity can and must change. We must not pretend for a moment that the journey will be simple, inevitably well received, or that it will ever end. Nonetheless, if we are to be faithful Christians, we must undertake it, accept the cost, and rejoice in our contribution to the worship life of God's new creation.

Both for those who are accustomed to a fixed liturgy and for those who worship with a free and varying liturgy, the changes we propose will be growth-producing and freeing and will open up new aspects of God's life with us. But the words may startle many, and we may find ourselves wondering if changes, such as in the Lord's Prayer or the baptismal formula, are even worth daring to consider in the real world of congregational life.

Paul Johnson, an English Roman Catholic historian and journalist, has movingly argued against changing the words of the liturgy. He acknowledges straightforwardly that language about God is anthropomorphic and that the Trinity is a "patriarchal concept" but insists that Christians do not think of God as masculine, "as opposed to feminine." The doctrine of the Trinity intimates that God is certainly not human as we are human. But because it is so difficult to think of God in the abstractness of the Trinity, many, among whom Johnson includes himself, prefer speaking of the Father.

Johnson does not launch into rigid or mean-spirited diatribes against feminism or female images or symbols for God, allowing that if women find it helpful for devotion, there is no reason why they ought not to think of God as She. He suspects that many saints, such as Monica, Catherine, and Teresa, knew God was neither male nor female. He does, however, attack feminists who "press for changes in the liturgy to make references to God non-gender-specific" and argues that it is wrong for ecclesiastical authorities to allow such changes, for they "upset most people." Let the liturgy, he pleads, "which has acquired the creative patina of age, so important in our devotions, stay as it is."[39]

Paul Johnson's eloquent plaint is heartfelt and perhaps the most effective in the argument among real church leaders about changing the language of the liturgy. He believes that people in the church depend on stable liturgy to form and sustain their identity as Christians. Thus, although they may use whatever language and forms they wish in private worship, public worship should be stable, and traditional masculine trinitarian language should not change. In brief, in the identity-forming balance between stability and the change of transformation, some are tempted to opt for liturgical stability in this chaotic world.

But every Christian (in truth, every human being) knows that change is essential and that it is an intrinsic element of life. The absence of tension and change equals death. The absence of change in the liturgy is as much a death sentence to the Christian life as is the total loss of stability and the absence of moorings. Both change and stability are necessary, and both elements are a part of our corporate worship. A mix of the familiar and the new evokes growth. The pastoral challenge is to balance the familiar and the new in liturgy. The Christian feminist critique and constructive approach to liturgy that we are advocating in this volume attempt to combine both.

A perusal of any historically oriented study of liturgy[40] demonstrates that in fact, liturgy is always changing. The pace may be glacial at any particular moment, but over the ages substantial changes do happen. To compare Hippolytus's eucharistic canon with that of Pius V's Roman Missal makes the magnitude of such change quickly and abundantly clear. Tracing those fourteen hundred years of changes and developments is most instructive. Patriarchal and more theologically abstract language comes to dominate over a more concise, historically oriented proclamation of God's deeds among us.[41]

Sometimes it is even possible to show that, not only did liturgical change happen but it did so in such a way as to weaken the position of women.[42] If liturgies have been changed to denigrate or marginalize women, can they and ought they not be modified in order to free and nurture women as part of God's new creation? Such change must, even in its more conservative forms, include some measure of inclusive language about the Trinity.

In the doctrine of the Trinity we express, as much as we can glimpse, the life of the God in whose image we are made, and whose life we are invited to share through our baptism and participation in the Eucharist. Through such liturgical change, the doctrine of the Trinity may be more adequately and fully expressed in our worship, and we will, as well as we are able, craft our liturgy to allow God's gracious and transforming grace to work in us. To this exercise we now turn.

2

Praising a Mystery

"O God, thy sea is so great and my boat is so small." So read a pewter trivet my parents displayed for forty years. Talk about the Trinity too often sounds as if we had analyzed one drop of water and thus knew all there was to know about the sea. In fact, the Trinity is the vast sea in which our small boats sail, intimately known to us, yet still mysterious.

The Trinity as mystery is not an unknowable abyss nor an unsolvable puzzle, but a living reality far beyond our experiences, our traditions, and our reason. Brian Wren explains in the preface to *Praising a Mystery*, a collection of his hymns:

> God is not one-dimensional, but a multi-dimensional mystery, decisively known in Jesus, active now as the Holy Spirit. The living God is a mystery, not a secret: secrets puzzle us, but lose their fascination when they are revealed. A mystery deepens the more it is pondered and known. At their best, worship, thinking and action are attempts to praise that mystery, to know God, and be known.[1]

As we analyze trinitarian language in the interest of fuller praise, we must recognize that the Trinity is unfathomable mystery, not because God is distant but because God is profoundly relational and thus not reducible to words. Further, though the story of God with us in Jesus Christ through the Spirit reliably reveals who God is, it does not exhaust all of who God is in the life of the universe. The Trinity remains mystery beyond all our words of praise, devotion, and reflection.

Christians worship a God who is mystery, yet is intimately involved with life. Indeed, those who originally formed and debated the doctrine of the Trinity did so out of a concern for human salvation and life in Christ. The Trinity is an eminently practical doctrine, as Catherine LaCugna has argued.[2] Christ, Spirit, and Source are one divine reality, who participate in a mutual life of love open to all people and all creation. Intentionally trinitarian worship witnesses to Jesus Christ, God incarnate with us. It testifies to the Spirit of life, the empowering presence who commissions the baptized for ministry and draws all people into the divine life. It witnesses to the mysterious Source of life—revealed through Word and Spirit, yet always greater than our imagining—who is our beginning and our destiny. The doctrine of the Trinity reveals a God who is intimately related to us and our everyday lives, values, and priorities. Christian worship is an invitation to join this dance of love by living in love, egalitarian community, and justice.[3]

Trinitarian language in worship grows out of the story of God with us to which scripture and Christian tradition witness. The center of Christian worship is growing relationship between God and the Christian community. In praise and prayer the community expresses its lament and longing for God, its joy and thanksgiving. Like the intratrinitarian relationship, this relationship between God and worshipers is not a closed system, but one which opens out in care for the world. Christian worship involves the stuff of daily life, where God has been, is, and will be revealed. Thus, through narrative and symbol coming out of fleshly existence, it evokes the story of God with us, God for us in the midst of life.

SOME FOUNDATIONAL CONSIDERATIONS

As we move toward developing practical guidelines for trinitarian language in worship, we must lay the groundwork by defining key issues and terms.

A good place to start is with "person," a term that has been central in naming distinctions within the triune God. Some characteristics of personhood do point to aspects of God: memory, will, conscious self-awareness, and above all, relationality. As many trinitarian theologians have noted, however, the term "person" itself, in reference to distinctions within the Trinity, is not without problems.[4] In the modern world, "person" tends to connote a center of individual human consciousness.[5] Thus, speaking of "persons" of the Trinity can give the impression that Christians worship three Gods, not one triune God. Despite the long tradition of using the word and the difficulty of finding adequate alternatives, complementing "person" with other terms may prevent confusion. At the same time, it is important to maintain the insight that the triune God is personal, in the sense of being relational.

In this chapter, I use "partner" interchangeably with "person," since this, at least, points to persons in cooperative relationship rather than individuals only. "Partner" is possibly less limited to human reality than "person." It coordinates with the metaphor of dance, which will be explored later in this chapter.[6] Of course, any metaphor has limitations; the chief drawback in a capitalist society is that "partner" also may point to business relationships dedicated only to economic profit. Finding new ways to name the distinct personal realities within the Trinity is an important future task, at least for English-speaking trinitarian theologians.

This is not the place to revisit in great detail the history of trinitarian thought and its distinctions of the economic Trinity (God revealed in relationship with humanity) and the immanent Trinity (the Trinity-in-itself, understood by extrapolation from human experience of God). Still, we must consider critical insights the church gained at great cost from the early trinitarian controversies. Trinitarian theology, as developed in Christian tradition, suggests some guidelines about what we can say (or cannot say) about the Trinity:

1. The ways we speak about the Trinity should reflect co-equality among the three partners, rather than a subordination of one to another. The triune reality is eternal; though the Word is begotten and the Spirit proceeds, this does not refer to a time sequence, but to the distinctive relationship of Word and Spirit to Source.
2. The unity of the trinitarian persons should also be lifted up in Christian worship.
3. The distinctiveness of each partner should not be blurred but recognized in Christian worship.

Reflection on the inner life of God has limits, for it is only possible on the basis of the revelation of God with us. Further, God *is* in relation to the world, so reflection on who God is apart from relatedness yields only a partial picture. Also, I believe that concrete language based in the economy of salvation (the economic Trinity) usually serves worship best, for the relationship between God and humanity is at the center of Christian worship. Still, theological clarifications about the relation among persons of the Trinity serve Christian faith and worship, helping us reflect on who God is and guiding the search for the best possible words for praising the trinitarian mystery.

Concern to represent the equality of the trinitarian partners provides a helpful caution when seeking alternative language for the Trinity. For example, though in some contexts "Creator" may appropriately name God, it is never good to imply that the Source creates Word or Spirit, which would deny the coequality of the divine persons. To do so would be to reaffirm the Arian position, rather than that of the Council of Nicaea which, according to Athanasius, acknowledged "that the Son is not from nothing but 'from God,' and is Word and Wisdom, and not creature or work, but proper offspring from the Father."[7] On the other hand, the search for alternatives opens the question whether traditional formulations such as the language of "Father" and "Son" tend toward subordinationism, whatever the original intent. The most challenging task in providing inclusive language for the Trinity is finding adequate language to represent the distinctiveness of persons, while affirming the unity and coequality of persons. One must attempt to describe the reality to which traditional words refer and to discover metaphors in scripture, tradition, and experience that point to the same reality. What follows is an attempt to describe the distinctiveness of each person of the Trinity.

The first person of the Trinity, "the Father" as traditionally named, is the unoriginate Source who begets Jesus Christ, breathes forth the Holy Spirit, and creates everything else in the universe.[8] ("Unoriginate" here means being without any prior source.) This living Source of life is revealed in the Hebrew Bible as creator of all nature and all humanity, and shaper of a people called to live to God's glory in love and justice toward all. This mysterious Source of life is never without a witness in any place or time, but seeks in holy love to draw all people into a life of communion and participation in the divine life through the Word and Spirit. Metaphors for this divine person include "Father," "Mother," "Source," "Creator," "Holy One," "Eternal, Living God," and "Mystery."

The second person of the Trinity, "the Son" as traditionally named, is the incarnate Word of God manifest in Jesus of Nazareth. As systematic theologian James Cone has argued, "Jesus is who he was."[9] That is, the Word is revealed in the concrete story of Jesus of Nazareth, in his ministry of preaching the good news of God's love for all, healing the sick, and welcoming the outcast. The death of Jesus Christ (experienced in solidarity with the shamed and outcast of his time) and the resurrection (the eternal Source's amen to the faithful and loving life of Jesus) reveal the Word, the communication of God in embodied form. Metaphors for this divine person include "Son," "Word," "Christ," "Sophia," "Redeemer," "risen One," and "incarnate One," and in the words of Julian of Norwich and others, "Mother."

The third person of the Trinity, "the Spirit" as traditionally named, is the eternal presence of God in life. The Spirit leads humanity into truth and reminds disciples of the words and deeds of Jesus Christ (John 14:25). In baptism the Spirit anoints Christians for ministry, bestowing gifts for the building up of the church in love for the world. The Spirit sanctifies, granting freedom in Christ and empowering Christians to grow in the image and likeness of Christ. This mysterious Spirit labors to restore all people and all creation to God's original intention (Rom. 8:18–25). Many metaphors have been used to describe the Spirit, particularly "wind" and "breath," which are the literal meanings of *ru'ach*, the Hebrew word translated as "Spirit." Other metaphors are "Giver of Life," "Sanctifier," "Comforter," and "Sustainer."

To speak of God as three persons or partners is not to speak of three gods, but one triune God existing eternally in a communion of shared life. The triune God is fundamentally relational, not only because the three partners exist in communion, but also because this communion opens out in love to incorporate all creation into the life of the triune God. Incorporation into the life of God supports an ethical life of love and justice based on the incarnation of Jesus Christ, who showed particular concern for those whom society neglects and marginalizes: women and children, the poor, the oppressed, the sick. Whether one contemplates the inner life of the Trinity (a shared life of love among equal persons) or the life of Jesus to which the Gospels witness, a trinitarian ethic promotes a lifestyle of love, justice, and concern for all persons.

To praise the Trinity is to praise a mystery, the mystery of relationship that always goes beyond words, known to us because God reveals God's self in the history of human life.

PRACTICAL GUIDELINES
FOR TRINITARIAN LANGUAGE

Many metaphors are available for each person of the Trinity and for the Trinity as a whole.

To be intentional about being fully trinitarian in worship means giving witness to the triune God and the distinct nature and action of each person of the Trinity. This means attempting to represent coequality by giving significant attention to each partner of the Trinity as the seasons unfold. Representing the triune unity means always integrating talk of one person of the Trinity into the whole. Some worship services may focus on one person of the Trinity; for example, Easter services center on the risen Christ, while Pentecost services emphasize the empowering Spirit. Yet a fully trinitarian approach means these emphases will be placed in a wider trinitarian context. Although the Spirit is central to Pentecost, so is the preaching of the gospel of Jesus Christ, intertwined with witness to the work of God the Source in sending, raising, and exalting Jesus and calling humanity to faith. Preaching and worship on Pentecost Sunday therefore center on the giving of the Spirit, while referring to the presence of Word and Source in this earth-shaking event. Thus, Source, Word, or Spirit, though the focus of a service, is not portrayed as acting alone. Using related images for each person, such as Tertullian's metaphors of "root, shoot, and fruit," can also communicate the unity of the Trinity.[10] Coordinated references to partners of the Trinity help to nurture wholesome trinitarian faith.

Most fundamentally, trinitarian language that nurtures faith portrays God as relational, because the doctrine of the Trinity concerns the relationality of God within God's self (the immanent Trinity) and with creation (the economic Trinity). Unfortunately, formulations since Augustine have tended to focus on the inner relationships within the Trinity, at the expense of the economic Trinity.[11] For example, Augustine's analogy of Memory, Understanding, and Will does help to illustrate the triune unity of God, but unlike his metaphors of Lover, Beloved, and Love, they are difficult to relate to creation.[12] The partners of the Trinity share in one life; they are distinct yet not separate, and equally to be praised. Some feminist and liberation theologians have argued that this shared life, which honors difference and exemplifies equality, is an ideal model for human community. As Catherine Mowry LaCugna has pointed out, however, human life is transformed not so much by contemplating the inner life of God as by participating in relationship with the triune God.[13] The trinitarian relationship is not a closed system, a mutual admiration society of three divine persons. The triune God lives in mutual and overflowing love moving outward toward creation and draws the life of all people and all created things into the divine life.

Relational images for God are often *personal* images for God, images based on personal human reality. Human life is by nature relational. Thus, metaphors based on human relationships ("Mother," "Father," "Friend," and "Lover") can help humans understand divine love. Such metaphors are best used with other metaphors, to avoid the impression that God is a human being writ large and to recognize that God's love is greater than human love. Yet metaphors for God based on human relationships will surely always be useful in Christian worship.

Using human metaphors raises the issue of gender, so central to human identity and relationality. Some have argued that images for God must be gendered in order to be personal and relational, because gender is such a fundamental aspect of human identity.[14] This argument does not, however, give adequate importance to the full range of human relationships and experiences, including those which transcend gender stereotypes. Once again, diversity is helpful: Removing all gendered language for God in worship limits the range of relational imagery; yet nongendered relational images such as Friend or Comforter also have a role to play in portraying how God relates to the world.

At the opposite end of the spectrum from relational language about God is language that portrays God as impassive, unmoved by human joy and sorrow, uninvolved in human life. By contrast, expressing a fully trinitarian faith in worship means showing God as involved in and affected by human life and struggle.

Language used to speak of the Trinity should reflect love, justice, and equality, which are the marks of ethical life based in trinitarian faith. This means that the language and images of Christian worship should not reflect a patriarchal culture of domination of women by men, which is suggested when God is always associated with masculine images such as "Father" and "Lord." Nor should it reflect racist culture by constantly portraying God as light and never dark. Fully trinitarian liturgical language is emancipatory, showing the Holy One at work bringing justice and communion among humanity in the continuing mission of Jesus the Christ through the power of the Spirit.

Biblical theologian Gerard S. Sloyan argues that more frequent repetition of trinitarian doxologies addressed to the Father through the Son in the communion of the Holy Spirit to close prayers and sung parts of the liturgy (with "no misconceived substitutes") would help the church recover trinitarian faith.[15] Liturgical tradition has focused on a formula naming God "Father, Son, and Holy Spirit" as the one way to speak about trinitarian reality. Constantly using this formula results in an imbalance of masculine language; moreover, it risks rote repetition of words that no longer inspire us toward growth in understanding or faith. Although, for reasons I will outline below, "Source, Word, and Spirit" is a good alternative when a short phrase is needed, compact formulas are not always the best way to express trinitarian praise. Constantly using the same short phrase reinforces the idea that the Trinity is a logical puzzle or a mathematical formula, not a loving and multifaceted reality to which we witness. By contrast, the triune God is the mystery of salvation—worthy of overflowing praise using varied images with poetic power that stretch to put into words the breadth and length and height and depth of the love of Christ that surpasses knowledge (Eph. 3:18–19). Let us turn, then, to some images that might be used in intentionally trinitarian and inclusive worship.

I AM: THE NAME BEYOND NAMES

Some persons claim that the phrase "Father, Son, and Holy Spirit" represents the revealed name of God and resist any other ways of speaking about the Trinity.[16] Actually, the biblical passage that claims most directly to reveal God's name is Exodus 3, in which Moses meets God in a burning bush. Moses asks to know the name of this God who is sending him to lead the Hebrew slaves out of bondage. God replies to Moses: "I AM WHO I AM. . . . Thus you shall say to the Israelites, 'YHWH, the God of your ancestors, . . . has sent me to you.' This is my name forever, and this is my title for all generations" (Ex. 3:14–15). YHWH, the divine name, is probably a form of the verb meaning "to be." Thus, "I AM WHO I AM," which might better be translated "I WILL BE WHAT I WILL BE,"[17] is a word play on YHWH. When the Jewish people came to believe that YHWH was too sacred to pronounce, a word that we translate as "Lord" in English was often used in its place; Christian translations of scripture have continued this practice. Other translations such as "the Eternal One" or "the Living God" are closer in meaning to the original, if biblical scholars are correct that YHWH grows out of the verb "to be." "Holy One" also points to the sacredness of God's name.[18]

Drawing on this linguistic background, Gail Ramshaw suggests that "the Living One" could be used to translate the name of God in worship, and that it would also be appropriate as a title for the risen Christ.[19] In this way, the church could mirror the practice of using "LORD" to speak both of God the Source and of Jesus. We could build on Ramshaw's proposal to praise the triune God:

> Praise the living One!
> Praise the risen Christ who lives among us forever!
> Praise the Spirit, the Giver of Life!

These are a few possibilities for trinitarian language in worship which the name God revealed to Moses suggests.

NAMING GOD "FATHER" OR "MOTHER"

Finding alternative language for "Father" is essential yet perplexing. For one thing, few metaphors other than "Father" have been used in Christian worship specifically to refer to the first person of the Trinity. God's self-revelation in Jesus Christ has inspired many metaphors, including many gender-neutral metaphors and some feminine ones. It is relatively easy to find scripturally based gender-neutral or balanced language for "Spirit," since it is a feminine word in Hebrew and a gender-neutral word in Greek and English (though masculine pronouns are often used to refer to "Spirit"). The Spirit has inspired many natural metaphors such as "breath" and "wind," though it is also good to seek language that portrays the Spirit as personal. But finding alternatives to use along with "Father," for reasons of gender balance and metaphoric richness, poses a far greater challenge.

"Parent" is an abstract category, not a name children speak to their mothers or fathers. Therefore, "Mother" would appear to be the most natural complement to "Father" language for God. Biblical scholar Johanna van Wijk-Bos demonstrates that the Hebrew Bible offers diverse maternal imagery for God, especially when translated without sexist bias.[20] God gives birth (Isa. 42:14 and Deut. 32:18) and writhes in labor (Ps. 90:2). Moses calls God to account for the hunger and thirst of the Hebrews in the wilderness by implying that not he but God has given birth to this unruly people

(Num. 11:11–12.) God never forgets her children, though human mothers may (Isa. 49:14–17). Yet though she comforts her children (Isa. 66:13), she also encourages them to full adulthood, rather than keeping them dependent.

The image of God as eagle (found n Ex. 19:3–6 and Deut. 32:10–13) shows how maternal and paternal imagery can complement each other, for as van Wijk-Bos writes:

> The comparison of God to the eagle is parental in nature, rather than maternal or paternal. Both mother and father eagle teach the young birds to fly. They do so by rousing the nest, by flapping their wings and stirring the young ones to flight. When the young birds are in the air, the parents fly under them, showing by example and at the same time ready to catch and carry the young ones when they fall.[21]

Deuteronomy 32:13 also speaks of God "suckling" the people with honey and oil, providing another feminine image for God. Surely if scripture can speak of God as an eagle or other animal (lion, lamb, or mother bear), as well as comparing God to human mothers, using "Mother" in trinitarian language is possible. It could legitimately be argued that in the Hebrew Bible maternal images for God are about as frequent as paternal images, which appear only fifteen times, according to New Testament scholar Joachim Jeremias.[22]

Despite evidence from scripture, many arguments have been advanced to oppose the idea of complementing the language of Father with that of Mother. For example, some charge that praying to Mother God brings sexuality into the divine life where it did not exist before — an argument only possible through the androcentric belief that women (mothers) represent sexuality whereas men (fathers) do not.[23]

Some call "Father" a revealed metaphor and argue that maternal language for God in scripture is simile, not analogy or metaphor.[24] A close look at the texts using feminine language about God shows, however, that they often function metaphorically. If Isaiah 66:13 speaks in simile ("as a mother comforts a child, I will comfort you"), Deuteronomy 32:18 is metaphor ("you forgot the God who writhed in labor with you").[25]

While most of these arguments are so weakly based as to reveal the misogyny of their proponents, some legitimate cautions arise from the critique of maternal imagery for God. First, the image of Mother should be used with sensitivity to cultural stereotypes about mothers. "Father" and "Mother" do not connote the same things in patriarchal culture. There is a tendency to use maternal imagery to speak of God's nurturing love, but not of God's great power to liberate the oppressed and guide the public life of humanity. In order to honor God and to honor woman as image of God, maternal imagery should be used in ways that balance divine immanence with divine power. Also, the experience of dependence on God as a parent should be balanced with the sense that God encourages us to grow toward maturity and shared responsibility.

"Mother" is one good way of speaking about the first person of the Trinity, but it should not be the only way, since people have varied experiences of their mothers. For one person, calling God "Mother" may encourage a close and loving relationship with God; for another, it may evoke painful associations of a troubled relationship. Moreover, when used constantly, "Mother," like "Father," tends to imply subordination of the "Son" or "Child" and to discourage Christian maturity. Overusing any particular metaphor implies that it is literal truth, not a limited human way of understanding God. Used carefully, along with other metaphors, "Mother" can provide a good alternative or complement to addressing God as Father.

PERICHORESIS: THE DIVINE DANCE OF LOVE

The Greek term *perichoresis* ("cyclical movement," "recurrence," "reciprocity," "encompassing"), made common in trinitarian theology by the eighth-century theologian John of Damascus, suggests an image to describe the mutual indwelling or coinherence of the persons of the Trinity.[26] John wrote:

> [The Father, the Son, and the Holy Spirit] are made one not so as to commingle but so as to cleave to each other without any coalescence or commingling. For the Deity is undivided amongst things divided. . . . it is just like three suns cleaving to each other without separation and giving out light mingled and conjoined into one.[27]

Perichoresis describes the unity of the inner life of God, in which the three persons of the Trinity intermingle in a ceaseless flowing of love and shared life that opens out toward creation. In an economic trinitarian theology, it also describes the communion of God with humanity and all creatures.[28]

This communion of sharing divine life has been compared to a dance; though the Greek word *perichoreuo* ("dance round") does not share etymological roots with *perichoresis*, it provides an apt metaphor for shared life.[29] Dancing together implies mutuality. Dancing partners move together;

the movements of one influence those of another. Dancing together implies unity, as the movements of all contribute to the pattern that is the dance. Yet the individuality of dancers is not absorbed into the whole; instead, the distinct movements of each contributes to the whole.

The concept of *perichoresis*—envisioned through the metaphor of dance—holds possibilities for praising the triune unity. The concept of dancing together provides a way of portraying the distinctiveness and unity of persons of the Trinity, as well as depicting an open Trinity that invites all creation to join the dance. Brian Wren uses the metaphor as follows:

> How wonderful the Three-in-One,
> whose energies of dancing light
> are undivided, pure and good,
> communing love in shared delight.[30]

And, in a different hymn:

> God is One, unique and holy,
> endless dance of love and light.[31]

If extended to portray God's invitation for all to join the dance, dance could be a very helpful image of the Trinity.

SOURCE, WORD, AND SPIRIT

When a short phrase is needed to praise God as Trinity, the images "Source," "Word," and "Spirit" have much to commend them.

Karl Rahner has written of God the Father: "This unoriginate God is experienced as <u>Father of the Son</u>, as 'generating principle,' as source, origin, and principle of the whole Godhead."[32] Leonardo Boff calls the paternal/maternal God "the Origin and Goal of All Liberation" and notes that official Roman Catholic documents speak of the Father as "the originated origin" and the "source and origin of all divinity."[33] In interpreting God as unoriginate source, Elizabeth Johnson speaks of the Mother as "primordial upwelling of the power of being and divine acts of giving life, sustaining it, encouraging it to grow."[34] "Source" is the one word in everyday speech that comes closest to expressing the same meaning as technical words such as "generating principle," "unoriginate origin," or "primordial upwelling." Further, "Source" can apply to generation, procession, and creation, so that it appropriately refers both to relation of Father/Mother to Word and Spirit, and (by appropriation) to the relation of Father/Mother to creation.

"Son" is useful as a name for the second trinitarian partner mainly when used in conjunction with a parental metaphor for the first, for the Son is "Son of the Father" or "Son of the Mother."[35] Theologians often acknowledge that describing the relationship between two partners of the Trinity as father and son tends to undermine the sense of equality among the partners (in patriarchal society at least). Coequality may be further undermined by replacing "Son" with "Child" in order to avoid gendered language. "Daughter" will rarely suffice as a term equivalent to "Son" in trinitarian language for worship, since the Word was historically incarnate in the male Jesus. For these reasons, "Son" cannot as easily be replaced by equivalents as close as "Mother" or "Source" are to "Father."

In many liturgical contexts, references to Jesus the Christ or the risen Christ are adequate to speak of the second partner of the Trinity, as our reflection on the divine name (YHWH) has shown. The naming "Jesus the Christ" is grounded in the story of God with us in Jesus (whose name means "God saves") as Christ (anointed one) to the people of earth. It serves less to complement or replace the formula "Father, Son, and Holy Spirit," which has been seen as referring especially to the inner life of God. Alternative formulas would best be capable of referring both to the relationship between divine partners and to the relationship between each person of the Trinity and creation. For that reason, "Word" presents itself as a helpful alternative. The Word made flesh in Jesus is both the self-communication of the Father and the "Word made flesh who lived among us"—the Word to us and for us.

"Word" is a familiar name for the incarnate one, because of the frequent liturgical use of John 1: "And the Word became flesh and lived among us" (v. 14). Metaphorically, it points to the self-communication of God to humanity, as well as reflecting the Hebrew tradition's emphasis on the written and spoken word. As humans, we reveal ourselves through our words and the way they interrelate with our embodied actions. In the same way, the words and actions of Jesus communicated the very self of God.

Although scripture and liturgy have used many names to refer to the second partner of the Trinity, "Word" is perhaps the best term for a short formula. It refers both to the relationship of partners of the Trinity and to the divine-human relationship. It points to the revelation of God as incarnate one, which is the most distinctive way the second person may be described.

It is familiar and has metaphorical resonance through its meaning in everyday speech as a means of self-revelation and growing relationship.

As noted above, "Spirit" does not present problems when seeking gender-inclusive alternatives to the trinitarian formula. In fact, as Elizabeth Johnson has noted, the experience of women in the church is closely tied with the work of the liberating Spirit breaking through established structures and worldviews.[36] On the other hand, it would not be helpful to identify Spirit as the "feminine" partner of the Trinity, while retaining masculine language for the other two, given the church's tendency to neglect and fear the work of the Spirit.

Few alternatives for a short formula using both masculine and feminine language appear to have promise for use in worship. Such alternatives as "Mother and son," "Father and daughter," "Source, Son, and Womanspirit" seem labored, calling attention to the attempt to balance genders rather than pointing beyond themselves to the triune God. At this point in history, churches are only slowly gaining comfort in calling God both "Mother" and "Father." For the time being, it seems more helpful to develop masculine and feminine images at greater length than to put them together in phrases that begin and end as quickly as a flash of lightning.

No human words, and certainly no short formula, adequately speaks the mystery of God, but "Source, Word, and Spirit" provides a good alternative when striving for economy of words.

OBJECTIVE IMAGERY

Metaphors based on human relationships are not the only way to speak of the relationality of God. Metaphors for God based on human relations (e.g., "Father," "Mother," "Friend") tend to be taken literally without regard for the limits of metaphorical language. Human relationships with family members, lovers, and friends can, at best, be our experiences closest to relationship with the triune God. Yet relationship with God goes beyond any of these human experiences, for God is not human. Gail Ramshaw has argued that "objective metaphors"—images from the world of nature or inorganic matter— have the advantage of avoiding anthropomorphism and literalism:

> In turning from anthropomorphic to objective metaphors for God, we discover that the greatest danger no longer threatens: although calling God a judge suggests to many people that God is literally a judge, and

although some people take comfort in imaging God to be like humans, no one in calling God a dove confuses the deity with a bird. When God is called after an object, the metaphor tends to remain a metaphor.[37]

In particular, metaphors from nature can reveal something about relationship with God. Jesus says in the Gospel of John, "I am the vine, you are the branches. Those who abide in me and I in them bear much fruit, because apart from me you can do nothing" (John 15:5). This organic metaphor pictures the living union between Jesus Christ and those who find the source of their life in Christ. The gospel of John, in particular, uses many objective and nonhuman natural metaphors: Jesus is living water, living bread, light, and lamb of God.

"Fount" or "fountain of life" (Ps. 36:9) is, in particular, a helpful metaphor for God as Source, since it is similar in meaning, yet holds richer potential as metaphor. It could be used in conjunction with the metaphor of the Word as giver of living water, and the Spirit as wellspring of new life.

Here again, the context of a particular worship service and its scriptural texts could suggest possibilities. For example, Ephesians 2:11–22 pictures Christ as cornerstone of the church built in the Spirit as a dwelling place for God; the image of Christ as cornerstone could be central in worship focusing on that text. The image of fire, suggesting the passionate and risky nature of life lived with God, could be explored when using texts in which Luke presents Jesus as bringer of fire (Luke 3:16; Luke 24:32) or the Spirit as flame (Acts 2:3). Objective metaphors usually serve best when they are intentionally developed based on the texts and themes of the day.

Reflection on the value of objective metaphors demonstrates how diverse images can point the triune reality and enhance Christian worship's witness to trinitarian life.

FUNCTIONAL LANGUAGE

"God" is a verb, some theologians have proclaimed, pointing to the dynamic, active nature of God as well as to the observation that we know the activity of God toward us, though we do not have cognitive access to the inner being of God.[38] Since trinitarian language in worship focuses on the economy of salvation, then the church might appropriately use verbs, or nouns such as Creator, Redeemer, Sustainer based on verbs, to speak about the Trinity. Indeed, praise for what God has done, is doing, will do is central to Christian worship.

For good reason, however, such theologians as Geoffrey Wainwright express reservations about accepting functional language (language based on verbs describing what God does) as an alternative for traditional trinitarian language.[39] The problem with describing the persons in terms of actions is that trinitarian theology since Augustine generally affirms that all actions of the Trinity (except those in the inner life of God) are done in concert. This safeguards the belief that the Trinity is one God. Since scripture attributes specific actions to God as Source, Word, or Spirit, however, the "doctrine of appropriations" became necessary. By that teaching, certain actions were "appropriated" as particular to one person of the Trinity, while recognizing that the whole Trinity participates in the work of creating, redeeming, and sustaining.

LaCugna noted that the doctrine of appropriations only became necessary when trinitarian theology focused narrowly on the inner life of God rather than on the economy of salvation, that is, the saving life of God with us. In the economy, each divine partner has a distinct mission; the shared life of the Trinity follows a triune pattern (so that unity need not obliterate distinction):

> The mission of the Son to become incarnate belongs properly to the Son as Son. The Spirit is the one sent to make the creature holy. The Father's role in sending the Son and the Spirit belongs to the Father alone. . . . A theology centered on the economy . . . affirms that God (Father) creates, redeems, and divinizes through the Son and by the power of the Holy Spirit.[40]

Her convincing argument suggests that using verbs to speak of the Trinity should be acceptable, if grounded in scripture and the life of God with us. Practically speaking, that would mean using verbs (or words based on verbs) that grow out of the text for the day, rather than always using the same words ("Creator, Redeemer, Sustainer") as abstracted from the story of God with us. Otherwise, functional language will tend toward abstraction, rather than presenting the triune God who acts in myriad ways to seek us in holy love.

Using context-sensitive verbs to describe the nature and work of the trinitarian partners also helps to address the charge of modalism. Constant use of terms such as "Creator, Sustainer, and Redeemer" tends to identify the persons of the Trinity narrowly with particular actions, as if the other persons do not participate or as if the nature of a trinitarian partner could be reduced to a specific action. Using diverse words that grow out of scripture texts and liturgical contexts can provide vivid language that avoids modalism and more adequately witnesses to the inexhaustible, mysterious reality of God.[41]

THE WORD "GOD": A CHALLENGE

At times, it is difficult to discern whether a term refers to the whole Trinity or to the first person of the Trinity; this is especially true of the very name "God." The triad "God, Christ, and Spirit" often appears in hymns and doxologies. Such use of "God" to represent the first person depends on traditions naming first Father, then Son, then Spirit, as well as on the time-honored practice of addressing prayer to the Father through the Son in the Spirit. Thus, in Latin collects one could infer that *Deus* referred to the first person of the Trinity because of the ending, "through Jesus Christ who reigns with you and the Holy Spirit." Today, as worship leaders sometimes change the sequence of persons or address prayer to Christ or Spirit directly, order and direct address are not always enough to clarify what "God" means. Further, "God" is used culturally, and in unitarian and non-Christian religions, as a name for the divine. Given all this, how can one distinguish between "God-in-general," the triune God as a unity, and the first person of the Trinity? Context can help. For example, a prayer spoken to "God who takes on human flesh" addresses the Word, to whom the incarnation is particular. On the other hand, the whole Trinity participates in creating, redeeming, and sustaining. Can we necessarily assume that "Creator" always refers to the first person of the Trinity?

While working on this chapter, I had a dream that lifted up another aspect of this dilemma. I dreamed I was in an ancient city with classical architecture like that which I have seen in Ephesus. I was visiting what had been a church complex. Part of it had been turned into a military museum. This disgusted my dreaming self, and it seemed on waking to symbolize the patriarchal and military captivity of the church. But what fascinated me most was a synagogue, more ancient than the church, embedded in the church complex. In the dream I kept trying to find a good position from which to photograph the synagogue, but I never could get a clear view from a great enough distance to take a picture of the whole. This dream points to another challenge about naming the first person of the Trinity: While Christianity is truly a new religion, Judaism is embedded in its very heart. Thus,

Christians claim to be monotheists and honor the Hebrew Bible as sacred scripture, even as they worship God as triune. At times, Christians find in the Hebrew Bible references to Christ or Spirit, while probably assuming in most cases that talk of God refers to the first person of the Trinity.

Long-standing tradition such as the Latin collects, as well as the use of Hebrew scripture in worship, probably means that Christians will continue to speak of both the whole Trinity and the first partner of the Trinity by the one word "God," yet it would be unfortunate to intensify the problem in the attempt to avoid overusing the name "Father." Particularly when worship focuses on the three partners of the Trinity, leaders should seek creative alternatives to naming only the first partner "God." For example, for the sake of inclusiveness, we might think of changing the trinitarian formula to "in the name of God and of the Child and of the Holy Spirit." But it would be better to use a formula such as "in the name of God the Source, Word, and Spirit" or "in the name of Source, Word, and Spirit, one triune God," so that "God" is used once to refer to the whole Trinity. Another possibility is "in the name of God the Father and Mother, and of Jesus Christ, God incarnate, and of the Spirit, God ever-present," so that "God" is used of each partner of the Trinity. Such approaches to developing inclusive alternatives to traditional language will support worship that is fully trinitarian.

OTHER POSSIBLE LANGUAGE
FOR THE TRINITY

Language witnesses to the height and depth and breadth and width of the love of God that cannot be bounded by human limits. No list could exhaust possible ways of praying to the triune God, though all ways should be subject to reason and critique in order to do the best we can. The language of Holy Wisdom is another way of praying to the Trinity; this is explored in a separate chapter, in order to give adequate attention to historical backgrounds and contemporary controversies. There are many more ways mystics, poets, and ordinary church folk have spoken to and about the triune God through the centuries.

To demonstrate the diverse possibilities for trinitarian language and to conclude this chapter, I turn to the Christian poets and hymn text writers from Wesley and Watts to modern writers such as Brian Wren, the British

Reformed writer described above, and Jean Janzen, a poet who draws on the writings of Christian mystics such as Julian of Norwich and Hildegard of Bingen. The following phrases stand out for me for their creativity and diversity of expression.

Some names for God as source and origin (Father) are:

> "Great God of all the ages" ("Come, Great God of All the Ages," Mary Jackson Cathey)
>
> "Only source of mind and body, star-cloud, atom, day or night" ("God Is One, Unique and Holy," Brian Wren)
>
> "God of love and mother-earth" ("God of Eve and God of Mary," Fred Kaan)
>
> "Eternal Light" ("Eternal Light, Shine in My Heart," Alcuin, para. Christopher Idle)
>
> [Our creator] "who dwells amidst the dazzling light of vast eternity" ("How Wondrous Great," Isaac Watts)
>
> "Mothering God" ("Mothering God, You Gave Me Birth," Jean Janzen, based on Julian)
>
> "Womb and birth of time" ("God of Many Names," Brian Wren)
>
> "Root of life" ("O Holy Spirit, Root of Life," Jean Janzen, 1991, from Hildegard of Bingen)
>
> "Great womb of wondrous love" ("O God, Great Womb of Wondrous Love," Harris J. Loewen)

Some names for Jesus Christ, Word of God, are:

> "Lamb of God . . . Incarnate Word . . . Savior" ("Behold, the Lamb of God," Matthew Bridges)
>
> "Sure foundation . . . head . . . cornerstone" ("Christ Is Made the Sure Foundation," seventh-century Latin hymn)
>
> "Christ our brother, human Son" ("God of Eve and God of Mary")[42]
>
> "Eternal Life . . . Eternal Brightness" ("Eternal Light, Shine in My Heart")
>
> "Mothering Christ, you took my form" ("Mothering God, You Gave Me Birth")

"Eternal Vigor, Saving One" ("O Holy Spirit, Root of Life")
"Rabbi of the poor" ("God of Many Names")

Some names for God as Spirit include:

"Creator Spirit, . . . the well of life, the fire of love" ("Come, O Creator Spirit, Come," medieval Latin, trans. Robert S. Bridges)

"Spirit of power" ("Come, Thou Almighty King," anonymous)

"Spirit, caring like a Mother" ("God of Eve and God of Mary")

"Holy Wisdom, Moving Force" ("O Holy Spirit, Root of Life")

"Life-giving Spirit, Comforter most gracious" ("Father, Most Holy, Merciful, and Loving," tenth-century hymn)

"O Holy Spirit, . . . rushing wind of heaven" ("O Mighty God," Erik Routley)

"Mothering Spirit, nurt'ring one" ("Mothering God, You Gave Me Birth")

"Hearth . . . heartbeat . . . dark light dance ("O God, Great Womb of Wondrous Love")

"Sacred energy" ("Maker, in Whom We Live," Charles Wesley)

Some phrases in hymns that describe the Trinity as a unity are:

"Three in a wondrous unity unbroken" ("Father, Most Holy, Merciful, and Loving")

"Blest Trinity, life's source and spring" ("The Royal Banners Forward Go," Venantius Fortunatus)

Or in the simple words of Wesley: "Eternal Triune God" ("Maker, in Whom We Live"). This illustrates the many metaphors that may speak of the triune God. Some are better than others; their diversity reveals how varying our metaphors about the Trinity could help us grow in our understanding and praise of God. In all this, we seek the living language of faith. We are praising a God who eternally seeks us in love!

We praise God as Trinity, simply because the Source of life comes to us in Jesus Christ and seeks through the Spirit to draw us into communion with God's self, all people, and all creation. Love is the mystery at the heart of creation. The only appropriate way for us to respond is in praise and in the offering of our very selves in love. And then, when we need to find words for this wondrous, all-encompassing relationship of pure unbounded love, we must apply heart, soul, and imagination to the task. "Father, Son, and Holy Spirit" is only one way of putting the mystery into words. Current and future generations face the task of finding additional words to praise the triune God, not only to avoid the pitfalls of exclusively masculine language but also to recover worship of the Trinity as the vital center of life and faith!

3

The Trinity in *Sunday Worship*

In chapter 2, I approached the task of renewing trinitarian worship by exploring varied and vibrant ways of praising the Trinity. This chapter points to opportunities to enhance trinitarian language and symbolism through specific parts of worship such as creeds and doxologies and liturgies of baptism, Eucharist, and healing, as well as through the way we celebrate the church year.

PARTS OF WORSHIP

Creeds

One dictionary defines "creed" as "a concise, accepted, and approved statement of the central beliefs held by an individual or community."[1] Most people probably think first of creeds when they consider how trinitarian faith is expressed in worship. Most Christian churches have affirmed faith in the Trinity, or "Father, Son, and Spirit," as a central belief. The earliest type of creed or affirmation of faith in Christian worship was used during baptism; indeed, the Apostles' Creed is based on three questions used in early Roman baptisms. Christians began using a creed as a regular part of worship in Antioch in 473 and in Toledo in 589, as a way of presenting those churches' positions in contemporary christological and trinitarian controversies. Rome and most of the Western church adopted liturgical use of a creed (the Nicene Creed) only in 1014, placing it following the reading of scripture and proclamation of the word.[2]

Ben Herbster, the first president of the United Church of Christ, said at UCC General Assembly in 1968, "We do not use theological doctrine as a test of faith, but as a testimony to our faith."[3] Creeds that best serve worship are testimonies; they seek to express the faith of the churches in a concise yet comprehensive way, in a mode of thanksgiving and praise. Creeds that focus on making academic distinctions, especially about the immanent Trinity, speak the language of secondary theological reflection and not the primary language of worship. Liturgical Theologian Michael Downey has written: "The Christian creed is at once a doxology that acclaims the glory of God, and a confession of praise and thanksgiving for what God has done in Christ Jesus."[4] As such, the creed should be expressed primarily in the language of praise and thanksgiving.

The pseudo-Athanasian creed, which some churches still use, exemplifies wording that reflects academic theology more than praise. Consider the language of this creed, given here only in part:

> We worship one God in Trinity and Trinity in Unity, neither confounding the Persons, nor dividing the Substance. For there is one person of the Father, another of the Son, another of the Holy Spirit; but the Godhead of the Father and of the Son and of the Holy Spirit is all one, the Glory equal, the Majesty coeternal. Such as the Father is, such is the Son, and such is the Holy Spirit. The Father uncreate, the Son uncreate, and the Holy Spirit uncreate. The Father incomprehensible, the Son incomprehensible, and the Holy Spirit incomprehensible. The Father eternal, the Son eternal, and the Holy Spirit eternal. And yet they are not three eternals but one eternal. As also there are not three incomprehensibles, nor three uncreated, but one uncreated, and one incomprehensible. So likewise the Father is Almighty, the Son Almighty, and the Holy Spirit Almighty. Yet there are not three Almighties, but one Almighty.[5]

This creed very carefully delineates trinitarian faith, yet it is not particularly appropriate for worship. What it gains in precision, it loses in the ability to inspire love and praise. The language is abstract, repetitive, and often multisyllabic. Yet translating "incomprehensible" or "coequal" into simpler terms would not yet yield appropriate doxological language. This creed focuses almost entirely on the inner life of God, with little attention to the way God is revealed in the economy of salvation.

By contrast, the Statement of Faith of the United Church of Canada (given here in its entirety) uses simple, poetic, gender-neutral language to speak of God's revelation among humanity as well as the believer's relationship with God:

We are not alone, we live in God's world.
We believe in God:
    who has created and is creating,
    who has come in Jesus, the Word made flesh,
        to reconcile and make new,
    who works in us and others by the Spirit.
We trust in God.
We are called to be the church:
    to celebrate God's presence,
    to live with respect to Creation,
    to love and serve others,
    to seek justice and resist evil,
    to proclaim Jesus, crucified and risen,
        our judge and our hope.
In life, in death, in life beyond death,
    God is with us.
We are not alone.
Thanks be to God. Amen.

While not particularly rich in metaphoric language, this statement of faith expresses trust in and thanks to God as one who is forever present. It is trinitarian in that it speaks of God as known as Source, Word, and Spirit and emphasizes the trinitarian lifestyle of love, justice, and concern for all people. It is a testimony of faith spoken with thanksgiving to God, whereas the pseudo-Athanasian creed is a test of faith spoken to one another in hopes of fostering correct belief.

Late Anglican Dean of York and scholar Alan Richardson has pointed out that in addition to baptismal affirmations and spoken creeds, the creedal hymn provides a third way to confess Christian faith.[6] The hymn to Christ in Philippians 2:6–11, which many New Testament scholars believe to be a liturgical hymn quoted by Paul, is an early example. Like creeds, hymns have sometimes been used to promote particular positions in theological controversies, but they also provide possibilities for affirming trinitarian faith in a doxological way. The role of hymns in expressing trinitarian faith is so important that it is explored in a separate chapter (chapter 5).

Affirmations of faith are important in worship to express the identity and beliefs of the worshiping community. The more these affirmations are expressed in the language of praise, the more they will nurture trinitarian faith.

Doxologies

Another common place for trinitarian language in worship is in doxologies. Doxologies are words of praise to God, usually with trinitarian content and structure. They play an important part in worship, as a way of focusing on the triune God as the center of worship. Doxologies are typically rather brief; they may serve to punctuate worship with a sense of reverent joy. As we shall see, most eucharistic prayers end with trinitarian doxologies, as do collects; Christian prayer characteristically begins and ends with words of praise to God. Hymns and responsorial psalms frequently end with doxologies.

For many Protestants, "doxology" brings to mind the following short metrical act of praise, penned by Thomas Ken in 1674 as the last stanza of two hymns, and usually sung to the tune called OLD HUNDREDTH[7]:

> Praise God, from whom all blessings flow.
> Praise him, all creatures here below.
> Praise him above, ye heavenly host,
> Praise Father, Son, and Holy Ghost.

In Roman Catholic tradition, however, the doxology is what many Protestants call the Gloria Patri:

> Glory be to the Father, and to the Son, and to the Holy Spirit;
> as it was in the beginning, is now and ever shall be, world without end.
> Amen.

In Eastern liturgies, the ending is "both now, and for ever, and world without end. Amen."[8] This doxology is also known as the "lesser doxology," in contrast to the Gloria in Excelsis, or the "greater doxology"[9]:

> Glory to God in the highest,
> and peace to God's people on earth.
>
> Lord God, heavenly King,
> almighty God and Father,
>   we worship you, we give you thanks,
>   we praise you for your glory.
>
> Lord Jesus Christ, only Son of the Father,
> Lord God, Lamb of God,
> you take away the sin of the world:
>   have mercy on us;

you are seated at the right hand of the Father:
   receive our prayer.

For you alone are the Holy One,
you alone are the Lord,
you alone are the Most High,
   Jesus Christ,
   with the Holy Spirit,
   in the glory of God the Father. Amen.[10]

The Gloria in Excelsis, even more than the other doxologies quoted so far, uses much masculine language for God. Furthermore, as an act of trinitarian praise, it attends very little to the Spirit. Yet it demonstrates the nature of a doxology: an act of praise glorifying God in exalted language centered on God and not the worshiper.

Doxologies tend to take on characteristic forms within liturgical traditions and local congregations. At times the wording of doxologies has incited controversy. One season of controversy was in the fourth century. At that time, the following form of doxology had been prevalent: "Glory to the Father *through* [in Greek, *dia*] the Son *in* [*en*] the Holy Spirit."[11] Arians claimed that the words "through the Son" indicated that the Son was a mediator subordinate to the Father; the Nicene party denied this. A few years later, those who denied the divinity of the Holy Spirit contested a wording of the doxology that Bishop Basil of Caesarea used in addition to the more common form.[12] They rejected his wording, "Glory to the Father *and* [or with; Greek, *meta*] to the Son *and* [or together with; Greek, *syn*] to the Holy Spirit," because it implied the coequality of Father, Son, and Spirit (which Basil affirmed and they denied). In his work *Of the Holy Spirit*, Basil shows that scripture uses these prepositions interchangeably of Father, Son, and Spirit and argues that either wording can give equal glory to the three persons.[13] After the Council of Constantinople affirmed the divinity of the Holy Spirit in 381, the "and/and" form became customary in the Eastern churches, while both wordings were used in the West. It could be argued that "in Christ through the Spirit" is at least as appropriate. Those who live in Christ participate in divine reality through the agency of the Spirit.[14]

Many local congregations today are seeking alternative language for doxologies, because of concern about using the masculine metaphors "Father" and "Son" when unbalanced by other metaphors. Some congregations sing different versions of the doxology in different seasons of the church year; content may reflect the season and the traditional wording may be sung during one season.[15] The Carmelite Monastery of Indianapolis uses this doxology in its services of morning and evening prayer: "Glory to you, Source of Being, Eternal Word, and Holy Spirit. As it was in the beginning, is now and ever shall be, world without end. Amen."[16] The United Church of Christ offers a version of the Gloria in Excelsis in its *Book of Worship* that is mostly gender-neutral, although it uses "Lord" to refer to Jesus Christ:

> Glory to God in the highest, and peace to God's people on earth.
> Holy One, heavenly God, sovereign God and Creator,
> we worship you, we give you thanks, we praise you for your glory.
> Lord Jesus Christ, God's only begotten one,
> Lord God, Lamb of God, you take away the sin of the world:
> have mercy on us; you are seated at the right hand of Majesty:
> receive our prayer.
> For you alone are the Messiah, you alone are the Lord,
> you are alone the Most High, Jesus Christ,
> with the Holy Spirit, in the glory of the triune God.[17]

This version raises questions: Was it necessary to undermine the trinitarian structure of the closing by leaving out reference to the first partner of the Trinity? Why was "Holy One" changed to "Messiah"? Was it because "Holy One" is so often the name addressed to the first person of the Trinity elsewhere in the book? Why delete "Father" and retain "Lord"? Still, this is a worshipful rewording of the Gloria in Excelsis that deserves consideration as an act of praise.

Alternative doxologies do not usually raise as much controversy today as they did in Basil's time, possibly because congregations have welcomed fresh language in this repeated part of worship or because doxologies do not evoke as much feeling as do such parts of worship as hymns. It seems relatively easy to change the pronouns: "Praise God from whom all blessings flow; praise *God,* all creatures here below." The following version from *The Presbyterian Hymnal* has been welcomed by many in that denomination and beyond: "Praise God from whom all blessings flow; praise Christ, all people here below; praise Holy Spirit evermore; praise triune God whom we adore."[18] One drawback to this form is that it appropriates the name "God" to the first person of the Trinity and to the triune God, but not to Christ and Spirit. This is a common worship practice, but carrying it further in the attempt to be inclusive might create confusion.

The purpose of doxologies is to give exalted praise to the triune God. Constantly using masculine language without also using feminine language reflects patriarchal social patterns, and thus is not adequate to praise. In response, churches in North America are using a great variety of alternatives. The best alternatives will name each person of the Trinity in ways that speak of the relationship of the Trinity to the life of the world, as well as relationship within the Trinity. They will lift up the unity of the Trinity. They will reflect the coequality of the trinitarian partners, attempting to attend to each in a balanced way. They will be poetic, accessible, and capable of expressing the faith of the congregation, so that they will truly be words of glory!

Beginnings and Endings

Christians often begin and end worship by witnessing to trinitarian faith. The first words spoken in worship are often, "In the name of the Father and of the Son and of the Holy Spirit" or "The grace of Jesus Christ, the love of God, and the communion of the Holy Spirit be with you all." Prayers or responsive calls to worship early in the service appropriately affirm that worship is in and through the triune God. The final blessing is often trinitarian. It is quite appropriate to begin and end by giving praise and honor to the triune God who has called us together to worship. The following benediction demonstrates the possibility of using non-gendered language for the Trinity:

> The blessing of God, fount of creation,
> the blessing of Jesus Christ, living one,
> the blessing of the Spirit, sacred breath of life,
> be and abide with us all. Amen.[19]

Often, a trinitarian blessing can grow out of images in the day's scripture texts and echo the preached word. The closing words of worship should characteristically express trinitarian faith, which, if genuine, must be lived in the world.

Preaching

Christian preaching proclaims the gospel of Jesus Christ in the power of the Spirit, to fulfill the purpose of God the Source to unite all things. Thus, by its very nature, preaching is trinitarian, and it also can be a means of interpreting trinitarian faith to a congregation. A separate chapter will address trinitarian faith and preaching, because of the importance of preaching in renewing trinitarian faith within the church.

TRINITARIAN LANGUAGE
AND SACRAMENTAL WORSHIP

Contemporary liturgical texts for the sacraments of Baptism and Eucharist and for liturgical healing are primary places where trinitarian language and symbolism are already used. Here we call attention to positive examples that worship leaders can emulate and enhance.

Baptism

In the twentieth century, the churches are recovering a fuller theology of baptism, as exemplified by the World Council of Churches document *Baptism, Eucharist, and Ministry*. The document begins by noting that "Christian baptism is rooted in the ministry of Jesus of Nazareth, in his death and his resurrection,"[20] thus grounding baptism in the incarnation. It goes on to say that "baptism means participating in the life, death, and resurrection of Jesus Christ," and that baptism is "incorporation into the body of Christ" (p. 2). This highlights the way baptism unites us to Christ and to the church, as a participation in the divine life. The document highlights "the gift of the Spirit," another primary meaning of baptism. It says that "God bestows on all baptized persons the anointing and promise of the Holy Spirit," and calls the church "the community of the Holy Spirit" (p. 3). Less specific attention is given to God as Father or Source, but the document, with its eschatological emphasis, assumes that baptism grows out of "the healing and reconciling love of God" (p. 3) and serves to gather persons into the life and the future of God (p. 3). This understanding echoes scriptural passages about baptism, such as 1 Corinthians 12:12–13: "For just as the body is one and has many members, and all the members of the body, though many, are one body, so it is with Christ. For in the one Spirit we were all baptized into one body— Jews or Greeks, slaves or free—and we were all made to drink of one Spirit." Baptism is an act of the triune God and a sign of our participation in the life of God.

Since about the eighth century, the words spoken with the administration of baptismal water are usually, "I baptize you [or, you are baptized] in the name of the Father and of the Son and of the Holy Spirit." These words provide a summary of Christian faith with its trinitarian structure. They echo words attributed to Jesus in Matthew 28:19: "Go therefore and make disciples of all nations, baptizing them in the name of the Father and of the Son and of the Holy Spirit," though it is likely that Jesus' original words may have been "baptizing in my name."[21] Several passages in Acts and the early Christian document called the Didache ("The Teaching of the Twelve Apostles") make it appear that baptisms were also done in the name of Jesus or in the name of Christ. It appears that for the first few centuries of the church, "baptizing them in the name of the Father and of the Son and of the Holy Spirit" was more a summary of the theology of baptism than a formula always used in baptism.

It is not only possible, but also desirable, to find alternatives to the traditional formula for baptism which continue to affirm trinitarian faith. One option is to emulate the early church's practice of asking three questions, to which those presenting themselves or others for baptism respond, rather than a declaratory formula spoken only by the presider. I have suggested using the following questions and answers:

> Do you believe in God, the Source, the fountain of life?
> I believe.
>
> Do you believe in Christ, the offspring of God embodied in Jesus of
> Nazareth and in the church?
> I believe.
>
> Do you believe in the liberating Spirit of God, the wellspring of new
> life?
> I believe.[22]

These questions are meant as an example rather than an unchanging pattern. The following short formula also affirms and summarizes trinitarian faith: "I baptize you in the name of God the Source of all being, of the Eternal Word of God, and of the Holy Spirit."[23] Some churches baptize in the name of Jesus or in the name of Christ alone. This is less desirable, despite its grounding in scripture, because it does not express fully trinitarian faith. The most common alternative, "in the name of the Creator, Sustainer, and Redeemer," has been widely criticized because it relies too much on functions that are appropriated to persons of the Trinity, but which are actions of the whole Trinity. Another option, which comes from New York's Riverside Church, especially helpful for churches whose denominations mandate using the traditional formula, complements masculine language with feminine language: "I baptize you in the name of the Father and of the Son and of the Holy Spirit, one God, Mother of us all."[24]

It is best to choose one of these alternatives rather than to continue using the traditional formula without changed or complementary language. Since the words spoken at baptism express the heart of Christian theology, using masculine images for God here without complementary images implies that Christian faith centers on a masculine God, and that feminine language may be used only at less important times or in peripheral ways. Using language at baptism that is not weighted toward either masculine or feminine imagery lives out the baptismal reality to which Paul witnesses in Galatians 3:27–28: "As many of you as were baptized into Christ have clothed yourselves with Christ. There is no longer Jew or Greek, there is no longer slave or free, there is no longer male and female; for all of you are one in Christ Jesus." At the same time, those seeking other options should take care to find alternatives that express trinitarian faith as fully as possible, both in the formula and in other parts of the baptismal liturgy, such as the prayer over the water.

Another way to enhance trinitarian faith as expressed by Christian baptism is to emphasize the importance of the Holy Spirit in baptismal symbolism. Ancient tradition includes an invocation of the Holy Spirit on the newly baptized, together with laying on of hands and anointing, rituals that embody the invocation of the Spirit. Many new denominational orders restore this ancient tradition. For example, in a baptismal order in *The United Methodist Book of Worship*, immediately after water baptism the presider (and perhaps the baptizand's family) lay hands upon the baptizand with the words, "The Holy Spirit work within you, that being born through water and the Spirit, you may be a faithful disciple of Jesus Christ. Amen."[25] The rubrics continue: "The pastor may trace on the forehead of each newly baptized person the sign of the cross in silence or with the words: 'Name, [child of God], you are sealed by the Holy Spirit in baptism and marked as Christ's own forever.' Olive oil may be used in this action."[26] Anointing is an ancient symbol pointing to the work of the Spirit in baptism, though it is optional in the *Book of Worship* and missing from *The United Methodist Hymnal*.[27] These acts of invoking the Holy Spirit, laying on of hands, and (one hopes) anointing, should not, in any case, be delayed until "confirmation" at a later age. It is beyond the scope of this book to explore the contemporary discussion of confirmation, but here it is important to say that the baptismal ritual should point to the meaning of baptism as the gift of the Spirit; this should not be delayed until confirmation, as is commonly done.[28] These signs of the Spirit (invocation, laying on of hands, and anointing) can be repeated when baptismal vows are later affirmed or reaffirmed, but they are an important part of baptism in that they highlight participation in the triune reality.

Baptism is a primary liturgical moment when Christians affirm that through the action of Christ and the gift of the Spirit, they are incorporated into the very life of God's overflowing love. By words, gestures, and ritual, chosen and administered with care, Christians express the heart of their trinitarian faith when they baptize.

The Eucharist

Eucharistic prayers growing out of the liturgical renewal movement of the twentieth century follow similar patterns, regardless of denomination. Typically, the first section of the prayer addresses the first person of the Trinity, highlighting God as source and destiny of all things, who reaches out to all people in holy love. Often this section recounts God's mighty acts with the Hebrew people. Then the prayer moves into giving thanks for the incarnation of Jesus Christ and his life, ministry, death, and resurrection. Sometimes at this point, the church gives praise for the outpouring of the Spirit on the church. Then, the prayer invokes the Holy Spirit on the gifts and on the community who celebrate the Eucharist and asks for the gifts of the Spirit in the life of the church, for the sake of the world. Often the presider points to the working of the Spirit by a gesture of holding hands palms down over the elements and extending hands over the people. The prayer concludes with a doxology praising the triune God, naming each person and pointing to the unity of the three. Then a congregational amen affirms the whole prayer. Before, during, or after the prayer, the liturgy remembers Jesus' final meal with the disciples.

The invocation of the Holy Spirit (also known as the *epiclesis*) has always been a part of Eastern Orthodox eucharistic prayers but has been newly recovered in Western churches. Presbyterian theologian Albert Curry Winn has explained why the *epiclesis* is essential, even though New Testament passages never directly link the Spirit with Holy Communion.[29] He finds the most direct link in 1 Corinthians 10:16–17: "The cup of blessing that we bless, is it not a sharing in the blood of Christ? The bread that we break, is it not a sharing in the body of Christ? Because there is one bread, we who are many are one body, for we all partake of the one bread." The word translated "sharing" here is the Greek word *koinonia*, also translated as "communion." The Holy Spirit is the One who creates *koinonia* in the church, as demonstrated by the trinitarian blessing, "The grace of the Lord Jesus Christ, the love of God, and the communion [*koinonia*] of the Holy Spirit be with all of you" (2 Cor. 13:13). Winn also supports his view by reference to Calvin, who said that secret working of the Holy Spirit brings about the real presence of Jesus Christ in the Eucharist by uniting Christ to us.[30]

While official eucharistic prayers include invocation of the Spirit, more elaboration or theological care would enhance the trinitarian character of the eucharistic prayer. Locally composed eucharistic prayers often do not include the *epiclesis*; correcting this omission not only acknowledges trinitarian faith but also expresses an appropriate eucharistic theology. Another sometimes-neglected opportunity to affirm trinitarian faith comes at the end of the eucharistic prayer: concluding with a trinitarian doxology serves to weave together all that has been said in the prayer.

Generally, the whole prayer addresses the first person of the Trinity, though a few prayers (including one by Janet Morley summarized later in this chapter) shift and address Jesus Christ in the second section, and then the Holy Spirit. Various acts of congregational praise punctuate the prayer; sometimes the Sanctus ("Holy, holy, holy") comes before thanksgiving for the incarnation in Jesus, sometimes in the midst of it.

Some traditions of eucharistic praying prescribe that the first part of the prayer be addressed to God as "Father," and that the second part begin by speaking of the "Son"; this is the pattern (with room for variation) in United Methodist eucharistic prayers. The United Church of Christ orders for Holy Communion offer four models of eucharistic prayers that do not use gendered language. These excerpts from Word and Sacrament II illustrate the possibilities:

> Holy God, our loving Creator, close to us as breathing and distant as
>   the farthest star,
> we thank you for your constant love for all you have made. . . .
> We thank you . . . especially for Jesus Christ,
> whom you have sent from your own being as our Savior. . . .

Come, Holy Spirit, come.
Bless this bread and bless this fruit of the vine.
Bless all of us in our eating and drinking at this table
that our eyes may be opened, and we may recognize the risen Christ in
our midst,
in each other, and in all for whom Christ died.[31]

The address to the first person of the Trinity, "Holy God, our loving Creator," is interesting in that it specifies "*our* loving Creator," thus alleviating any connotation of "Holy God" being the creator of Christ or Spirit. The ascription of praise metaphorically brings together the intimate presence of God in human life ("close to us as breathing") and the transcendence of God ("distant as the farthest star"). The thanksgiving for Jesus Christ expresses "begottenness" without the language of Father and Son. Another interesting move is the direct address of the Holy Spirit, not a frequent practice in liturgical tradition.

Some recent eucharistic prayers draw on wisdom traditions to provide feminine allusions or imagery. Janet Morley, in her book *All Desires Known*, addresses all eucharistic prayers to "Eternal Wisdom." Most of her prayers address the second person of the Trinity, referring to the kenosis of the Word and the experience of the cross. A prayer for Christmas Eve begins:

O Eternal Wisdom,
we praise you and give you thanks,
because you emptied yourself of power
and became foolishness for our sake;
for on this night you were delivered as one of us,
a baby needy and naked.[32]

A prayer for ordinary use begins in what seems to be an address to the first person of the Trinity:

Eternal Wisdom, source of our being,
and goal of all our longing,
we praise you and give you thanks
because you have created us, women and men,
together in your image
to cherish your world and seek your face.[33]

Immediately following this, the prayer shifts to address the second person of the Trinity:

> Divided and disfigured by sin,
> while we were yet helpless,
> you emptied yourself of power,
> and took upon you our unprotected flesh.[34]

The Sanctus follows; then the prayer recalls Jesus' Last Supper and connects remembrance of Jesus with remembrance of other "victims of tyranny and sin":

> Come then, life-giving spirit of our God,
> brood over these bodily things,
> and make us one body with Christ;
> that we may labour with creation
> to be delivered from its bondage to decay
> into the glorious liberty of all the children of God.[35]

The prayer ends with an invocation to the Spirit. Its transitions addressing God first as source, then incarnate one, and then as life-giving spirit, are somewhat abrupt. Oddly, the prayer ends without a trinitarian doxology. Despite these limitations, Morley's prayers suggest interesting possibilities for eucharistic prayers that express trinitarian faith with little gendered language.

Another possibility, demonstrated by the opening of the United Methodist eucharistic prayer "for use with children," is to add address to God as "Mother" to the traditional address to God as "Father": "We thank you, God, Mother and Father of us all." Later Jesus is called "your only child."[36]

The eucharistic prayer is the epitome of Christian prayer. It gives thanks to God for the sweep of God's love for all people throughout time. It remembers the incarnation in Jesus Christ and the table communion he shared. It calls upon the Holy Spirit to create *koinonia* and to empower the church for ministry in the world. Because this prayer summarizes the whole of Christian faith, it is by nature trinitarian. Though the triune God may be named in a variety of ways in eucharistic prayers, always the God made known in the economy of salvation is praised: God as Source, Word, and Spirit.

Liturgies of Healing

We find the theological grounding for liturgies of healing in the reality of the triune God of overflowing love for all creation: God the Source who seeks the good of all creatures, forgives our sins, and heals our diseases (Ps. 103:3); Jesus Christ, who healed many people of their diseases; and the Holy Spirit, through whom the church continues Jesus' ministry of healing. Since the ministry of Jesus reveals how God is with us and for us, telling the stories of healing from the Gospels is an important part of this ministry. An adequate theology of the incarnation and the Trinity leads us to affirm healing as an ongoing aspect of God's relationship with humanity, and not merely a historical fluke present during Jesus' ministry on earth. Healing liturgies also invoke the ongoing work of the Holy Spirit, as this prayer over the oil from an order for healing by Timothy Crouch of the Order of Saint Luke illustrates:

> O God, the giver of health and salvation,
> we give thanks to you for the gift of oil that,
> as your holy apostles anointed many who were sick and healed them,
> *your Holy Spirit may come upon us and on this gift,*
> *so that those who in faith and repentance receive this anointing*
> *may be made whole;*
> through the name of Jesus Christ our Lord. Amen.[37]

Laying on of hands and anointing at healing services (as well as baptism) are signs of the Spirit's work within and among us; these powerful symbols are an expression of trinitarian faith.

Services of healing are, above all, an expression of the profound love the triune God has for all people and all creation. Theologian David James Randolph, in his book *The Power That Heals: Love, Healing, and the Trinity*, explores healing as an expression of God's love, saying, "The power that heals is love: divine love expressed through creation, redemption, and sustenance interacting with human love in which persons care passionately and compassionately for God, neighbor, and self through awareness, acceptance, action, and affirmation."[38] Services of healing that focus on the power of the triune God to heal will avoid the pitfalls of some healing ministries that focus too much on the charismatic gifts of individuals. Instead they will emphasize what is most important to healing ministry: The well-being that results from strengthening and renewing human relationships with God, one another, and self.

THE CHURCH YEAR, THE LECTIONARY, AND THE TRINITY

The book introducing the *Revised Common Lectionary* emphasizes the centrality of Jesus Christ in the three-year lectionary cycle:

[The three-year cycle] allows the sequence of gospel readings each year to lead God's people to a deeper knowledge of Christ and faith in him. It is the paschal mystery of the saving death and resurrection of the Lord Jesus that is proclaimed through the lectionary readings and the preaching of the church.[39]

The book states that the lectionary is "a liturgical way to lead the faithful followers of Christ through his birth, baptism, ministry, death, and resurrection."[40] From Advent to Pentecost—six months—the story of Jesus unfolds, providing a pattern of worship. Indeed, the lectionary has helped many churches recover the centrality of Jesus Christ in worship, and in this sense to be more fully trinitarian in worship.

A closer look shows that, while the lectionary is organized around the story of Jesus the incarnate Word, key texts point also to the Holy Spirit. On the Fourth Sunday of Advent, Year A, the reading from Matthew speaks of the Holy Spirit as actor in the birth of Jesus. The angel announces to Joseph: "the child conceived in [Mary] is from the Holy Spirit" (Matt. 1:20). Similarly, on the Fourth Sunday of Advent, Year C, Mary is told that Jesus will be "the Son of the Most High," and that though a virgin, she will bear a child, for "the Holy Spirit will come upon you, and the power of the Most High will overshadow you" (Luke 1:35). In other Advent and Christmastide readings, Zechariah (John's father) and Simeon both prophesy about the meaning of Jesus' birth through the power of the Holy Spirit (Luke 1:67 and 2:25–27). The readings for the baptism of the Lord reflect a trinitarian pattern, for they all show the Holy Spirit descending on Jesus and a voice from heaven saying, "This is my beloved Son" (Matt. 3:13–17; Mark 1:4–11; and Luke 3:21–22). The Spirit is sometimes central to readings during the Sundays after Epiphany (for example, in Year A: John 1:29–34; in Year B: 1 Cor. 6:12–20; in Year C: Luke 4:14–21). A number of Lenten readings portray the Spirit as a main actor, leading Jesus to the wilderness where he experienced temptation (Matt. 4:1; Mark 1:12; and Luke 4:1), as well as giving life (Rom. 8:6–11), imparting new birth (John 3:1–17), and resurrecting dry bones (Ezek. 37:1–14). The first reading for Easter Day tells how the Spirit comes upon Gentile and Jew alike (Acts 10:34–48); on the Second Sunday of Eastertide, Years A, B, and C, the readings tell how Jesus breathed the Holy Spirit on the disciples (John 20:19–23). Throughout Eastertide, readings from Acts show the Spirit at work in the earliest church. The readings for Pentecost celebrate the gift of the Spirit to the young and old, women and men, of all nations.

Several New Testament texts that demonstrate a beginning form of trinitarian theology (such as Matt. 28:16–20; 2 Cor. 13:13; and Eph. 1:3–14; 3:14–21; 4:3–6) appear in the *Revised Common Lectionary*. Taken as a whole, the lectionary, while centering on Jesus Christ, is potentially a resource for forming the church in trinitarian faith.

The readings for the Easter Vigil, which sweep through salvation history, witness to the triune God. The first reading (from Genesis 1) witnesses to the work of God in creation (and the mighty wind, or Spirit, who swept across the waters). The second reading (from Genesis 22) speaks of God's covenant with Abraham, while the third reading (from Exodus 14) speaks of God's mighty deeds in bringing the Hebrews out of Egypt. Two readings from Isaiah describe the enduring covenant love of God (Isaiah 54 and 55). A reading from Baruch describes God as "the fountain of wisdom" and uses both male and female pronouns in English. In the reading from Ezekiel 36, the Holy One promises to put a new spirit within the people of Israel; Christians have identified this with Christ's gift of the Spirit. The epistle reading (Rom. 6:3–11) speaks of baptism into Christ, and the Gospel witnesses to the resurrection of Christ (from Matthew in Year A, Mark in Year B, and Luke in Year C). Taken together, the readings point to the trinitarian reality and lend themselves to preaching and hymnody that point to the pouring out of God's love in human history.[41]

Trinity Sunday is, for many Protestant churches, the only day in the church year dedicated to a doctrine or an abstract idea. Trinity Sunday became an official part of the church year for the Roman church in 1334, though its roots date back as far as the eighth century. Several popes refused proposals for an official celebration of the Trinity, including Pope Alexander II (d. 1073), who "refused the petition for a special feast and remarked that the Roman church daily honored the Trinity" in its worship, especially in psalmody and the Gloria Patri.[42] It was Pope John XII who approved the feast, during the exile of the papacy in Avignon.[43]

Though Trinity Sunday is a doctrinal feast, its celebration need not use abstract language. As Catherine LaCugna writes:

> The focus should be the mystery of redemption by God through Christ in the power of the Holy Spirit, as well as its consequences for Christian life. Preachers need not use the technical language of dogmas (e.g., *hypostasis*) nor is it necessarily desirable to explain particular trinitarian theories. . . . Since liturgy is the ritual celebration of the events of the economy of

salvation, preaching on Trinity Sunday should concentrate on the concrete reality of grace and divine love in the economy of salvation.[44]

The texts appointed for the day provide intriguing possibilities for preaching and liturgy. In Year A, the Gospel is Matthew 28:16–20; this might be the time to explore in preaching and worship the meaning of baptism and the baptismal formula. Since the epistle reading includes the trinitarian blessing quoted above (2 Cor. 13:13), different ways of speaking of the triune God could be explored. In Year B, the Gospel is John 3:1–17; in this passage Jesus tells Nicodemus he must be born of water and the Spirit—another good opportunity to consider how humans enter into the life of God through Jesus Christ in the Spirit. Or, the epistle reading (Rom. 8:12–17), which affirms that "all who are led by the Spirit of God are children of God," could inspire worship and preaching centering on the role of the Spirit in the lives of Christians, or on what it means for Christians to call God "Abba." In Year C, in the Gospel reading from John 16:12–15, Jesus says the Spirit will guide Christians into the truth and declare to them what the Father has given Jesus. Although this is a challenging text, it provides the opportunity to speak of the trinitarian relationship between Word, Spirit, and Father, as it relates to the lives of believers. Or, by drawing on the reading from Proverbs 8:1–4, 22–31, the worship leader could speak of Jesus as Word and Wisdom of God. As LaCugna argues, preaching and worship on Trinity Sunday is not so much a time to reflect on a doctrine as a time to wonder at the way the triune God reaches out to humanity in love.[45]

Trinity Sunday, the Easter Vigil, and other occasions when lectionary readings point to the triune God provide many opportunities for trinitarian language to echo through worship and preaching, witnessing to the ways Christians can participate in the life of God in Jesus Christ. While words such as "Trinity," "triune," or "trinitarian" may never be mentioned, liturgy can point worshipers toward praise and relatedness to God known as Source, Word, and Spirit.

SUMMARY

Witness to trinitarian faith is a natural part of many dimensions of Christian worship. Some traditions of worship bring out these inherent trinitarian dimensions more explicitly than others. Becoming more intentional in affirming trinitarian faith in elements of Sunday worship, including Baptism, Eucharist, and healing, and in the celebration of the church year, leads to fuller praise and a clearer invitation to participate in the life of God.

The Trinity and Preaching

In all Christian traditions, preaching is probably the activity that allows preacher and congregation the most freedom to experiment with language about the Trinity. In traditional Protestant circles, the "freedom of the pulpit" provides opportunity for exploration of the Trinity in more expansive ways than congregational prayer, which is often bound by congregational expectations and willingness to change its language. In more liturgical churches, the bishop, priest, or deacon who preaches the sermon or homily is free to explore the trinitarian aspects of scripture and liturgy, as well as to introduce new themes and new language.

These opportunities derive directly from the nature of the sermon itself. The sermon[1] links and articulates the interweaving of various parts of the service of worship, offering new language and new perspectives for our faith's encounter with today's world. It is that moment of the liturgy in which our life with God in the world today is connected with and illumined through humanity's history with God in the past. Whether it be a eucharistic liturgy or a service of the Word, all liturgy is the worship by the people, for the transformation of the whole people; all activity of the liturgy is the community's prayer to and before God. The sermon articulates our faith, our lives' intersection with the divine presence and activity to us in our world, and our own hopes and expectations for transformation through the recreating grace of God.[2]

Homiletician Christine Smith rightly describes preaching as a theological act because preachers wrestle with the "ultimate religious questions in life." These questions include the nature of God and of humanity, as well as the relationship between humanity and God, and humanity and the world. Furthermore, preaching is "an act of naming," articulating and disclosing truths, "redeeming and transforming reality."[3] Articulating the key questions of life for a congregation and naming the issues in such a way as to evoke transformation make preaching a powerful action in the community. In the context of trinitarian theology and language, preaching has particular power to nourish, stifle, or mislead the living trinitarian faith of a community.

From a positive perspective, within the realm of the freedom and responsibility of the pulpit, the preacher can do much to empower a deeper and truer encounter of the congregation with the trinitarian God of the Christian faith. The root of this power is in our unflagging effort to proclaim the interconnection of the scriptures and our contemporary life. The sermon is at the crossroad of our universe, where God, humanity, and the world meet. In each sermonic encounter, we discover a dimension of who we are in relationship to God and the world and what we are created and called to become and do.

Such discourse cannot be abstract or imperative; its intention is to attract and to lead us into a new way of life. The faith and doctrine we articulate must be commensurate with that task, but so also must be the actual language we use. Only language that addresses the whole self and offers a vision and perception of our interconnection with God and the world is suitable for preaching. The phrasing that we responsibly can use is that which makes such an interconnection in words, images, metaphors, and analogies. This type of language recasts, reframes, and reimagines both past and present in today's words. It also invites our whole selves into new modes of being.[4] It is imperative that our God-language in worship be used and shaped in today's words through our reinterpretation and further development of biblically given or rooted beliefs and words.

In order to speak more adequately of the Christian God in our sermons, we will want to examine the language we use, ask how the trinitarian reality of God is expressed in the themes of our preaching, and consider the ways we consistently include the exploration of the Trinity in our sermons. As we have asserted in previous chapters, our doctrine of the Trinity has been inadequately presented in theology, liturgy, and popular devotion. We can certainly say the same of preaching. The Trinity scarcely appears in our preaching, except on Trinity Sunday for those traditions which observe it. When the Trinity is mentioned, it tends to be as a puzzle to be solved, not a divine relationship to be apprehended for our life with God. How can we improve our preaching about the Trinity as nourishment and inspiration for the Christian life?

Because of the power of preaching to connect the belief of the community with its everyday life, genuine change in preaching about the Trinity could make substantial difference in shaping and nurturing the life of a people in community with the trinitarian God. Two issues seem especially important: what experience and belief about the Trinity is most important to communicate in congregational worship, and what inclusive language, images, metaphors, and analogies are most helpful in this endeavor. At the end of this discussion, I include the text of a Trinity Sunday sermon to suggest what such preaching might offer in a parish setting.

WHAT DO WE SEEK TO COMMUNICATE?

The doctrine of the Trinity has never been easy for Christians to understand or to explain. Who is the Trinity? We know the undeniable truism that the doctrine was formulated in the early church to explain who Jesus Christ is, who Jesus is in relationship to God (YHWH, Abba), and who the Holy Spirit is in relationship to Jesus and God / YHWH / Abba. Even in the very early church, Christian communities struggled to express their faith in the Trinity. As early as the second century, theologians and the "ordinary Christian" did not see eye to eye about the Trinity.[5]

Tertullian's *Against Praxeas*, written in 213, is cited by historical theologian H. J. Carpenter as an example of the difficulties theologians found in popular understandings (or misunderstandings) of the Trinity. Tertullian notes that the simple faithful are always the majority, and that they find it hard to understand the divine economy (*oikonomia*). They believe that God is one, and God's rule is one. For the ordinary Christian, the struggle was to preserve the belief in one God, in contrast to pagan beliefs. Tertullian insisted on the economy, the relationship of God, Jesus Christ, and the Holy Spirit, and explained that their interrelationship does not destroy the divine unity and monarchy of that Triunity.[6]

Tertullian's fulminations against the inadequacies of ordinary Christians to express a trinitarian faith points to a continuing challenge among theologians and ordinary Christians alike—what is the heart of trinitarian doctrine and how do we talk about it? We identify one God and Father / Abba /

Source, Jesus Christ / Word / Son, Holy Spirit / Advocate / Comforter. The key issue is their relatedness. Is God's unity one in which the distinctions are just names for one God in sequentially different modes—Creator, Redeemer, and Sanctifier? Is God really three separate Gods united by an agreement to act together? How do we talk about God as three and one?

It is important for the preacher to have a basic grasp of the development of the Christian doctrine of the Trinity.[7] It is equally important to base one's efforts in a clear understanding of the Trinity as a mystery. Unfortunately, all too often use of the word "mystery" suggests a puzzle that we have not solved, like the solution we seek as we read a detective novel. However, the mystery of the Trinity is of quite a different sort. It is rooted in God's nature as a living reality infinitely greater than our comprehension.

One of the most helpful books of the twentieth century in articulating this aspect of God's reality for us is Rudolf Otto's *The Idea of the Holy*. Otto wrote of God as numen, the "holy," a *mysterium tremendum et fascinosum*.[8] My purpose is not to deeply explore Otto's analysis of human comprehension of God, but to point to the starting point of any word about God—awe. God is a mystery, not in the sense of a puzzle, but as a profound living incomprehensibility. Of course, any great reality, a flower, tree, animal, person, is incomprehensible, in the sense that we understand bits and pieces, enough to be in a relationship, but we do not fully understand the reality of that other one. We do not even fully understand ourselves. We can apprehend enough to live with others and with ourselves, but we never understand the totality of everything, by itself and interconnected with others. "Ah, sweet mystery of life" is not just a sentimental song; it is a razor sharp truth for every human being about all of life.

The Trinity as mystery is analogous to ourselves as mystery—who we are, the depths of our feelings, the surprise of our thoughts, the intensity of our relations to others, our deep connections with the world around us. The mystery of ourselves suggests the true but partial grasp we gain of the height and depth and breadth of the infinite love that creates, redeems, and makes holy the world. Such divine mystery is, as Otto observes, *tremendum*, of a holiness that evokes awe, dread, wonder, rapturous astonishment at the incomprehensible divine life and power. At the same time, the divine is *fascinosum*, desirable, beautiful, lovable, the fulfillment of all wants and hopes. Like Moses encountering the burning bush, one humbly takes off one's sandals before the mystery, and at the same time, eagerly draws near to address it and seek its name.

Today the loss of a sense of mystery in religion and society is a common theme; one of the services that preaching about the Trinity can offer contemporary Christianity is to lead us face to face with the mystery of God's life among us. God is not the distant searching Judge, seeking to condemn, nor the sentimental curly-haired Jesus of Sunday school art. The trinitarian God is the unfathomable holiness of the God who is Creator, who has sent the Word incarnate, Jesus Christ, and who, with the Holy Spirit, dwells among us.

Reginald Heber's popular hymn to the Trinity takes the song of the cherubim in Isaiah, which was introduced early into Christian liturgy, and addresses God as "Holy, holy, holy."[9] His focus on God's holiness, expressed in trinitarian life, is a useful and important center for our own preaching about the Trinity. The preacher's work is to evoke for the congregation an experience of the trinitarian God as Holy, both awe inspiring and utterly desirable. We can understand something of God's holiness but never the whole. At the same time, the invitation of the Christian life is to know and experience this God more deeply and fully. The preacher constantly balances our desire to grasp the holy God, our fear of the consequences of knowing God, and our sense of human fulfillment as obtainable only in mutual relationship with this God.

We are not unique in a struggle to apprehend God's trinitarian life. The mystery has been apprehended by believers in every age, and the experience is shaped and expressed by each generation's (and perhaps even each congregation's) concerns. The scriptural rooting of our faith, its articulation through the ages, and our own perceptions, discoveries, and questions, must all be constantly reconfigured to ask our age's questions about who the trinitarian God is and what that God offers and asks of us. Sermons of past ages show concern in other times with the divinity of Jesus and of the Spirit, the role of the divine Spirit in the rebirth by grace, the relationship between sacrament and divine grace.[10] Our great twentieth-century question of the Trinity is about human relationships: What does it mean to be a person in relationship with others? How do we live with each other? As never before, we want to recognize our interconnections with each other and learn how to live in peace together. We believe that the Christian notion of the Trinity has much to offer to this contemporary quest.[11] The Trinity is a relationship; the uniqueness of Christian belief in God is that we claim that God's unity is a relationship.

That element of trinitarian life responds to our global search to live together just as profoundly as the third- and fourth-century search to discern the saving divinity of Jesus the Savior and the Holy Spirit shaped earlier trinitarian theology and preaching. The religious seekers of late antiquity sought deliverance, healing, and wholeness from a world that seemed alienated from them. Christianity answered their plea with God the Creator, sending Jesus to reconcile them and the Spirit to transform and to sanctify the world. We today, in a fragmented, disconnected world with yet so many technological and economic connections, seek life-giving relationships and true community. The Christian doctrine of the Trinity articulates a divine response to our quest.

Thus our preaching about the Trinity must remain constantly aware that God is a mystery, and that the Trinity is not a puzzle to be explained. Rather, it is our opening into God's life, which God chooses to share with us. Catherine LaCugna, in an article about preaching on Trinity Sunday, outlined her understanding of the God of salvation history: God created the world and established a covenant relationship with Israel; spoke through the prophets to recall the people to their covenant relationship; sent the only begotten Son, who lived, died, and is raised from the dead by God; God and the incarnate Son sent the Holy Spirit "to dwell among us."[12]

She offers a brief history of the origins of the feast of Trinity Sunday and the ways in which the liturgy and preaching about the Trinity became increasingly abstract and dissociated from the biblical immediacy of "God who is 'nearer to me than I am to myself.'"[13] In her eyes, and in those of most theologians and preachers, these abstractions are a source of confusion and distancing of the congregation from the living God of the scriptures.

The Collect for Trinity Sunday in the Episcopal *Book of Common Prayer* is essentially the same as that of the medieval Sarum Rite, and it was also used in the Roman Missal until the reforms of Vatican II.

> Almighty and everlasting God, you have given to us your servants grace, by the confession of a true faith, to acknowledge the glory of the eternal Trinity, and in the power of your divine Majesty to worship the Unity: Keep us steadfast in this faith and worship, and bring us at last to see you in your one and eternal glory, O Father; who with the Son and the Holy Spirit live and reign, one God, for ever and ever. Amen.[14]

The first collect for the feast in the Roman liturgy is a modern adaptation of that prayer. The prayer endeavors to praise God as the trinitarian God; it employs the abstract language of doctrinal definition of Trinity and Unity, as we profess our adoration to God's Trinity in Unity, to the God whom we worship as Father, with the Son and Holy Spirit. The language of the collect focuses us on the theological puzzle—that God is three in one, that Father, Son, and Holy Spirit are equal persons in one deity.

The second collect for Trinity Sunday in the Roman liturgy is much closer to the kind of biblical immediacy that LaCugna proposes:

> God, we praise you:
> Father all-powerful, Christ Lord and Savior, Spirit of Love.
> You reveal yourself in the depths of our being,
> drawing us to share in your life and your love.
> One God, Three Persons,
> be near to the people formed in your image,
> close to the world your love brings to life.
> We ask you this, Father, Son, and Holy Spirit,
> One God, true and living, for ever and ever.[15]

The tone of this collect, not, alas, echoed in the Preface, is much closer to the salvation history roots that LaCugna seeks for worship. The connection is made immediately between God as Father, Savior, and Spirit, in relationship to creation. The prayer is not directed to a God enthroned beyond the world but to the God revealed to us "in the depth of our being." God is addressed as the one in whose image we are made, and who made the world in love. The language of theological explanation is not used; instead the collect uses scriptural language of God's relationship to humanity and to the world.

The contrast between the two collects illustrates quite clearly the issues that have hampered our preaching in the Western church. When preaching on the Trinity we have assumed that we have to explain to the congregation the technical theological statements formulated to set boundaries against certain heresies. We have ignored the deeper reality that we do not need to preach theological technicalities from the pulpit; we need to preach the word of the living God, a word that relates the living God to humanity and to the world.

The key to good preaching about the Trinity is to focus on the relationship of God to the world, the trinitarian God who shares the divine life with us. The preacher's responsibility is to evoke in the congregation a sense of the mystery that is both awe inspiring and enticing, luring us to the infinite divine love. Thus relationship is the key for expressing the divine life and God's invitation to us. How do we express this relationship in preaching? I have three specific suggestions: (1) use prayers and invocations in preaching which express the trinitarian relationship to us; (2) preach with awareness and clarity about the trinitarian God in all the scriptures during all the Sundays, not just Trinity Sunday; and (3) connect God's trinitarian life explicitly with our life.

HOW TO PREACH ABOUT THE TRINITY

Trinitarian Invocations and Prayers in the Sermons

In some preaching traditions, the preacher is expected to begin the sermon and perhaps end it with an invocation or prayer to the Trinity. The use of such a reassuring formula at the beginning provides a transition for the congregation between the Gospel and the sermon; it also announces the sermon as an effort to interpret God's word to the congregation, rather than simply human speculation or an effort to offer practical advice.

"In the name of the Father, the Son, and the Holy Spirit" is traditional, but not always helpful in terms of inclusive language, nor in expressing God's relationship to us. It is certainly true that through Jesus, God is our Father, but the "Father" of the trinitarian formula designates Jesus' relationship to the Creator and Source who sent him into this world. The hardy but inadequate formula "Creator, Redeemer, and Sanctifier" is also inadequate to express the biblical Trinity. Where such a formula is expected, something as simple as "In the Name of God. Amen" may be adequate to the liturgical or pastoral needs. One might say: "In the Name of God, Source of all being, of the Eternal Word, and of the Holy Spirit. Amen." Or "Abba, Servant, and Paraclete," as suggested by the Prayer Book of the Anglican church in New Zealand.[16]

I find the trinitarian invocation that follows, from the *New Zealand Prayer Book*, both orthodox and inclusive in its language:

> God, Creator, bring us new life.
> Jesus, Redeemer, renew us.
> Holy Spirit, strengthen and guide us.[17]

If it is not used elsewhere in the service, the blessing from 2 Corinthians expresses well the name of the Trinity in relationship to us: "The grace of the Lord Jesus Christ, the love of God, and the communion of the Holy Spirit be with all of you" (13:13).

These invocations, used regularly, can provide a familiar language about the Trinity in relationship to us which acts as a touchstone and reference for a community's prayer and reaffirms the sermon's intention to speak in the name of the triune God, who creates, redeems, and saves us. A prayer that concludes the sermon can offer the same liturgical interconnection and worship language to the congregation.

In many traditions it is customary to end the sermon with a prayer. While this may not always be appropriate, it is often a helpful part of the sermon. A prayer can gather up various aspects of the sermon and focus on the particular transforming grace sought from God in this liturgical action. It also can provide a time of personal and prayerful reflection about the sermon and its connection with the individual's and the congregation's life.

For example, suppose that you are preaching on the Sunday nearest July 13, in Year B of the Episcopal lectionary. The texts for the day are: Amos 7:7–15; Psalm 85; Ephesians 1:1–14; Mark 6:7–13. Assume that you focus on the Gospel, which tells of Jesus sending the disciples out two by two, ordering them to cast out unclean spirits, to take nothing with them, to proclaim repentance where they are welcomed, and to leave those who will not receive them. The prayer at the end of the sermon might be:

> Jesus, our savior and our brother, you sent your disciples to proclaim good news, that the God who made us in love sent you to reconcile us to be holy and blameless in love. May the Holy Spirit who is sent by God to us in Holy Baptism draw us ever nearer to you in the life-giving power of your death and resurrection. May we, adopted by your gracious love, forever praise and share your glorious life, O God who created us, Jesus who reconciles us, and Holy Spirit, font of all blessings.

Such prayers are best composed by the preacher for a specific congregation at a particular time. There are also many collections of prayers that can be used or adapted, with attention to both the language and the theological issues. The Trinity is not added as an afterthought, but the prayer articulates the intrinsic connection between the particular sermon and the life of the Trinity with us.

Lifting Up the Trinitarian Themes from the Scriptures

Two streams flow from the scriptures as source for worship. The first is to lift up the trinitarian themes in the readings from scripture which are part of the liturgy each Sunday. The second is to take the opportunity to expand the congregation's perspectives which Trinity Sunday offers, if you belong to a denomination—United Church of Christ, Lutheran, Episcopalian, Roman Catholic—that celebrates the feast.

Every preacher has the opportunity to highlight trinitarian themes in the readings every Sunday and to expand the congregation's language and imagery for the Trinity. The divine mystery that reveals itself to us is revealed as a trinitarian God—the creator and source of all, YHWH of the covenant with Israel; the eternal Word of God, incarnate as Jesus of Nazareth, child of Wisdom and Wisdom incarnate; and the Holy Spirit, indwelling spirit of communion of humans with God. This Trinity speaks in the scriptures each Sunday. Yet often we do not even speak of the Trinity or identify the interrelationship of the persons of the Trinity to us.

By and large, preachers who preach about the readings focus on one text, usually the Gospel, and preach about Jesus and his relationship to us. If on occasion the preacher chooses another text, it is usually not chosen to deepen our trinitarian theology. But such could be done. For instance, in the Episcopal lectionary, on the Sunday closest to August 15 (Proper 15) in Year B, the readings are from Proverbs 9:1–6, Psalm 147, Ephesians 5:15–20, and John 6:53–59. These readings have rich trinitarian aspects that a preacher might well use.

The first reading, from Proverbs, tells of Lady Wisdom, who has built her house with seven pillars, prepared her meat and wine, and set the table. Then her servants go out to invite people from the town, calling them to come and eat her bread and wine, and walk in the way of insight. Quite possibly John wrote his Gospel with this Wisdom passage in mind; certainly Lady Wisdom is embodied as a figure offering saving insight at her table. This is a foreshadowing of eucharistic imagery, as is the femininity of Wisdom, with whom John's Gospel identifies Jesus. Lady Wisdom is eternally with the creator; the Word incarnate in Jesus is eternally in God.

So overt and surprising is this image to many Christians that after I preached on this one Sunday a few years ago, at the church door one of the parishioners accused me of making up this reading. We did a bit of quick Bible study. I remain convinced that an eye open to trinitarian theology sees in Wisdom's banquet some of the Hebrew roots both of the Trinity and of the Eucharist. Wisdom is the Wisdom of God, eternally creative before God and offering saving insight to those on earth who will follow her.[18]

The selection from Ephesians is concerned with living the way of wisdom in the Christian community. Wisdom and foolishness are contrasted, and the Christian is admonished to live wisely. This way is doxological and trinitarian: to be filled with the Spirit, thanking God the Father in the name of our Lord Jesus Christ. The preacher thus has the opportunity to connect the persons of the Trinity directly to the worship life of the community, but also to connect the persons of the Trinity in relation to each other as they relate to us. God is the Father of Jesus, who sent him; Jesus is the Lord of the community and of the creation; Jesus is also the Lady Wisdom, whose way is salvation, and through whom we are able to pray to God; the Spirit is given by God through Jesus, and through the Spirit we live in the way of wisdom and are empowered to pray and give thanks to God.

In the reading from John, set in the context of Jesus' synagogue teaching in Capernaum, the imagery of Lady Wisdom's banquet is pronounced. Jesus is Wisdom, sent from God. In the Gospel, Jesus is both Wisdom and the banquet, who provides life for the people. The Spirit is not mentioned here but is implied as the one who will be sent, according to the discourse at the Last Supper, by Jesus to give the disciples the capacity to live as Jesus has taught them.

Just this brief example shows ways in which the trinitarian theology of the Christian scriptures may be identified and proclaimed to the congregation and the imagery for the persons of the Trinity can be expanded from "Father, Son, and Holy Spirit." In this set of readings, Wisdom is the crucial new image. In many congregations this new image will need to be carefully introduced, in the face of ignorance or misconceptions. The effort will be well repaid if Wisdom imagery is integrated into Christians' trinitarian theology to make it more inclusive and empowering.

In a Trinity Sunday sermon certain issues can be even more directly addressed. Several important efforts have been made in the past few years to suggest ways preachers can work with the readings for Trinity Sunday to offer a more lively and experienced-based Trinity theology.[19] The preacher in a liturgical church lives in the reality that we do celebrate Trinity Sunday. Not to preach about the Trinity merely reinforces the notion that the Trinity is a silly or irrelevant religious puzzle, unrelated to life, and impossible or unworthy of the effort to understand and appreciate.

Thus the preacher wisely attempts to preach about the readings, to connect them with our experience of life with God, and to use language not bound by an abstract, patriarchal, or authoritarian framework. Biblical theologian Gerard Sloyan remarks: "The biblical riches available to us on the feast of the Most Holy Trinity over three years are not only the source of our faith in this mystery but also the most fitting way to preach, teach, and reflect on it."[20] The sermon that follows is an example of one way a Trinity Sunday sermon can address a congregation's search to deepen its worship of the trinitarian God.

SERMON FOR TRINITY SUNDAY, YEAR B

I preached this sermon on Trinity Sunday of 1997 at the Eucharist in a parish in Brooklyn. Both the congregation and the building were small, but the enthusiasm and energy were significant. The parish is mixed, ethnically and racially, and has a high level of loyalty to Anglicanism and the Episcopal church. The adult education program had been weak, and the congregation had expressed a desire to experience sermons that would help them understand more about their faith. I tried to balance the doxological and the educational dimensions of the sermon. In a practical vein, this sermon was directed to the congregation in the liturgical context of Trinity Sunday, when a significant number of the congregation would be present, and we would be sharing an obvious occasion for preaching about the Trinity.

May you have a happy and holy Trinity Sunday! We have together prayed, studied, and prepared ourselves to participate in the mystery of the Passion during Lent. We have rejoiced in the cross and resurrection of Jesus, welcomed those newly baptized, and renewed our own baptismal promises. Last Sunday, on Pentecost, we remembered with great thanksgiving how God sent the Holy Spirit, thus calling us into the new people of God, the church. Today we celebrate Trinity Sunday, a great "Thanks be to God" for all the gifts of God which we have received during Lent and Eastertide!

Who is our God? Trinity Sunday responds to that basic question as all good worship does, as a celebration of God's goodness and life-giving love for us. Sometimes our catechism and prayers make it hard for us to keep our eyes focused on the joy of God's trinitarian life for us. How many of us remember the catechism questions about God, the Trinity? Catechism lessons? Sermons?

Did it sometimes seem as though the Trinity was a puzzle, intended to be hard to comprehend? Three-in-One, One-in-Three. True as these words may be, the scriptures offer us a better way to grasp the God who created us, became incarnate among us, and gives us the Holy Spirit to live in us and draw us closer into eternal communion with God.

Even though we often treat our trinitarian God like a puzzle, God is really a mystery. The Greek word for mystery comes from language meaning something enclosed, not left open and exposed to everyone. This kind of mystery is familiar to us because we are mysteries, and so are all those we know and love. At depth, everyone and everything is mystery, that is, a reality richer and fuller than that which we can understand. Mystery is at the heart of life, for none of us can fully understand life—our own, that of others, and certainly not the source and great expanse of life.

The trinitarian God of life is a mystery who chooses to live with us and share the eternal divine life with us. We know God not as a puzzle to solve, or a catechism formula to explain, but as an immeasurably holy friend who has slowly, over the course of our history, shared more and more of this divine life with us. Today, as we celebrate this feast of the Most Holy Trinity, we are rejoicing in the story of God's self-giving and self-revealing life among us.

Our readings for the day speak to us of God's life for us: Exodus reveals God's holy name, spoken to Moses from the burning bush in the desert; in the letter to the Romans, Paul proclaims the work of the Spirit of God, sent to dwell in us by our baptism into the death and resurrection of Jesus; and in John's Gospel Jesus tells Nicodemus about the Spirit from whom we are reborn from above, and about the Son of Man, who will be lifted up to give eternal life to everyone who believes in him. Each of these readings shows us something more of God living among us.

The story of Moses hearing God's call from the burning bush is deeply moving. In a recent art exhibition, I saw large icon from the eleventh century, now at Saint Catherine's monastery in Mount Sinai. The young, clean-shaved Moses stood on the rock, reverently removing his sandals before the burning bush. In the barren desert, with only stones and sand surrounding, the bush stood elevated on the rock of the holy Mount Horeb, burning yet not consumed. As in the biblical story, the atmosphere of the painting is quiet, reverent, anticipatory.

In the story, Moses' anticipation of divine self-revealing is met by a heavenly voice speaking from the fire of the bush. We remember that often fire is a sign of God's action on earth—the pillar of fire that guides the people during the wandering in the desert of the Exodus, the fire over the heads of the disciples in the Upper Room at Pentecost. Moses, standing humbly on holy ground, hears God's voice declaring: "I am the God of your father, the God of Abraham, the God of Isaac, and the God of Jacob."

Moses is, we remember, an exile. He was adopted by Pharaoh's daughter to save him from the death fated for him as an Israelite, and then as a young adult he fled Pharaoh's court after killing an Egyptian official to save one of the Israelites. God's name, introduced here, not given in full, expresses God's faithfulness to Moses, the fugitive among the Kenites in the desert. Moses' own identity, shaken and changing during his youth, is now rooted in God, the covenant God who called Abraham and Sarah; Isaac and Rebecca; Jacob, Rachel, and Leah.

The God of Moses' ancestors is also Moses' God. Moses' identity depends not on himself or what he can win by his efforts but on the Holy One, who loved him, created him, and chose him. Moses' encounter with God, along with the divine name spoken to Moses, is also for any of us the root of our relationship with God. God is the God of our people and the God of each of us; divine compassion chooses this relationship with us because of infinite love. God is ours even when we are not yet aware of the relationship, have turned away from it, or are ignorant of what is offered to us. God, in holiness, will seek and claim us. God's name, which connects us with the chosen people throughout all time, affirms divine faithful love as the source of infinite and all-encompassing life with us.

Paul wrote his letter to the Romans to introduce his ministry to them in his own words and assure them that he was proclaiming the true gospel of Jesus. Admonishing his hearers to seek the way of life, he reminds them that, through their baptism into the death and resurrection of Jesus, they have received the Spirit of life to make them children of God. To be a child of God is to be empowered to call God "Abba," just as Jesus did. "Abba" is a child's word for father, expressing great respect, awe, and intimacy. Through the Spirit, received through Jesus, we are God's children and can call

God "Abba," because as children, we are heirs of God and joint heirs of Christ.

The Spirit is God's active agent, who incorporates us into the life of Jesus the Christ. We are, by the grace of adoption of baptism, children just as Jesus is God's child, in a close and intimate relationship with God, through Jesus, by the indwelling Spirit. Paul reminds the Romans that this relationship of adoption includes our following of Jesus' way of life, in order that we may share in his eternal life: "we suffer with him that we may be glorified with him." Through the Spirit we are baptized into Jesus' way of life, now enabled to share God's eternal life.

In John's Gospel, we hear of the same relationship, described in emphatic imagery. By chapter 3 of John's Gospel, Jesus has already begun his public life and is making enemies among the political and religious establishment. Nicodemus, a leader in the Sanhedrin, comes to Jesus by night. The circumstances of his conversations with Jesus seem true to life and also are set in the time of quiet, rest, and rebirth. Nicodemus is himself earnestly seeking a new perspective on God's word to Israel, and he even is willing to study with this controversial new figure, Jesus of Nazareth.

As was customary in rabbinic study, the seeker poses a question for the rabbi. Nicodemus draws together the elements of Jesus' ministry: we know you are a teacher come from God; only God could give you the power to work these signs. The "signs," such as the miracle of Cana, are not wonders, but rather indicators of God's purpose for us, and are part of the revealing of God's will for us. Jesus' response appears at first not to be related to Nicodemus's opening comments, but it is; Jesus affirms that to see the realm of God you must be born from above. In other words, you must be remade by God in order to participate in God's realm here.

Nicodemus then seizes on the obvious imagery: how can anyone be born again? Jesus' reply focuses on the heart of the matter, which is that he is not speaking of a second earthly birth, but of rebirth in a spiritual and analogical sense. Rebirth is a comparison, not a literal statement. To belong to God's realm requires a remaking of the self which is as radical as going back into the womb and being born again. One has to be reborn of water and the Spirit. The Spirit is as unknowable and uncontrollable to worldly people as the wind is to us. If we seek God's realm, we must be reborn of the Spirit.

Nicodemus then asks the next obvious question: how can this rebirth by the Spirit take place? Jesus, after poking a bit of fun at him, addresses him directly: I have seen God in heaven and am testifying to you directly about what God is doing in this world to give humanity eternal life. Jesus asserts that he has been sent by God, and for that reason, his ascension, his being lifted up on the cross like the serpent in the wilderness by Moses, will give eternal life to those who believe in him. The eternal life, the new life in God's realm, is God's gift to us through Jesus Christ by whom the Holy Spirit acts in us to bring us to new birth.

Each of these readings is rich and resonant of many meanings for us. But today, this Trinity Sunday, each of them deepens in us our relationship to the trinitarian God who invites us to be God's friends, to share God's own companionship, God's own life. On this Trinity Sunday, the scripture readings have led us through a journey of discovery of God's face, a growth in appreciating the love of God for us made known in time and space.

Because we know more about who God is, we understand more about who we are and what God gives us and asks of us. In Exodus we hear that God's creative love is faithful and seeks us out, even in the barren desert. God gives us our identity, which is bound together with the divine life and love. Our creator God is our covenant God and graciously recalls us to live in the way of life and truth.

In Jesus Christ, we see God's face and experience God's will for us. Jesus is sent by God, to live among us, die, and rise for us. Through Jesus, the Holy Spirit of God comes to live among us, that we might be reborn, remade to life in the pattern of Jesus' life. Can we understand the height and breadth and depth of God's love for us? Can we understand the Trinity? No.

But we can understand and respond to God's love for us. We can offer our own yes to the faithful love of our creator and covenant God. We who are baptized into the death and resurrection of Jesus can accept with joy our rebirth in water and the Spirit, and in the power of the Spirit suffer and be glorified with Jesus. We can live our lives in the grace and love of the trinitarian God, who calls us to the feast of eternal life.

This Sunday we celebrate that God made us, redeems us, and makes us holy. This creator and covenant God, incarnate in Jesus Christ the Word, active as the indwelling Spirit, is our God, God for us. In the church we grow in the life of this God who made us, loves us, and calls us to live as one people in eternal life. Let us pray that we may be God's people, in the fullness of life, now and forever.

I believe that God's ways are not our ways, and that God's love can encompass us, even when we are still seeking and stumbling toward God. I believe that God always knows and finds us through Jesus, in the Holy Spirit, and that through this trinitarian life, God fills us with beauty, peace, truth, and love. Amen.

5

Trinitarian Language in Hymns

Christian worship is at its very heart trinitarian. In its rituals, its proclamation, and its singing, the church testifies to the triune God. Baptism is immersion into the Holy One in union with Christ through the power of the Spirit; the Eucharist gives thanks to God the Source, remembers Jesus the Word, and prays for the gift of the Spirit. In preaching, through the power of the Spirit, we proclaim the presence of the Eternal God in the life, death, and resurrection of Jesus Christ and in our daily lives. And, for many of us, as for Christians in the past, hymns are the wellspring and witness of trinitarian faith.

The earliest Christian hymns probably centered on Jesus Christ. Several New Testament passages may be fragments of early hymns about Christ (John 1:1–14; Phil. 2:6–11; Col. 1:15–20; 1 Tim. 3:16; and Rev. 5:12–13, for example.) In about 112 C.E., Pliny, a Roman official, wrote Emperor Trajan that "on an appointed day, they [Christians] had been accustomed to meet before daybreak, and to recite a hymn antiphonally to Christ, as to a god."[1] Prayers and hymns addressed to Christ in this early period were among the seeds from which trinitarian theology grew; later, they supported the orthodox position on Christology.

Gnostic, Arian, and orthodox groups used hymn texts to express and promote their approaches to Christian faith. In Edessa, Syria, Bar-Daisan and his son Harmonius wrote hymns to support Gnostic Christian thought. Later, also in Edessa, Ephraem of Syria (306–373), known as the "Harp of the Spirit," wrote hymns to promote orthodox Christology, emphasizing the incarnation: "A central theological theme [of Ephraem's writings] is the incarnation as the miraculous self-abasement of God out of love for humankind and the consequent intimacy between the creator and human beings both collectively and individually."[2] His hymns use rich imagery that draws on scripture yet express the poet's imagination. For example, in an extended hymn of thanksgiving for the incarnation, Ephraem speaks imaginatively of the relation between the first and second persons of the Trinity:

> Glory to that Silent One Who spoke by means of His voice. . . . Glory to that Sublime One Who was seen by means of His dawn. . . . Glory to that Hidden One Whose Child was revealed. . . . Glory to that Living One Whose Son became a mortal.[3]

His works greatly influenced the liturgy and theology of the Syrian churches.

The Arian controversy strongly influenced the development of hymnody in the Eastern church. Sacred songs were written, using popular tunes, to promote the teachings of Arius, who denied the full divinity of Christ.[4] The Arians may in fact have been the first to set their beliefs to music and sing them to defy other Christians with whom they disagreed.[5] Orthodox Christians such as Gregory of Nazianzus countered with hymns to support emerging trinitarian theology. In late fourth-century Constantinople, when forbidden a place to worship, the Arians paraded through the streets at night singing hymns that expressed their position and ridiculed trinitarian thought. Bishop John Chrysostom, concerned lest the faithful be led astray, countered with processions of people singing hymns promoting the orthodox position. When this well-intended strategy ended in violence, with people killed on both sides, the emperor prohibited the Arians from singing their songs in public.[6] To understand these intense trinitarian conflicts, which raged even in the marketplace, one must recall that ordinary Christians of the fourth century believed these issues to bear directly on their salvation.

The first Christian hymn for which we have musical notation is a fragment in the Oxyrhynchus Papyri XV.1786.[7] Written in Greek in the third century, it praises the Trinity: "We sing a song of praise to the Father and the Son and the Holy Spirit."[8] John of Damascus, well known today because of his term *perichoresis* to describe the Trinity, also expressed the orthodox position through well-written hymns.[9] Use of trinitarian language continued to pervade later Greek hymnody.

Although Hilary of Poitiers (c. 310–366) wrote anti-Arian Latin hymns before him, Ambrose of Milan (340–397) is known as the father of Latin hymnody.[10] As Bishop of Milan, Ambrose popularized hymn singing in order to comfort and strengthen orthodox Christians, who were in bitter conflict with the Arians. Through his influence, use of the hymnic form now called Long Meter (four lines of eight syllables in iambic meter) became common; in fact, hymns in this meter came to be called "Ambrosian," no matter who wrote them.[11] As we learn in Augustine's *Confessions*, Ambrose's hymns encouraged his followers (including Augustine's mother) for several days while they defended the newly built basilica in Milan from forces of the Arian emperor Valentinian and his mother the empress Justina.[12]

Perhaps it was through Ambrose's influence that trinitarian doxologies became common in Latin hymnody. Besides concluding his hymns with doxologies, Ambrose also wrote entire hymns of praise to Christ or the Trinity. Only four hymns survive which scholars agree were written by Ambrose: *Aeterne rerum conditor, Iam surgit hora tertia, Intende que regis Israel*, and *Deus creator Omnium*.[13] The latter ends with the trinitarian doxology "Christum rogamus et Patrem, Christi Patrisque Spiritum, unum potens er omnia; foue precantes, Trinitas."[14] This may be translated: We pray to Christ and the Father and the Spirit of the Christ and the Father, only power in all things; sustain those who pray to you, Trinity.[15] The full trinitarian expression of this doxology is interesting, given the fact that only in 382 did a synod at Constantinople specifically affirm "the consubstantiality and the full divinity of the Holy Spirit," also identifying the Spirit as a separate *hypostasis*.[16]

Such Christian leaders as Prudentius (348–c. 410 C.E., on whose poetry "Of the Father's Love Begotten" is based) and Fortunatus (c. 540–c. 609 C.E., author of "Sing, My Tongue, the Glorious Battle") also wrote hymns in Latin expressing orthodox trinitarian theology.

For as long as five centuries (the seventh to the twelfth), however, the Roman church used only psalmody and a few approved hymns and responses in public worship. According to hymnologist Louis Benson, this happened because the monastic practice of chanting psalms began to predominate in public worship.[17] Hymnody survived longer in the monasteries themselves; several hours of daily prayer allowed time for hymns as well as songs. Monks often sang the hymns of Ambrose or hymns imitating his style, as well as psalms ending with trinitarian doxologies. Meanwhile, congregational singing became rare in the Roman mass.

Not only monastic practice but also concern about orthodox doctrine motivated some churches to approve for worship only psalms and a few well-known hymns such as the Te Deum and the Gloria in Excelsis. Even though Arian and Gnostic challenges had inspired some excellent orthodox hymnody, some churches grew wary of the power of hymns to promote heresy. At times some church leaders in both East and West banned all nonscriptural songs. A synod in Laodicea (Asia Minor) did so in 363, as did a council in Braga (Spain) in 563.[18] Another approach was to accept only a few hymns with approved trinitarian theology. The Council of Toledo in 633 supported the singing of some nonscriptural hymnody, such as the hymns of Ambrose and Hilary, the Gloria Patri, and the Gloria in Excelsis, all very trinitarian in emphasis.[19]

New hymnody written in the Roman church from the fourth century through the medieval period often included trinitarian doxologies at the end of hymns and psalms. If not part of the original compositions, doxologies sometimes were added.[20] Latin metrical doxologies often varied to reflect the seasons of the church year.[21]

Various churches of the Reformation answered the question of psalms and hymns differently. Luther encouraged the singing of both psalms and hymns. His original hymns addressed to Jesus Christ, the Spirit, and the Trinity as a whole express a hearty trinitarian faith. Some of his psalm paraphrases conclude with doxologies, and the hymns he translates from Latin into German sometimes focus on the Trinity. Luther did not neglect expressions of trinitarian faith in his great efforts to reform hymnody;[22] in fact, the last hymn he wrote was a German version of an ancient hymn to the Trinity, *O lux beata Trinitas*.[23]

Calvin believed that psalms were the most appropriate texts for Christians to sing:

> When we have looked thoroughly everywhere and searched high and low, we shall find no better songs nor more appropriate to the purpose than the Psalms of David through which the Holy Spirit made and spoke through him. And furthermore, we are certain that God puts the words in our mouths.[24]

Calvin's views on psalm singing influenced Reformed churches; for example, the Christian Reformed Church, U.S. used only psalms for congregational singing until 1934; their 1987 *Psalter Hymnal* includes 491 hymns but also at least one metrical setting of all 150 psalms.[25]

HYMN SINGING IN ENGLISH-SPEAKING CHURCHES

During the first centuries of the English Reformation, Anglican and Separatist churches (both influenced by Calvin) mainly sang psalms and a few ancient hymns such as the Gloria in Excelsis. Metrical psalters such as the seventeenth century *New Version* by Nahum Tate and Nicholas Brady, as well as the Psalms of David versified by Isaac Walts (1674–1748), included trinitarian doxologies for use at the end of psalms. The doxologies, collected in a separate section, were matched to sing with psalms of the same meter.[26]

The practice of singing trinitarian doxologies, including those of Watts, became a matter of hot debate during the dispute between unitarian and trinitarian parties in early eighteenth-century England.[27] Later in that century, the Wesleys responded to similar controversies by publishing collections of trinitarian hymns by Charles Wesley, *Gloria Patri . . . or Hymns on the Trinity* (1746) and *Hymns on the Trinity* (1767).[28] According to United Methodist theologian Barry E. Bryant, these hymns served three main purposes: To teach orthodox doctrine, especially the unity of the Trinity; to nurture believers in saving and sanctifying relationship with the triune God; and to offer right praise.[29] Of these, the soteriological purpose was primary. Bryant observes that for the Wesleys,

> The doctrine of the Trinity was not simply a speculative doctrine. . . . It was to influence "hearts and lives," ultimately affecting the way people lived. Obviously, to the Wesleys, the doctrine of the Trinity had far-reaching and pastoral implications.[30]

Note that, in contrast to modern assumptions that the Trinity is an abstract doctrine of import only to theologians, the Wesleys took pains through hymnody to nurture trinitarian faith in workers without much formal education.

By the first half of the nineteenth century, English-speaking Christians who were not Anglican often sang hymns in worship, such as those written by Watts and Wesley. The Church of England, influenced by the

Oxford movement, looked to other sources for hymns. Oxford movement leaders wanted to promote orthodox theology and recover the hymnody of the past. Persons such as John Mason Neale labored to provide excellent translations of the Latin hymnody or to provide more objective hymns in similar style. These hymns, collected in *Hymns Ancient and Modern* (1859–61), provided an Anglican alternative to psalm singing and became the mainstay of Anglican hymnody.

The editors and text writers of *Hymns Ancient and Modern* continued the Latin and early Reformation practice of ending hymns with doxologies. At times they added doxologies to hymns, including the Latin hymns they translated;[31] on at least one occasion they altered a text someone had submitted in order to promote more orthodox trinitarian theology.[32] The editors of the hymnal were well aware that hymns can promote adequate Christian doctrine, and their use of doxologies was a case in point,[33] even if later generations are not as enthusiastic about this strategy. The Anglican churches have continued to set high theological, musical, and literary standards in hymnody.

Since 1970, there has been a new flourishing of trinitarian hymnody, as text writers seek to discover ways to express trinitarian faith without using traditional male-dominant metaphors. Brian Wren is a noteworthy example, for he has written several hymns concerning the Trinity, as well as exploring trinitarian language in hymnody in his book *What Language Shall I Borrow?*[34] A number of other authors, including Carl Daw, Thomas Troeger, and Mary Jane Cathey, have written trinitarian hymns experimenting with new language. An excellent example is Jean Janzen's text based on the writings of Julian of Norwich, which addresses God as "Mothering God," "Mothering Christ," and "Mothering Spirit." This text will be discussed in more detail below.

A survey of hymns listed in hymnal indexes under the subject "Trinity" revealed that the fourth through eighth centuries and the years after 1970 produced the most vivid and original trinitarian hymnody among hymns churches still sing. Thomas Troeger has observed that times of theological controversy spark creativity in hymn writing.[35] The trinitarian controversies of the fourth and fifth centuries produced some of the world's most beautiful hymns. Today's debates about the Trinity—provoked by disputes about inclusive language—may well inspire more creativity in writing trinitarian hymns than the church has seen in more than a thousand years.

TYPES OF TRINITARIAN HYMNODY

To consider the way hymns express trinitarian theology, I examined eight hymnals published by Protestant denominations in the United States since 1982, attending to but going beyond hymns listed under "Trinity" in the subject index: *Hymnal 1982* (The Episcopal Church, U.S., 1982); *Rejoice in the Lord* (Reformed Church in America, 1985); *United Methodist Hymnal* (United Methodist Church, 1989); *The Presbyterian Hymnal* (Presbyterian Church, 1990); *The Baptist Hymnal* (Southern Baptist Convention, 1991); *Hymnal: A Worship Book* (Church of the Brethren, General Conference Mennonite Church, and the Mennonite Church of North America, 1992); *Chalice Hymnal* (Disciples of Christ, 1995); *New Century Hymnal* (United Church of Christ, 1995).[36] I identified five categories of hymns expressing trinitarian theology through study of the hymnals: (1) hymns including one stanza that was a doxology praising the Trinity; (2) hymns with a stanza about each person of the Trinity, and perhaps another stanza—often the last, sometimes the first—praising the whole Trinity; (3) hymns directed to the Trinity as a unity, often expressing exalted praise and wonder at God's very nature; (4) brief pieces of service music such as the Gloria; and (5) hymns that express an economic trinitarian theology—that is, that focus on the relationship of the believer with the triune God. Hymns of this fifth type clearly mention each person of the Trinity, as fits the hymn's flow of thought, more than in formulas, technical trinitarian language, or threefold structures.

Considering the ways traditional and contemporary hymns have witnessed to the Trinity can help us be aware of options for new and revised hymnody. Let us then consider examples from each category, to discover how hymns express trinitarian faith.

Many traditional and modern hymns end with a trinitarian doxology, the first category. Some of these are older psalm paraphrases ending with trinitarian doxologies as a vehicle for Christian praise. In general, metrical psalms today do not end with trinitarian doxologies; for example, none of the texts in the psalter section of *The Presbyterian Hymnal* does so.[37] Some Christian thinkers today argue that it shows more respect for the integrity of scripture and for God's continuing revelation to the Jewish people not to inject christological elements into psalms sung in worship.

Sometimes stanzas with trinitarian doxologies are part of hymns that address Christ or Spirit. An ancient example is a hymn to the Spirit, "Come,

O Creator Spirit, Come," translated from Latin by Robert Bridges, which concludes:

> May we by thee the Father learn,
> and know the Son, and thee discern,
> who art of both, and thus adore
> in perfect faith forevermore.[38]

Doxologies as final verses of hymns addressed to Christ or Spirit safeguard the theological insight that God is one, even though we may focus on one person of the Trinity at a given time.

Trinitarian doxologies serve best in hymns when they sum up and form a seamless whole with the rest of the text. Adding trinitarian doxologies to psalms and hymns in order to promote orthodoxy is of limited usefulness, especially when the language is technical or stereotyped. Further, adding a doxology unrelated to the whole may undermine the text's poetic integrity.

Hymns in the second category (hymns addressing one stanza to each person of the Trinity) often begin or end with another stanza praising the whole Trinity. "Come, Thou Almighty King" follows a familiar pattern; first it praises the Father, then the Son, then the Holy Spirit, and finally the whole Trinity. Stanza 1 invokes the "Almighty King," "Father all-glorious," and "Ancient of Days"; stanza 2 invokes Christ as "Incarnate Word"; stanza 3 calls on the "Holy Comforter" and "Spirit of power." The final stanza addresses God as "Great one in three" and speaks of God's "sovereign majesty." Another hymn, "All Glory Be to God on High," places the doxology first, then sings to Father/Lord (stanza 2), then to the Lord Jesus Christ/Son of God (3) and the Holy Spirit (4). "O God, Almighty Father" provides an interesting alternative. Stanzas address God as Father and "Creator of all things," Jesus as "Word incarnate, Redeemer most adored," and the Holy Spirit as one "who lives within our soul." A chorus follows each stanza: "O most holy Trinity, undivided unity, Holy God, mighty God, God immortal be adored." This structure helps to hold together the unity and the diversity of the triune God.

Of the inclusive-language trinitarian hymns by modern authors listed in Trinity indexes, most fit into this second category. A hymn by Mary Jackson Cathey invokes each person: "Come, great God of all the ages . . . Come, Christ Jesus, flesh and spirit, sure foundation, cornerstone . . .

Come, great Spirit, in and with us." A hymn by Jeffery Rowthorn, "Creating God, Your Fingers Trace," has stanzas addressed to "Creating God," "Sustaining God," "Redeeming God," and "Indwelling God." Another by Jane Parker Huber addresses "Creator God, creating still" (stanza 1), "Redeemer God, redeeming still" (2), and "Sustainer God, sustaining still" (3), and ends, "Great Trinity, for this new day we need your presence still. Create, redeem, sustain us now to do your work and will." One observer notes that these three hymns focus on the activities or functions of the persons of the Trinity.[39] Another agonizes whether Rowthorn's hymn is trinitarian, or whether it is, despite the author's intention, a "Unitarian (Sabellian?) hymn, dwelling on four aspects of divine activity."[40]

Jean Janzen's innovative 1991 hymn "Mothering God, You Gave Me Birth" draws on the writings of Julian of Norwich to speak of each person of the Trinity in a separate stanza:

> Mothering God, you gave me birth
> in the bright morning of this world.
> Creator, source of ev'ry breath,
> you are my rain, my wind, my sun.
>
> Mothering Christ, you took my form,
> offering me your food of light,
> grain of life, grape of love,
> your very body for my peace.
>
> Mothering Spirit, nurt'ring one
> in arms of patience hold me close,
> so that in faith I root and grow
> until I flow'r, until I know.

This text is interesting because it not only uses maternal images for each person of the Trinity but also uses vivid metaphors throughout and puts the Trinity in intimate relationship with the believer.

Hymns in the third category address the Trinity more generally, rather than emphasizing divine threefoldness. It is challenging to write such a hymn as a vivid faith expression and not a pedantic exercise in scholastic theology. Louis Benson accuses Reginald Heber of abandoning poetry in the hymn "Holy, Holy, Holy":

The opening, "Holy! Holy! Holy! Lord God Almighty," gives perfect poetical expression to the doctrine of the Trinity. The closing line, "God in three persons, blessed Trinity," instead of attaining a poetic climax, is not poetry at all but simply a reversion to Nicene definition.[41]

Some other hymns, such as "Holy God, We Praise Thy Name," tend toward abstraction rather than poetry. The last stanza of "The Royal Banners Forward Go," a hymn written originally in Latin around 574 C.E. by Fortunatus, is better: "Blessed Trinity, life's source and spring, may every soul thy praises sing!" This aptly combines a technical term ("Trinity") and strong metaphors ("source and spring") in the context of the Christian's response of praise.

Brian Wren has written one of the few modern inclusive trinitarian hymns that emphasizes the oneness of the Trinity:

> God is One, unique and holy,
>   endless dance of love and light,
> only source of mind and body,
>   star-cloud, atom, day and night:
>   everything that is or could be
>   tells God's anguish and delight.
>
> God is Oneness-by-Communion:
>   never distant or alone,
> at the heart of all belonging:
>   loyal friendship, loving home,
>   common mind and shared agreement,
>   common loaf and sung Shalom.
>
> Through the pain that loving Wisdom
>   could foresee, but not forestall,
> God is One, though torn and anguished
>   in the Christ's forsaken call,
>   One through death and resurrection,
>   One in Spirit, One for all.[42]

Each stanza describes actions closely associated with one person of the Trinity (creation, communion, death and resurrection), while picturing the whole Trinity acting together. Wren follows an unusual order—Source, Spirit, Christ—which may well help to move people's imagination past formulas. He expresses these profound theological insights while scarcely resorting to technical trinitarian terminology. With its lively metaphors, the hymn worthily expresses trinitarian faith.

We are familiar with trinitarian witness in service music (short sung liturgical pieces). One of the best-known examples in the English language is Thomas Ken's (from 1674 C.E.):

> Praise God, from whom all blessings flow;
> praise him, all creatures here below;
> praise him above, ye heavenly host;
> praise Father, Son, and Holy Ghost.

These doxologies, which sometimes served as the final verses of sung psalms, are now often used alone as service music.

New trinitarian doxologies have been composed for use as service music; for example, this doxology written by Wren to the tune REGENTS SQUARE:

> Praise the Lover of Creation,
> Praise the Spirit, Friend of Friends,
> Praise the true Beloved, our Savior,
> Praise the God who makes and mends,
>   strong, surrendered, many splendored,
> Three whose Oneness never ends.[43]

> Copyright 1989 Hope Publishing Company

This is some of Wren's finest work on the Trinity to date. While speaking quite adequately of the internal relationship of the Trinity, he here strongly emphasizes the work of God in the economy of salvation—in our human lives. This refines the "Lover-Beloved-Mutual Friend" metaphor system he proposes elsewhere.[44] The Spirit now is "Friend of Friends"—a relational metaphor stronger than "mutual friend" (who could be a "third wheel"). Even the divergence from usual order avoids the connotation that the Spirit is subordinate to Lover and Beloved. A variation of this form is the chorus, or *corito*, that names each partner of the Trinity, for example this Latin American *corito*:

> Somos uno en Christo . . . un solo Dios, un solo Señor, una solo fe, un solo amor, un solo bautismo, un solo Espiritu, y ese es el Consolador. (We are one in Christ . . . with only one God, only one Lord, only one faith, only one love, only one baptism, only one Spirit, who is the Comforter.)[45]

This *corito* gives another alternative for expressing trinitarian faith.

An "economic" trinitarian hymn uses names associated with the three dimensions of the Trinity in a way that assumes their participation together in the divine life. Such a hymn points to the activity of God in human history, in the church, and in the life of the singers. It centers on praise, thanksgiving, and Christian commitment in the life of the world, thus using the language of metaphor and of devotion. Often, its central metaphor is love—God's love toward us, and our love of God and one another, and the work of love in reconciling and recreating the world. Not all these hymns can be found in hymnal indexes under "Trinity," yet they express trinitarian theology.

"I Bind unto Myself Today" (or "St. Patrick's Breastplate," attributed to Patrick [372–466] and translated by Cecil F. Alexander [1818–1895]) is a vivid example of a traditional economic trinitarian hymn. The singer calls on the name and power of the Trinity for guidance, comfort, and wisdom:

> I bind unto myself today the strong Name of the Trinity,
> by invocation of the same, the Three in One and One in Three.

The singer recalls the incarnation, baptism, death, and resurrection of Christ, and then the love of the angels, the virtues of nature, the wisdom of God, and the presence of Christ. The hymn closes by once again invoking the Trinity, "Of whom all nations hath creation, eternal Father, Spirit, Word." This hymn, patterned after Celtic invocations more than trinitarian formulas, relates all it says of the Trinity to the life of the believer. Language is vivid and compelling.

Several well-known hymns express an economic trinitarian theology. Fanny Crosby speaks of God/Jesus/Spirit in "Blessed Assurance"; Luther speaks of God/Christ Jesus/Spirit in "A Mighty Fortress Is Our God." In "Love Divine, All Loves Excelling," Charles Wesley speaks of God, Christ, and Spirit in such varied ways that one cannot always tell which person of the Trinity he is addressing. Some modern hymns also sing of the Trinity in an economic way. "Glorious Is Your Name, O Jesus," by Robert J. Fryson, speaks beautifully of relationship with Christ and Spirit. Jaroslav Vajda's powerful communion hymn "Now the Silence" tells of Christ's self-giving and resurrection, "the Spirit's visitation," and the "Father's arms in welcome." Ronald Cole-Turner's hymn, "Child of Blessing, Child of Promise," speaks of the triune God acting in the Christian's life through baptism. The singers say the child is "baptized with the Spirit's sign" and ask the child to "live as one who bears Christ's name" as a "child of God your loving Parent." Wren's "There's a Spirit in the Air" focuses on how we identify the presence of Christ and the Spirit: people are reconciled, the hungry are fed, and justice is done.

Each of these five approaches to trinitarian congregational song plays a part in giving voice to the faith of the church.

HYMNALS AND THE TRINITY

Because hymns express and form the faith and spirituality of worshipers, and because the Trinity is a central Christian doctrine, hymnal committees should consider how adequately hymns express trinitarian theology.

British Methodist liturgical historian David Tripp extensively studied the 1989 *United Methodist Hymnal*, comparing it with the 1780 *Collection of Hymns for the Use of the People Called Methodists*. He counted economic trinitarian hymns, but not doxologies used only as service music or last stanzas. He found that 70 of 734 (11.41 percent) items in the *United Methodist Hymnal* are explicitly trinitarian and concludes: "Since 1780, the proportion of explicitly Trinitarian hymns has dropped by slightly more than half."[46] He expresses alarm that this change in hymn texts may indicate that United Methodists embrace trinitarian theology less wholeheartedly than in the past, because of theological shifts, such as the emphasis on inclusive language.

Tripp also worries that inclusive language adaptations may obscure or even subvert the trinitarian theology of traditional texts. For example, he laments the *United Methodist Hymnal*'s alteration of Charles Wesley's "Father, in Whom We Live" to "Maker, in Whom We Live."[47] In his view this destroys the way the original text relates theological terms such as "Father," "Incarnate Deity," and "Triune God" with economic language expressing the faith experience of believers. The hymn's classic four-stanza structure (Maker/Incarnate Deity/Spirit of Holiness/Eternal, Triune God) leaves no doubt that the altered first stanza addresses the first person of the Trinity. Still, it is fair to ask how extensive hymn alteration will affect trinitarian theology. How much can the relational language of "Father" be replaced by the functional language of "Maker" or "Creator" without undermining the formation of Christians in trinitarian spirituality?

In a caustic review of the United Church of Christ's *New Century Hymnal*, Richard L. Christensen argues that "the most theologically questionable change in the new hymnal is the near-elimination of classical Christian language for the Trinity."[48] He objects to the hymnal's use of "Mother" to replace or balance "Father" as a name for God, since in his view, using "Mother" in trinitarian language "implies that the act of creation involves giving birth, which makes creation of the same substance as God."[49] (Note that if the name "Father" were taken this literally it would imply that every human bears the DNA of the Father—and thus is of the same substance as God). Rejecting the idea that changing words can contribute to justice for women, Christensen appears to reject all alternatives to "Father" in trinitarian hymnody, whether in adapted or new texts.

Though these critiques merit consideration, nurturing trinitarian faith calls for a far more nuanced approach. What if Christians held traditional expressions of trinitarian faith in tension with new expressions, including some hymns using feminine language for God? What if committees considered adaptations text by text, without insisting on keeping or changing every reference to Father, Son, and Spirit? In each case they could consider how proposed changes integrate with the theology and language of the original text, seeking poetry that is at least as good as the original. Several strategies, such as using new hymns with feminine language for God or avoiding pronouns when using gendered names, might help to reduce any imbalance of masculine language in the hymnal. Committees should seek to provide a rich and vivid diversity of ways of talking about the triune God, drawing on the best traditional and modern hymnody. Most important, committees should consider how the overall body of hymns serves to nurture living faith in the triune God.

WRITING NEW HYMN TEXTS ON THE TRINITY

Hymn text writers bear a weighty theological responsibility, for hymns are one of the main ways that Christian faith passes from one generation to the next. Hymn writers are responsible not only for continuing the tradition, but also for renewing and transforming it: for providing fresh words that ring true for Christians living with the challenges and opportunities of their own time and place.

Hymn writers continue and renew theological traditions through the use of poetic language. In chapter 2 I argue the importance of using vivid metaphorical language in expressing trinitarian faith. Nowhere is this so important as in hymnody. Hymn writers must complement or provide alternatives to the traditional language of "Father, Son, and Spirit," alternatives that are more inspiring than "Creating, Redeeming, and Sustaining God," even though these terms do describe what God has done, is doing, and will do for us. Hymn writers have already been using a plethora of fascinating metaphors to sing to the triune God. I hope that many more new hymns about the Trinity will renew the vocabulary of Christian praise.

As we have seen, trinitarian hymns can take several forms. Short trinitarian doxologies are useful as service music and as stanzas that harmonize with the thoughts of the whole hymn. Some beautiful and exalted hymns praise the triune unity. Hymns with one stanza devoted to each person provide a sturdy structure in which to give equal honor and praise to each partner in the divine dance; an additional stanza or chorus can serve to lift up the divine unity as well. The structure may vary: Why not sing first to Spirit, then to Christ, then to the Source of all?

Hymn writers could also seek forms to express the perichoretic (intermingling) nature of the Trinity. I attempted to create such a structure in the following hymn, by anticipating in the last line of stanzas 1 and 2 the person of the Trinity to be addressed in the next stanza:

> God, who made the stars of heaven,
> God, who spread the earth,
> breath of ev'ry living being,
> source of life and birth,
> you have formed us as your people,
> led us by your hand.
> Light of nations, shine in us,
> brighten ev'ry land.
>
> Living Christ, the light of nations,
> radiant as the sun,
> build us up, a growing body;
> knit your church as one.
> May our loving be a witness
> all the world may see.
> Send your Spirit, bond of peace,
> source of unity.
>
> Spirit God, equip your people,
> all with gifts to share:
> messengers to speak the gospel,

ministers of care.
So may valleys rise to greatness,
mountains be a plain.
Come, surprise us; change our lives;
heal the hearts in pain.

So may peoples praise your greatness,
do your will on earth,
free the captives from their prisons,
treat the poor with worth.
So may desert, coast, and village
sing new songs to you.
May your Spirit fill the world,
making all things new.

Words by Ruth Duck,
Copyright 1998 Pilgrim Press[50]

The last stanza addresses the Trinity as a whole; the phrase "do your will on earth" recalls the prayer of Jesus to the Father; and "Light of nations" recalls the second stanza, addressed to Christ. This exemplifies a form that attempts to highlight the interrelation of the triune partners.

Texts that are strongly grounded in the economy of salvation have great potential for nurturing trinitarian faith. Focusing not only on the inner life of God, but also on God's life with humanity, such hymns need not depend only on formulaic language of "Father, Son, and Spirit." They can grow out of the scripture witness to God with us, as well as reflecting contemporary experience. The root metaphor is love—God's love reaching out to humanity and all creation to unite all things in love—which may engender other relational metaphors such as Father, Mother, Lover, Beloved, and Friend.

The potential subject matter for new trinitarian hymnody is as broad as any hymnal index. Vital new trinitarian hymns of praise for the beginning of worship and for the celebration of Baptism and Eucharist will enhance the church's worship. The churches need good new trinitarian hymns in particular subject areas, judging at least from the *United Methodist Hymnal*.[51] It appears that few hymns focusing on Jesus Christ refer to the Spirit; those that do are mostly gospel hymns and choruses of the nineteenth and twentieth centuries (e.g., "Standing on the Promises" and "Spirit Song"). Resurrection and communion hymns that speak of the gift of the Spirit, as well as the life, death, and resurrection of Jesus, are in short supply. Surprisingly few hymns about Christian mission in the *United Methodist Hymnal* refer to the Spirit, though most of the baptism and ordination hymns do. Hymns for liturgies of Christian marriage and burial do well to express faith in the Source of love and life known in Jesus Christ and at work among us through the Spirit. Yet no hymns in the *United Methodist Hymnal* sections on "Marriage" or "Funeral and Memorial Service" and very few in the section on "Death and Eternal Life" explicitly express trinitarian faith. A living trinitarian faith is an impetus for concern for the life of the world. LaCugna, for example, emphasizes the ethical dimension of trinitarian faith: the whole Trinity labors for love, peace, and justice within all creation.[52] New hymns about justice, peace, and mission expressing a fully trinitarian faith might help mend the breach between spirituality and justice Christians sometimes experience. All these areas are fertile ground for new trinitarian hymns.

SUMMARY

In response to theological controversies in the early church, the language of theological reflection came to dominate the words Christians have sung in worship. My survey of trinitarian language in hymnody suggests that when Christians sing about the Trinity, they often do so in formulaic ways that do not inspire feeling, imagination, or reflection. The current concern about gender language in liturgy need not threaten trinitarian theology; rather, it is a crucial opportunity to witness to trinitarian faith with greater expressive power.

The primary human response to the love of the triune God is doxology — praising God and living to God's glory.[53] Singing hymns is a crucial part of praising God and expressing commitment to live to God's glory. The current debate about gender and liturgical language provides the opportunity for a new outpouring of hymns of praise and love to the Trinity.

6

Sophia and the Trinity

The Re-Imagining gathering of November 1993 made public what was already a prominent theme in Christian feminist theology and liturgy: the use of "Sophia" as a name for God. This naming was based especially on images from Proverbs and on the deuterocanonical books of the Wisdom of Ben Sirach (Ecclesiasticus) and the Wisdom of Solomon. *Sophia*, of course, means "wisdom" in Greek. The Septuagint uses it to translate the Hebrew *Hokmah*; in English it may be translated "Holy Wisdom." Though the names *Hokmah* or "Holy Wisdom" might create less confusion, for some the name "Sophia" inspires the imagination; for others, it provokes wrath. Like *Hokmah*, *Sophia* is a grammatically feminine word.

Using Wisdom imagery for God is attractive to biblically oriented Christians who seek feminine imagery for God in order to complement the masculine and gender-neutral terms of liturgical tradition. Most feminine images for God in scripture, such as midwife, mother bird, and human mother, portray God in roles that females play in patriarchal societies. Feminine metaphors for God to complement tradition should draw on a *broad* range of activities—such as Creator, Architect, Eternal One, and Gracious Hostess. Metaphors for Holy Wisdom in scripture draw on all these roles and more, rather than on a single human activity, even one as profound as giving birth. Further, unlike other feminine images for God used once in passing, Wisdom imagery pervades later biblical literature. Thus, this whole tradition, too diverse for a one-size-fits-all theological interpretation, offers rich resources for expanded liturgical practice. Yet, as I will argue, using Wisdom imagery calls for theological, pastoral, and linguistic care.

A good starting point is to survey some biblical and apocryphal material to consider how the image of divine Wisdom developed.

THE DEVELOPMENT OF THE IMAGE
OF DIVINE WISDOM

The wisdom tradition, with personified feminine images of divine Wisdom, emerged as a major stream of biblical tradition in early postexilic Israel. Wisdom spirituality is found not only in what is called wisdom literature, but also in the literature of Jewish apocalyptic and Qumran.[1] It influenced diverse social classes, though sometimes obviously addressing elite males.[2] The tradition is practical, giving advice for daily life. It is open-ended, not theologically exclusive; it seeks to tolerate or absorb the best of world religious traditions, rather than urging isolation.

Several theories attempt to explain how Wisdom imagery emerged. The first emphasizes social and political context. Feminist biblical scholar Elisabeth Schüssler Fiorenza notes that Wisdom imagery emerged at a time when the household was replacing the monarchy as administrator of Judah's way of life.[3] In this social context, Lady Wisdom, pictured as teacher, mother, sister, and lover, replaced the king as divine mediator between God and Israel.

Others, emphasizing the influence of world religions, hold the theory that *Sophia* may have emerged to respond to popular worship of one or more Near Eastern deities. Barbara Newman, a scholar of English literature well known for her work on Hildegard of Bingen, is researching the history of *Sophia*. With several other scholars, she believes that "Since the attractions of Asherah's cult could not be denied, the sages of Israel decided to fight a goddess with a goddess, introducing the figure of Hokmah or Sophia in their teaching as a counterweight to the pagan deity."[4] Later, when Isis worship spread throughout the Hellenistic world, sages of Israel may have developed "their portrait of *Sophia* still further, introducing many features of Isis."[5] *Hokmah* was not just a carbon copy of Isis or other deities; the sages carefully related her being and work to that of the Holy One, avoiding bi-theism.

A third approach, more psychological, theorizes that whenever religious traditions exclude the feminine from the divine, sooner or later it reemerges—from the exalted Mary to the gentle, "feminine" Jesus of nineteenth-century hymnody and Salmon portraits. Thus *Sophia* emerged as a psychological balance to the masculine Lord of Hebrew tradition. This explanation is less helpful than the others are, to the extent that it collapses history and human personality into masculine and feminine stereotypes, for instance, by presuming that gentleness is only feminine. It is possible that, along with socioeconomic and interfaith influences, the unconscious desire for feminine images might have played a part in the development of the wisdom tradition.

For whatever reason, Wisdom imagery became more prominent in biblical literature, beginning after the exile and continuing through the first three centuries of the Christian era. Let us now briefly trace the historical development of the Wisdom image in scriptural literature.

The first personified use of Wisdom imagery is in the book of Proverbs, chapters 1–9. Key passages include chapter 8, where Wisdom appears as teacher, and as one who was present with God at creation, and the beginning of 9, where Wisdom prepares a rich feast (Prov. 8:1–5, 22–31; 9:1–6). Though here the use is modest, so that Wisdom can be said to personify an aspect of God's nature, she is already a complex character who provides an alternative to feminine deities because of her preexistence, her part in creation, and her offer of life. Scholars generally find Egyptian influence in this portion of Proverbs, and perhaps some hints of the Isis cult—one of many African influences in scripture.[6]

The Wisdom of Solomon is an apocryphal book that is part of the scriptural canon for Roman Catholic and Orthodox Christians. It may have been written around 100 B.C.E., and it contains some exalted Wisdom imagery. Chapter 7:22b–28 is striking:

> There is in her a spirit that is intelligent, holy,
> unique, manifold, subtle,
> mobile, clear, unpolluted,
> distinct, invulnerable, loving the good, keen,
> irresistible, beneficent, humane,
> steadfast, sure, free from anxiety,
> all-powerful, overseeing all,
> and penetrating through all spirits
> that are intelligent, pure, and altogether subtle.
> For wisdom is more mobile than any motion;
> because of her pureness she pervades and penetrates all things.

> For she is a breath of the power of God,
> and a pure emanation of the glory of the Almighty;
> therefore nothing defiled gains entrance into her.
> For she is a reflection of eternal light,
> a spotless mirror of the working of God,
> and an image of his goodness.
> Although she is but one, she can do all things,
> and while remaining in herself, she renews all things;
> in every generation she passes into holy souls,
> and makes them friends of God, and prophets;
> for God loves nothing so much as the person who lives with wisdom.

Here we have moved past simple personification to what biblical scholar David Winston has called a "divine eternal emanation."[7] This emanational theology parallels Egyptian and Akkadian sources in which hypostases represent characteristics of the high deity (characteristics such as "righteousness" or "creative word"). Sometimes these hypostases are called children of the deity and have their own myths and cults. Wisdom 8:3–4 pictures what Winston calls "a symbiotic relationship with God, a condition of unbroken intimacy with the divine":[8]

> She glorifies her noble birth by living with God,
> and the Lord of all loves her.
> For she is an initiate in the knowledge of God,
> and an associate in his works.

But perhaps Holy Wisdom is most exalted in Wisdom of Solomon 10, which attributes to her the saving activities of God: giving Adam "strength to rule all things," saving humanity from the flood, bringing the oppressed out of Egypt. In one striking passage she does what God does in Exodus 15:

> She brought them over the Red Sea,
> and led them through deep waters;
> but she drowned their enemies,
> and cast them up from the depth of the sea.

> (Wisd. Sol. 10:18–19)

Here *Sophia* is fully developed as a divine presence, ambiguous though her role as destroyer of Egyptian armies may be.

Philo, the first-century Jewish philosopher, also considered *Sophia* to be an exalted hypostasis of God and the daughter of God, but he believed that feminine language was "weak" and inadequate to speak of the emanation of God. As he developed his theological system, he transferred scriptural attributes from *Sophia* to *Logos*. He retained a role for *Sophia* in the heavenly spheres but described *Logos* as mediator of God on earth.[9] Philo's thinking and language may have influenced John's Gospel.

The apostle Paul refers to wisdom theology, using *Sophia* imagery for Christ, especially in 1 Corinthians. Here Paul appears to respond to theologies that exalt wisdom as a secret possession of an elite who considered themselves superior to other community members. Paul subverts such theologies by applying wisdom theology to the cross of Christ. Notice how Paul twice calls Christ the "wisdom of God" in 1 Corinthians 1:18 and 22–31:

> For the message about the cross is foolishness to those who are perishing, but to us who are being saved it is the power of God. . . .
>
> For Jews demand signs and Greeks desire wisdom, but we proclaim Christ crucified, a stumbling block to Jews and foolishness to Gentiles, but to those who are the called, both Jews and Greeks, *Christ the power of God and the wisdom of God.* For God's foolishness is wiser than human wisdom, and God's weakness is stronger than human strength.
>
> Consider your own call, brothers and sisters: not many of you were wise by human standards, not many were powerful, not many were of noble birth. But God chose what is foolish in the world to shame the wise; God chose what is weak in the world to shame the strong; God chose what is low and despised in the world, things that are not, to reduce to nothing things that are, so that no one might boast in the presence of God. He is the source of your life in Christ Jesus, *who became for us wisdom from God*, and righteousness and sanctification and redemption, in order that, as it is written, "Let the one who boasts, boast in the Lord." (my emphasis)

According to Paul, then, Christ is most fully revealed as *Sophia* on the cross—a caution to any modern wisdom Christology that might become merely self-serving.

Especially since 1970, studies of Matthew's Gospel have uncovered much influence by wisdom traditions.[10] That Gospel identifies Jesus with Holy Wisdom, at times adapting material from previous sources which shows Jesus as Wisdom's messenger and prophet.[11] For example, in Luke 11:49, Jesus says, "*the Wisdom of God* said, 'I will send them prophets and apostles, some of whom they will kill and persecute,'" but in Matthew 23:34 Jesus himself says, "Therefore *I* send you prophets, sages, and scribes, some of whom you will kill and crucify."[12] The Gospel of Matthew also applies imagery from apocryphal wisdom literature to Jesus. For example, in Matthew 11:28–30, Jesus says,

> Come to me, all you that are weary and are carrying heavy burdens, and I will give you rest. Take my yoke upon you, and learn from me; for I am gentle and humble in heart, and you will find rest for your souls. For my yoke is easy, and my burden is light.

These words echo Ben Sirach's words about *Sophia*: "Put your neck under her yoke, and let your souls receive instruction" (Sirach 51:26) and "Put your feet into her fetters, and your neck into her collar. Bend your shoulders and carry her, and do not fret under her bonds. Come to her with all your soul, and keep her ways with all your might. . . . For at last you will find the rest she gives, and she will be changed into joy for you" (Sirach 6:24–26, 28). Given many such references, Elisabeth Schüssler Fiorenza says that Matthew pictures Jesus "as *Sophia* herself . . . [for] Jesus does what *Sophia* does."[13] Or as Jack Suggs, one of the first modern New Testament scholars to highlight Matthew's development of wisdom traditions, writes, for Matthew, "Jesus is Sophia incarnate."[14]

John's Gospel also draws on wisdom traditions, but where Matthew speaks of *Sophia*, John speaks of *Logos* ("Word"). What John's prologue attributes to the Logos, postexilic Jewish literature had attributed to *Sophia*: her preexistence, activity in creation, and identity as offspring of God. Just as *Sophia* makes friends for God (Wisd. Sol. 7:27, quoted above), Jesus calls his disciples friends (John 15:12–14). John echoes Wisdom traditions in talking about Jesus; for example, the "I am" sayings resemble the way Wisdom talks about herself. Like *Sophia*, Jesus offers his followers bread and living water, and the light, way, and truth. Obviously, the language of *Logos* (a masculine grammatical term) attracted the Gospel writer, given Jesus' maleness and perhaps the influence of Philo, but this choice has made Christians less aware of the influence of wisdom traditions in the fourth Gospel.

Early church theologians such as Justin, Origen, Tertullian, and Augustine of Hippo often identified Jesus Christ with *Sophia*; in fact, one of the first ways early Christians sought to explain how God was made known in Jesus Christ was through Jewish *Sophia* traditions of the last centuries B.C.E. Tertullian identifies the Son with *Logos* ("Word") and *Sophia* ("Wisdom"), citing Proverbs 8:22 and 25 to show how even at creation there was a distinction between the Father and "Wisdom."[15] In this way he refutes Praxeus's claim that Father and Son are one and the same. Tertullian writes that both Proverbs 8 and John 1 speak of the same power who "became the Son": "It is one and the same power which is in one place described under the name of Wisdom, and in another passage under the appellation of the Word."[16] Origen expresses a Wisdom Christology, saying that "the only-begotten Son of God is God's wisdom hypostatically existing."[17] He identifies the wisdom and Word of God, thus arguing that the Son is eternally begotten. For support he cites Colossians 1:15, Hebrews 1:3, and Wisdom of Solomon 7:25, quoted above ("she is a breath of the power of God"). In discussing the incarnation, he expresses wonder at how

> this mighty power of the divine majesty, the very word of the Father, and the very wisdom of God, in which were created "all things visible and invisible," can be believed to have existed within the compass of that man who appeared in Judaea; yes, and how the wisdom of God can have entered into a woman's womb and been born as a little child and uttered noises like those of crying children.[18]

Origen's identification of Jesus Christ with Wisdom is quite striking.

Identification of Jesus Christ with the Wisdom of God was hardly rare in the early church. In fourth-century debates about the nature of Christ, both sides assumed that Christ and *Sophia* were one and the same but interpreted the same scriptures differently. According to Gregory of Nyssa, his opponent Eunomius used Proverbs 8:22 ("The LORD created me at the beginning of his work, the first of his acts of long ago") to argue that Jesus Christ was a creature. Gregory characterizes Eunomius's position: "Because these words are spoken by Wisdom, and the Lord is called Wisdom by the great Paul, they allege this passage as though the Only-begotten God Himself, under the name of Wisdom, acknowledges that He was created by the Maker of all things."[19] Gregory responds by quoting Proverbs 8:25 ("Before the mountains had been shaped, before the hills, I was begotten"),[20] and saying that "creature" refers to the humanity of Christ, while "begotten" refers to the Godhead of the Lord Jesus Christ.[21] He says "Christ is Wisdom," who participated in the creation of the world, "being always in the Father, not waiting to arise in Him as a result of creation."[22] Although he finds it necessary to explain the passage from Proverbs, Gregory assumes that the reader would readily accept the identification of Christ with Wisdom. During the first four centuries of the church, it was commonplace to identify Jesus Christ with the Wisdom figure of Proverbs, Ben Sirach, and Wisdom of Solomon. This tradition has continued in the churches of the East; the church of *Hagia Sophia* (Holy Wisdom) in Istanbul is just one example of their esteem for Holy Wisdom.

As Western theology continued to develop, use of Wisdom imagery for the divine became rare; at times Mary, Lady Philosophy, or nature were portrayed using the figure of Wisdom.[23] The mystics, however, provide striking examples of Wisdom imagery for God. Lady Wisdom (*Sapienta*) appears in diverse and dazzling ways in the visions and writings of Hildegard of Bingen (1098–1179), in reference to Word, Spirit, and Father. In one hymn she addresses the Trinity as "the energy of Wisdom . . . encompassing all in one path that possesses life, having three wings."[24] Julian of Norwich (1342–c. 1423), who characteristically calls Christ "Mother," associates the Son with Wisdom as she describes the Trinity: "The almighty truth of the Trinity is our Father, for he made us and keeps us in him. And the deep wisdom of the Trinity is our Mother, in whom we are enclosed. And the high goodness of the Trinity is our Lord, and in him we are enclosed and he in us."[25] Henry Suso (1295–1366), in the "Little Book of Eternal Wisdom," continually speaks of the incarnate one as "eternal Wisdom," alluding to biblical wisdom texts. The way he identifies eternal Wisdom with the story of the incarnate, crucified, and living One, and not his use of other titles such as "Christ," "Son," or even "Jesus," reveal to whom he is speaking. Suso expresses the believer's thirst for the joy of divine presence; eternal Wisdom replies to his desire by saying: "If you want to see me in my uncreated Godhead, you should learn to know and love me here in my suffering humanity."[26] Although the public liturgy did not often use Wisdom imagery for the divine, these and other mystics kept the tradition alive.

Wisdom imagery, in its various forms, is far more widespread in scripture and tradition than most of us have supposed. With good reason, many Christian feminists are exploring uses for this previously neglected imagery in worship. I believe this is an essential undertaking, for this imagery is a rich tradition that may provide helpful biblical feminine naming for God. The task of recovery is not, however, as simple as it might seem. If neglected and unfamiliar symbols are not to subvert a theological system, they must be related to the existing system. This task is theological but also pastoral. When we introduce new or neglected imagery to Christian worship, we must do it in a way that expands, rather than undermines, the faith of believers.

Like postexilic Jews who spoke of Wisdom with care in order not to contradict monotheism, so Christians who wish to recover Wisdom imagery should take care to relate such imagery to the Trinity. Using Wisdom imagery in worship, and especially using *Sophia* as a name for God or Christ, presses the trinitarian question. Is Holy Wisdom or *Sophia* a fourth person of the trinity, a new Godhead to replace the Trinity, or something else? A popular book about Wisdom in scripture, tradition, and present-day worship speaks of *Sophia* as having "co-equal status with God," and advocates giving her "full divine status."[27] Because the authors did not develop this claim in relation to the Trinity, they seemed to exalt *Sophia* as a new goddess, rather than as a recovery of feminine imagery to praise the God of Jesus Christ (as I believe they intended).

Fortunately, some recent authors who propose wider use of *Sophia* or Wisdom imagery in Christian theology and worship have labored to integrate such imagery with trinitarian theology.

Elizabeth Johnson, in *She Who Is*, a magnificent work of systematic theology, relates *Sophia* and the Trinity by drawing connections between each person of the Trinity and *Hokmah/Sophia* in various scripture passages.[28]

She begins by considering Spirit-Sophia, since the ever-present Spirit supports women's work of reconstructing church and theology. The apocryphal book of Wisdom closely connects Spirit and Wisdom, starting with chapter 1: "Wisdom is a kindly spirit" (v. 6). Johnson explains her understanding of Spirit-Sophia: "Spirit-Sophia is the living God at her closest to the world, pervading the whole and each creature to awaken life and mutual kinship."[29] Along with others, she notes the close affinity of Spirit and *Sophia* in Pauline theology.

Johnson connects Jesus and *Sophia* easily, drawing on the material from 1 Corinthians, John, and Matthew discussed above, as well as the prologues to Colossians and Hebrews. She cites biblical scholars Jack Suggs, who says that for Matthew, Jesus is *Sophia* incarnate, and Raymond Brown, who says that for John, Jesus is personified Wisdom. Johnson argues for a corporate Christ: Not only Jesus but the whole community of disciples constitutes Jesus-Sophia, who is God-incarnate, involved in the world.[30]

Johnson's search to build a "Mother-Sophia" image draws more on theology than scripture. She says that "Holy Wisdom is the mother of the universe, the unoriginate, living source of all that exists."[31] Though she warns against using "Mother" as the only female image of God, she notes that, despite errors of medieval biology, both "Mother" and "Father" originate life.

Johnson summarizes her theology by referring to the Trinity as the "Spirit's universal quickening and liberating presence, the living memory of Wisdom's particular path in the history of Jesus, and inconceivable Holy Wisdom herself who brings forth and orients the universe."[32]

Jann Aldredge-Clanton, by contrast, focuses on "Christ-Sophia" in her proposal for integrating *Sophia* imagery into trinitarian Christian theology.[33] She believes Sophia-Christ is a good way to portray God incarnate. "*Sophia*" has female associations, "Christ" has male associations, but "Sophia-Christ" models female-male mutuality.

She believes the wisdom tradition helped early Christians express who Jesus was. She cites scriptures speaking of Christ's preexistence that echo earlier passages speaking of *Sophia*. She points to passages in which Jesus identifies himself with *Sophia* and argues that "the image of God in the Hebrew Scriptures that had the most pervasive influence on the early church's understanding of Jesus was the feminine figure of Holy Wisdom."[34] She believes that the Father/Son language eclipsed Wisdom imagery partly because of the influence of the fourth- and fifth-century theological debates. Yet Jesus valued women, treating them as equals, using female figures in parables, calling female disciples, and using feminine images about himself. In the incarnation Jesus took on humanity in its fullness, and the image "Christ-Sophia" makes it clear that both females and males are redeemed in Jesus.

Aldredge-Clanton's most distinctive contribution is in developing a feminist theology of the resurrection emphasizing the continued presence of Christ-Sophia "incarnate in the individual believer and in the church."[35] Christian feminists sometimes dismiss belief in resurrection as a prideful wish to survive death. By contrast, Aldredge-Clanton affirms the centrality of the resurrection to liberating Christian faith, for through the Spirit of the resurrected Christ-Sophia, the church may incarnate a mutual ministry of justice, love, and peace.

This proposal is promising, if one rethinks one troubling feature: Aldredge-Clanton's tendency to identify Christ more with the historic person of Jesus, and *Sophia* more with the resurrected Christ active in the world. This subverts her goal of mutuality by implying Jesus is truly *hu-man* as male and truly *divine* as female. By implying that the resurrection, more than the ministry of Jesus, reveals the divine nature of Christ-Sophia, and toying with the idea that Jesus became Messiah only after the resurrection, she falls short of a full theology of incarnation.[36] This subverts her own claims about the preexistence of Christ and denies the co-eternity of the Trinity. With further work, however, the model of Christ-Sophia could achieve the goal of integrating Wisdom imagery into a fully trinitarian theology, by absorbing *Sophia* into the second person of the Trinity.

Johnson's proposal has much to commend it, when integrating Wisdom imagery into all three persons of the Trinity is possible liturgically. Aldredge-Clanton's proposal to use Wisdom imagery to speak of Christ is perhaps more likely to gain support, because of the wide range of sources in scripture and church tradition which speak of Christ as Wisdom. Both proposals advance the task of relating Wisdom theology to the Trinity.

USING WISDOM IMAGERY IN WORSHIP

Exploring the broad range of sources in scripture and tradition and theological proposals by Johnson and Aldredge-Clanton gives support to the possibility of using Wisdom language for God in worship. It remains for us to develop practical approaches to using Wisdom imagery in fully trinitarian Christian worship.

Since to many church people the wisdom tradition is unfamiliar or even suspect (given the attention the religious press and conservative Christian groups have given the "Sophia controversy"), worship leaders must proceed thoughtfully in introducing Wisdom imagery to worship. The wisdom tradition could be the focus of a fascinating adult education series, with sessions on Proverbs, the apocryphal literature, the Gospels, Paul, the early church, and the mystics. A concluding session could relate Wisdom imagery to trinitarian faith and contemporary concerns, including its use in worship. Including study of wisdom traditions in Christian education curricula for children and youth is a part of providing future generations with a broader range of imagery for God. Since not all worshipers would attend education sessions, it would also be helpful to explore the wisdom tradition through preaching coordinated with other parts of worship. This could be a series, possibly planned to coordinate with a study program.

The lectionary also provides opportunities to highlight aspects of this tradition. The whole of Matthew 11 is suffused with Wisdom imagery applied to Jesus. We have already commented on Matthew 11:28–30, which appears in July of Year A, together with Matthew 11:16–19, which is also a key passage applying the *Sophia* tradition to Jesus:

> "But to what will I compare this generation? It is like children sitting in the marketplaces and calling to one another, 'We played the flute for you, and you did not dance; we wailed, and you did not mourn.' For John came neither eating nor drinking, and they say, 'He has a demon'; the Son of Man came eating and drinking, and they say, 'Look, a glutton and a drunkard, a friend of tax collectors and sinners!' Yet wisdom is vindicated by her deeds."

Exegesis of the whole chapter will provide insights to those preaching on Matthew 11:2–11 (Third Sunday of Advent, Year A), as I discovered in preparing for the sermon with which this chapter concludes. Matthew's use of Wisdom/*Sophia* imagery for Jesus could be more or less central to the development of the sermon and worship service, as worship planners are led by the Spirit and the needs of the congregation.

On Trinity Sunday, Year C, Proverbs 8:1–4, 22–31 appears in the lectionary, providing the opportunity to center worship and preaching on the integration of wisdom tradition with trinitarian thought, as Saint John's United Church of Christ, Lansdale, Pennsylvania, did one year. In this context they introduced my hymn, "Come and Seek the Ways of Wisdom," which speaks of each person of the Trinity using Wisdom imagery, with some feminine pronouns. The pastors developed the theme of wisdom so well in worship and preaching that the hymn text was natural to the worship service; the congregation accepted it without comment.[37]

When Proverbs 9:1–6 appears during August of Year B, worship leaders could relate Jesus' table communion to the feast of *Sophia*, who sets her table and invites the simple to come and eat of her bread and drink and to walk in the way of insight. Obviously, it would be good to celebrate Holy Communion as part of this service.

The passage in which Paul speaks of Christ as the Wisdom of God, 1 Corinthians 1:18–25, appears in the lectionary on the Fourth Sunday after the Epiphany, Year A. Interpretation of this familiar passage becomes even more poignant when one recognizes the *Sophia* tradition to which Paul alludes: through Jesus Christ, Wisdom incarnate, God makes foolish the wisdom of the world.

The second Sunday of Christmas (A, B, and C) invites exploration of the influence of *Sophia* traditions on John's portrayal of Jesus as the Word; the Gospel is John 1:1–18 (10–18), and Sirach 24:1–12 and Wisdom of Solomon 10:15–21 are optional readings. Wisdom of Solomon 7:26–8:1, which appears as an option in September of Year A, includes a portion of the exalted passage about Wisdom quoted earlier in the chapter; it would be good to begin at verse 22. The Gospel is Mark 8:27–38. This is during "ordinary time," when texts do not necessarily coordinate, but the early church's attempt to find words and images such as "Messiah" and "Sophia" to describe who Jesus was could possibly provide a focus. Although most Protestant churches do not use the readings from the Apocrypha, use of passages from Wisdom of Solomon and Ben Sirach could help churches better understand the world of thought in which the Gospel writers lived. Education sessions on the intertestamental literature could provide not only a fascinating Bible study topic but also a preparation for occasional readings from the Apocrypha in worship.

One drawback to lectionary-based worship is the tendency to take texts out of context, and this is a particular danger with the wisdom literature. Although the passages just named can be a source of feminine images of the divine, Proverbs and other wisdom literature often portray human women in unfavorable ways, for example, as a temptation to the young man who would be wise. Linking worship and education also gives the opportunity to explore this tradition honestly, realizing that it is only partly retrievable for justice-seeking Christians.

Scripture provides a good starting point for introducing wisdom traditions. The hymnal is often another resource for gently introducing Wisdom imagery, because it indicates that others in one's denomination are using Wisdom imagery. The following order of morning prayer, developed from the *United Methodist Hymnal*[38] and scripture, has been positively received by groups of United Methodists:

> Call to praise and prayer:
> > One: Let us raise our voices and glorify the living God.
> > All: Thanks be to God.
> Morning hymn: "Morning Has Broken," number 145, stanzas 1 and 3

Scripture readings (by three readers):
    Proverbs 8:1–5, 27–31
    1 Corinthians 1:26–30a
    Matthew 11:16–19, 28–30
Silence
Canticle of Wisdom, number 112, response 2
    (Response 2 from "O Come, O Come, Emmanuel":
    "O come, thou Wisdom from on high, and order all things
    far and nigh.")
Prayers of the people
    Conclude each prayer with: God, in your wisdom,
    All respond: Hear our prayer.
Hymn: Come and Seek the Ways of Wisdom

While the words "God, in your wisdom," were designed to coordinate with the theme of the service, I now prefer it as an alternative to the popular, "Lord, in your mercy." "Mercy" seems to imply that we must beg God to hear our prayers, but "wisdom" hints that God in wisdom knows better what we need than we know how to ask. The *Chalice Hymnal* includes Patrick Michael's bold hymn to Wisdom, "Who Comes from God, as Word and Breath?" in which almost all the words are drawn from the scriptures (including the Apocrypha).[39] The *New Century Hymnal* includes the Latin chant "O Wisdom, Breathed from God," adding a new stanza addressed to the Trinity.[40] As with all congregational song, these musical resources will only serve well when appropriate to the liturgical context.

If we consider the worship suggestions so far in light of the proposals of Aldredge-Clanton and Johnson, we find that many of the texts, such as John 1:1–18, Matthew 11:16–19, 26–28, or 1 Corinthians 1:18–25, lend themselves most naturally to application of Wisdom imagery to the Christ. The added third stanza of "O Wisdom, Breathed from God" admirably gives the ancient antiphon to *Sapientia* a context in praise of the Trinity. The hymn "Who Comes from God, as Word and Breath" and some of the scripture passages it quotes are not as specific; worship leaders should make a conscious effort to put texts and hymns in a context that relates them either to one trinitarian partner or to the Trinity as a whole.

Given the breadth of the wisdom tradition in scripture and Jewish and Christian history, there are many other ways to integrate Wisdom imagery in worship. For example, each of the three major sections for the presider in the Great Thanksgiving (the eucharistic prayer before communion) speaks of one trinitarian partner, and the prayer ends with a trinitarian doxology. Weaving Wisdom imagery into the prayer (in an appropriate liturgical context) provides one more window into the inexhaustible reality of the Trinity. A central feature of the wisdom tradition is the way it shows God present in the midst of daily human life and of nature. Thus, to preach about the Trinity using wisdom traditions is immediately to relate the Trinity to life and issues such as restoring the natural environment and dealing with relationships wisely. Readings from Julian of Norwich, Hildegard of Bingen, or Henry Suso—or prayers based on their writings—could also help worshipers relate the wisdom tradition to their individual spiritual journeys.

To speak of the triune God as "Holy Wisdom" or "Sophia" broadens the range of our trinitarian metaphors by including feminine and nongendered imagery. Since the goal is a range of metaphors to inspire the imagination, reach a variety of people, and ultimately to enliven trinitarian faith and praise, Wisdom imagery should be used together with many other images. Feminine Wisdom imagery can be used along with masculine language in speaking of the Trinity, as a way to resonate with male-female mutuality. One hundred years from now, it may be possible to speak of God throughout a worship service exclusively as Father (with masculine pronouns) or Wisdom (with feminine pronouns or the word *Sophia*). Such gender imbalance would be insensitive today, except perhaps on rare, carefully planned occasions. A visitor hearing only masculine language for the divine might get the impression that the congregation has no sensitivity to gender justice; worshipers hearing only feminine Wisdom imagery for God might fear that reversal from masculine to feminine images, rather than mutuality, was the goal.

Speaking of God as "Sophia" presents particular challenges, because Christian and Jewish traditions avoid speaking of God with a proper name, such as Artemis or Zeus. And "Sophia" is often a proper name. In a *Family Circle* cartoon, a child asks who the Gloria is that they keep singing about. Like "Gloria," "Sophia" is a proper name in our culture, but the biblical Greek of *Sophia* is much less well known to English speakers than the liturgical Latin of *Gloria*. Thus, "Holy Wisdom" (perhaps with feminine pronouns) may serve better in worship than *Sophia*, except where congregations are familiar with biblical wisdom traditions.

Expanding imagery for God in worship is a pastoral task, for worship leaders are charged with nurturing congregations' faith and spirituality.

This means using care about traditional imagery (such as "Father") and unfamiliar imagery (such as "Wisdom"), in order to avoid placing stumbling blocks on the path of faith. A heavy, unbalanced load of masculine imagery can make the traveler falter or turn back from the journey. Careless introduction of new imagery can be like a sudden explosion that leaves pilgrims wounded by the roadside. Careful trail guides on the journey of faith consider the well-being of all companions, with their varied abilities and needs.

Wisdom traditions offer rich resources for expanded imagery in Christian worship of the triune God. Together with other metaphors, they enrich the language of praise, that Christians may glorify the Trinity in our worship and in all of life.

SERMON: WISDOM'S INCARNATION

Texts: Matthew 11:2–19, 28–30, and Wisdom of Ben Sirach 6:18–31

I preached this sermon on December 2, 1995, for the Women of the Word worshiping community of Chicago, Illinois. This is a group of women consciously seeking to renew Christian tradition from an emancipatory feminist/womanist/mujerista perspective, to whom the word of Christ-Sophia is indeed good news. The sermon would be different if preached in another context.

I am fascinated with the figure of Holy Wisdom, or Sophia as some
    call her,
simply using the term for wisdom found in biblical Greek.
In Proverbs she seems to personify an aspect of God,
but in later writings she appears as a divine emanation.
I have been pursuing her through sacred page,
including apocryphal scriptures I've never heard in church.
I want to "search out and seek," that Wisdom "will become known"
    to me (Sirach 6:27),
because, like many women, I need to see myself in religious symbols,
especially in this season when masculine symbols are everywhere.
A graduate of our seminary once said she couldn't see herself in the
    chapel windows.
No African American served as stained-glass icon, and the only
    woman was Mary.

Now, because of a senior class gift, Leontine Kelly and Georgia Harkness shine in our windows,
along with Martin Luther and John Wesley,
but we still long to see ourselves in images of God.
When women use feminine images of God—such as Holy Wisdom—
this is not projection or idolatry (as some charge),
for both women and men are made in God's image.
And, although it's a well-kept secret,
the image of Wisdom was commonly used of Jesus in the early centuries of the church.
The way Matthew 11 shows Jesus as Wisdom's incarnation,
echoing the Wisdom of Ben Sirach 6, is just one example.

The first thing to notice is that Matthew 11:2–19 is a unit,
although the lectionary reading for the Third Sunday of Advent stops
  at verse 11!
  [Did any of you bring your Bibles?
  I love the thought of Bible-toting feminists.
  Perhaps then we really would be dangerous!]
The passage begins with John the Baptist hearing about the *deeds* of
  the Messiah
and asking if Jesus is the one who is to come.
Jesus answers by describing what is happening in his ministry,
in language that echoes Isaiah's words about the Messiah.
(The lectionary reading ends here.)
Then Jesus speaks of John the Baptist's ministry,
and tells the parable about children calling out in the marketplace,
as a way of considering how people rejected both John and Jesus.
And Jesus says, "Wisdom is justified by her *deeds*."
Where have we heard the word *deeds* before?
Yes, in verse 2, John had wondered about the *deeds* of the Messiah.
The same Greek word is used to begin and end the section,
though English translations tend to hide the fact.
Wisdom is justified by her *deeds*,
the same deeds John has heard about in prison.
John asked from prison, "Are you the one who is to come, or shall we
  wait for another?"

Why this confusion from one who was so sure
when the sun was glistening on the River Jordan
as Jesus came up from baptismal waters?
Perhaps Jesus doesn't fit with John's image of the Messiah;
John has said that the Christ will come as a judge
who burns the chaff in unquenchable fire (Matt. 3:12b).
Jesus doesn't fit that image, and even less the popular image of a po-
    litical or military hero.
These aren't the deeds Jesus is doing.
Or, perhaps John is asking, "If you are really the Messiah, why am I
    in prison?
Why are so few responding to your message?"
If this is of God, then why are we in so much trouble?
Not an uncommon human question.
So Christian feminists may ask themselves these days!
How does Jesus respond to John?
[*I asked the group to give input here.*]
    Yes, there is healing.
    Good news is being preached to the poor.
    The dead are being raised.
Jesus talks about himself, echoing words Isaiah used to describe the
    day of the Messiah:
    the eyes of the blind shall be opened,
    the ears of the deaf will be unstopped,
    the lame shall leap like a deer,
    and the tongues of the speechless sing for joy (Isa. 35:5–6).
He says the Messiah is present when these things happen,
when people find healing, not judgment.
He adds that the Messiah is present when the poor,
the powerless, the marginalized, the excluded,
hear good news for a change
and new life comes from death.
These are the deeds of the Messiah, and of Wisdom incarnate.
There seems to be consensus in contemporary scholarship
that the Gospel of Matthew here identifies Jesus with the figure of Holy
    Wisdom.
This is most explicit when Jesus says,

"Wisdom is justified by her deeds,"
yet Matthew identifies Jesus with Sophia several times.
The only question is whether Matthew *lifts up* Sophia
or whether, like John the evangelist,
he absorbs her almost totally into the male person of Jesus.
Whatever the author intended,
here is an image of Jesus as Christ-Sophia we can integrate into fully
    Christian faith.
Unlike some other wisdom passages,
this one suggests a Sophia-ethics we can live by.
Though we may be doing something new in bringing the image and
    ethics
of Christ-Sophia to our own context,
Matthew 11 gives us a starting point.
Here Holy Wisdom appears, incarnate in Jesus.

She was before all things,
yet she is taking on flesh in Jesus.
We meet Christ-Sophia when people find the fullness of healing which
    is *shalom,*
when hope comes to the homeless
and new life comes from death.
Holy Wisdom then is more than an ethereal image
to comfort those who are weary of speaking of God as only male.
Sophia takes flesh
and in her union with the human Jesus,
she embodies mutuality between male and female.
She comes with healing, hope, and new life.
These are the deeds of Christ-Sophia.
This is the incarnation we seek in the season of Advent.

And we are invited to share her deeds and shoulder her yoke.
John the Baptist expected a power-over Messiah.
The Wisdom-Christ portrayed in Matthew 11
walks beside us and shares the labor of living, saying:

"Come to me, all you that are weary
and are carrying heavy burdens,

and I will give you rest.
Take my yoke upon you, and learn from me;
for I am gentle and humble in heart,
and you will find rest for your souls.
For my yoke is easy, and my burden is light."

In Ben Sirach chapter 6 (and also chapter 51)
Holy Wisdom invites the wise to share *her* yoke with very similar words.
By putting Sophia's words of invitation into Jesus' mouth,
Matthew again identifies Jesus and Wisdom.

The yoke both passages picture is the wooden yoke
placed on the shoulders of two oxen,
enabling them to share in common labor.
To be yoked to Christ-Sophia is to share
the yoke of discipline,
the yoke of simplicity,
the yoke of the Torah,
a law that is demanding, yet brings life,
the law that Jesus fulfills as Wisdom's incarnation
as he heals, proclaims good news, and brings new life out of death.
This is the yoke Jesus invites us to share,
a yoke that seems harsh to the undisciplined,
but which is a glorious robe to the wise,
a yoke that Jesus calls easy.
How can Jesus say his yoke is easy and his burden is light,
when John is in prison, awaiting death?
How can he say this, following his own words of lament (in verses we
    didn't read)
about people who won't hear him?
The answer, I think, is in how we interpret
"for I am gentle and humble of heart" ("meek and lowly of heart" in
    the King James Version).
This is not, I believe,
a meekness that causes us to retreat to tradition at the first accusation
    of heresy
or to relinquish our God-given role as those who pass on and reshape
    tradition.

It is a meekness and lowliness that repents with John,
and rejoices with Jesus,
that casts its lot with the outcast.
It is a meekness and lowliness
that weeps with those who mourn,
and dances with those who dance,
moving to the sound of the pipe in the marketplace.
It is a meekness and lowliness
that walks beside rather than exercises power from above.
Walking with Christ-Sophia, we no longer fear the fate of faithful
    prophets,
knowing that the poor have walked this path before us.
If some of us find our jobs threatened or our orthodoxy questioned,
we can be glad to share the yoke of others
who have little access to recognized ministries in the first place.
This is how we find rest for our souls,
sharing the yoke and the common labor.
As we share the labor of bringing good news, healing, and life,
the yoke of Christ-Sophia becomes a glorious robe,
and *we* become the body of Christ, Wisdom's incarnation.

Christ-Sophia calls again
in the *StreetWise* vendor bringing good news to the city.[41]
Wisdom cried out for justice
when one of the *StreetWise* was shot down.
I heard Christ-Sophia calling last Martin Luther King day
when hundreds of members of Saint Sabina's church
went to the frosty home of the homeless in Lower Wacker Drive
with gifts of clothing, food, and sleeping bags.
Wisdom sang in the choir bringing gospel sounds to Lower Wacker.

A few weeks ago Christ-Sophia came to me in a dream
to bring healing from the words of patriarchs
who claimed the right to define me out of Christian tradition.
She came as a sister they had also condemned,
offering her hand and prayer
in the hospital where [in the dream] I sought healing.

Wisdom is at work bringing new life out of death
when a prisoner becomes president,
when bullets fell a peacemaker
but a people still pledge themselves to peace,
when victims become survivors and survivors begin to thrive.

Wisdom calls out to us, "Share my yoke!
Labor with me in bringing healing, good news, and life!
Yes, this yoke seems harsh to the undisciplined,
for the powers of violence, bad news, and death are strong
in the marketplace, the home, the school, the church.
But I share the yoke with you,
and invite you to share the yoke of those who suffer,
to give your labors to the life of the world.
Embody Wisdom in the world, and you will know joy, and rest for
   your souls."
Christ-Sophia has already come, is always present, calling, "Share
   my yoke!"
The whole world is waiting for an Advent people to become Wisdom's incarnation,
to share the tears of those who mourn
and the joy of those who dance.
So may we respond, not only in ritual,
but with lives that sing with Wisdom,
and hearts that are clothed with robes of praise.
In the name of Christ-Sophia. Amen.

7

Living the Trinitarian Life:
Ethics and Worship

The Trinity is a vital Christian belief; worship is crucial to the Christian life; and ethics are necessary to an authentic Christian existence. It would thus seem that the trinitarian dimension of ethics ought to be plain and obvious in our life and worship. In this chapter I explore this presumably overt interconnection between the Trinity and ethics as it is expressed in worship.

Liturgy is a drama of the development of our communion in God and also a pattern of how we are called to live and to act in God.[1] We would assume that liturgy, as an embodiment of the world's (and our) relationship with God and of each other with God would express in its structure and movement the trinitarian implications of our moral life as Christians. Episcopal priest and liturgical scholar Richard D. McCall contends that the "Trinity, in [its] ceaseless relationship of procession and offering, its acts of love, is a more fitting model of reality than any metaphysical absolute."[2] Even if one does not concur with his process-oriented metaphysics, one must wholeheartedly agree with his assertion that the Trinity is the appropriate liturgical model for creation and recreation, for the interconnection of divine and human in the liturgy.

How is the Trinity incorporated into our life of worship? Some of the most significant expression is in liturgical art, in images adorning the church walls, windows, statues, books for worship. In the words (rites) of liturgical prayer, we find in a different medium specific images of the Trinity, which also directly or indirectly interconnect the Trinity with human moral behavior and ethics.

Visual art and the repeated words of community prayer affect the whole of our personhood, not just our reason, aesthetic sense, or physical enjoyment of what we see and hear. Our minds and hearts are drawn into these forms of expression, and the whole human responds to and reflects on liturgical expression in visual and aural form. As we return again and again to specific pictures and words, they permeate our psyches. These words and images powerfully and subconsciously form our theological perspectives and ethical views. They have been important throughout Christian history, and they remain important today because of their psychological and pedagogical influence.

TRINITY AS ICON

In order to gain a clearer idea of how the Trinity serves as a model or pattern for Christian life in the liturgy, let us begin with the Trinity as pictured in Christian art. I make no pretense of being complete, but I believe that the images discussed are suggestive of the Trinity as imagined by liturgical worshipers. Art, of course, is visual, not auditory like text, or kinetic like the movement of the liturgy. Images are found on walls, in windows, in liturgical books, and sometimes in statuary and bas-relief. They become a part of worship as a nonverbal, conscious and unconscious influence on our actions and our meditations at worship. Because of their pervasiveness, these images have been and can be a vital formative influence in the shaping of the Christian community's sense of the Trinity.[3]

The presence of such images in our churches and common worship is often as important as the words of our liturgy for suggesting the relation of the Trinity to our life and thus to our behavior. Compare the relation suggested at Our Lady of Pompei Roman Catholic Church, with its large plaster statue of the Trinity, Father bearded and robed, holding the cross with Jesus, with the Spirit as a dove between them, and rows of votive lights and prie-dieux for the faithful, with that suggested at First Presbyterian Church, with its large window showing the Good Shepherd above the communion table, and in small windows beside it, a trefoil and interconnected circles.

One way to categorize the images of the Trinity found in Christian liturgical art is to divide them into those directly involved in the biblical history of redemption, and those not so directly involved with the world. Both kinds of images can be found in liturgical or devotional books or in churches and thus both are directly involved in the formation of the worshiping community and its life. All of these images are common at different times and places and thus clearly play their role in shaping people's imagination of the Trinity.

The Trinity in Salvation History

Three kinds of image are most common. The first is what the early church and Middle Ages regarded as an Old Testament type of the Trinity: the appearance of the three angels to Abraham and Sarah under the tree at Mamre. The second is the baptism of Jesus, and the third is the crucifixion. Each suggests a different dimension of a trinitarian life and of the interconnection of the Trinity with the world.

Early liturgical art depicted the Old Testament Trinity as the three angelic figures appearing to Abraham and Sarah. In Genesis 18, the angels (the messengers of God) come to tell Abraham and Sarah that Sarah will give birth to a son, who will be called Isaac. Before they deliver their prediction, Abraham welcomes them under the oaks of Mamre. He prepares a meal of bread, milk, curds, and a calf. After his hospitality is accepted, they predict the birth of Isaac. The three angels were interpreted as the Trinity in the early church because Genesis 18:1 describes the Lord appearing to Abraham, and verse 2 tells of "three men." Not surprisingly, Christian commentators who believed firmly in the unity of the scriptures regarded this as a manifestation of the Trinity.

In the first half of the sixth century, a mosaic of this event was placed on the walls of San Vitale, a church in Ravenna, Italy. We see Sarah in the house, smiling, perhaps in anticipation of the angels' prediction. Abraham stands under the oaks, offering a calf to the three men who are seated at a table under the same tree. Their faces and clothing are similar, and each sits in front of a loaf of bread that is formed like the bread of the Eucharist. The center person faces us, while the two others look at Abraham and Sarah. The Trinity is sharing among itself, as the intertwined hands suggest, and also being attentive to Abraham and Sarah and the vital importance of the covenant promise to them. They are also very much present to the creation, seated beneath a flourishing tree, with grass and flowers growing beneath the oaks. The persons of the Trinity each have a slightly different expression and posture, suggesting not only a unity and interconnection of equals (*perichoresis*) but also distinction among themselves and distinguishable relations to humans and their world.[4]

The Old Testament Trinity became popular in Russian iconography. The image of the three figures in the context of their encounter with Abraham and Sarah by the trees of Mamre was common. Often the busyness of the event was emphasized, and the same icon will contain scenes from other events of Abraham and Sarah's life, such as the three angels approaching, the birth of Isaac, and his sacrifice on the mountain of Moriah. The appearance of the Trinity in this development of the iconography is even more clearly connected with God's saving work in the covenant with Abraham; we see Abraham and Sarah's response, Abraham's hospitality, his obedience, and God's fulfillment of the covenant promise.[5]

A later version, popularized by the Russian artist Andrei Rublev, shows the three angelic figures seated at the table, under the oak, with bread and perhaps a cup. A building in the background is the only reminder that this scene is part of a human drama. Instead, the focus is on the interrelationship of the persons of the Trinity itself; their hands are open and extended to each other. The eucharistic resonances of the Trinity, both heavenly and of this earth, at the table sharing with one another, invite the beholder into this same perfect communion into which the children of the new covenant are invited. The typological or contextual dimension of the image as the Trinity of Christian worship is emphasized, and the historical event—the angels/men meeting Abraham—is minimized. The sacramental and liturgical typology became central to the image.[6]

Two historic events in Jesus' life are most frequently depicted in visual presentations of the Trinity: the baptism and the crucifixion.[7] The presence of signs for the Father and the Spirit is explicitly required by the baptismal narratives; the crucifixion stories often do not picture the Spirit.

In the theophany, or baptism of Jesus, Jesus is portrayed in the water of the Jordan, with John the Baptist pouring water over his head. God the Father, shown as an old man blessing the world, holds a globe and is breathing forth the Holy Spirit, which is embodied as a dove. The event at hand is Jesus' baptism, which is the occasion of his being revealed to the world as its savior by God, the voice from heaven, and the Spirit, who appears as a dove above Jesus in the water. The voice from heaven asserts Jesus' role as the divine savior sent by the Creator and Father; the Holy Spirit as dove is both an affirmation of Jesus' messianic mission and the sign of the re-creation of the world by Jesus' redemptive life, death, and resurrection.[8]

The crucifixion, in both Greek and Latin tradition, is portrayed as a historic event, with the crucified Jesus, Mary, John, and other figures (such as the other condemned, the soldiers, the women who followed Jesus) who were or may have been present at the event.[9] Occasionally in Latin manuscripts the hand of God is pictured above the cross, in blessing or acceptance.[10]

Cosmic and Devotional Images of the Trinity

In some Russian icons, God the Father is portrayed above the top cross bar, in the heavens, sometimes with the Holy Spirit as a dove descending.[11] In a nineteenth-century Russian crucifix in my possession, the Father, adored by angels, is pictured above the cross, holding a globe, which is topped by a cross. The Holy Spirit is moving toward the cross, descending from the Father. This explicit presentation of the Trinity in the activity of the crucifixion connects the role of Father, Jesus the incarnate Word, and the Holy Spirit in the saving of the world in the life-giving work of the cross.

At first in the West, and later in the East, the Trinity was depicted separately from specific biblical events. It was represented by symbols of the divine, intended for our contemplation, "expressions of human inadequacy in the face of a mystery."[12] In the early medieval West, these figures include a throned human figure, a lamb, and a dove, which symbolize the mission of the persons of the Trinity, not any intrinsic relationship to one another.[13]

In the West, the Trinity was also portrayed as an older man in rich robes, Jesus on the cross, and the Spirit as a dove between the Father and the crucified Jesus. This image shows the divine working together for the world's redemption, with the crucifixion an action of the whole Trinity rather than an appeasement of God the Father by Jesus the Son.[14] Sometimes the Trinity, with this configuration of Father, crucified Jesus, and Spirit as a dove, is pictured responding to the prayers of a human being, contemporaneous to the portrayal, who is obviously interceding for him- or herself and others.[15] This medieval image provides another way to show the salvific activity of the Trinity ongoing in the life of believers.

In the Eastern tradition, the figures of the three persons are together, triumphant in heaven, usually enthroned amid the angels and saints, with God the Father and King, Jesus the glorified Ruler, and the Spirit as a dove.[16] In the Byzantine tradition, the cosmic dimension of the re-creation of the world by the work of the Trinity is of particular importance. Occasionally in the West, the three persons are depicted as either three persons or one person with three heads.[17]

On rare occasions, the Spirit is portrayed as a woman emerging between Father and Son, as the dove or third male person might otherwise do.[18] There is no evidence that this female figure is related to the much earlier Syrian written tradition that uses feminine language about the Spirit as female.

Symbols of the Trinity

Numerous symbols of the Trinity are found in the Western church, in all but the most visually iconoclastic of churches. These symbols include the triangle, the circle with triangle within it, trefoil, three fish in a triangular arrangement, and three interconnected circles.[19] Although these symbols depict no persons, the images imply relationship, equality, and interconnection.

THE TRINITY IN LITURGICAL PRAYERS

What richness do we find in our verbal icons and references to the Trinity, and what connection articulated between the Trinity and our human behavior is evoked or required of us because of our trinitarian worship? Although there are many references to the Trinity in our worship, prayers to the Trinity are of three major sorts: prayers in baptism; eucharistic prayer; and in doxologies that are part of invocations, collects and prayers, and blessings.

The Trinity in Baptism

Because baptism must be done in the name of the Trinity, the Trinity has remained central to the baptismal liturgy. The creed, whether in interrogative or declarative form, was always necessarily trinitarian. The immersion, or pouring of water, was always in the name of the Trinity. If there was an anointing, it was also trinitarian in form. It was not, however, until the twentieth century that liturgies began again to make explicit the moral implications of trinitarian baptism, a connection that had often been expressed in the early church through the catechumenate, which led to baptism, as well as the exorcism and renunciations by the candidate before baptism.[20]

The Trinity in the Eucharistic Prayer

In the early Greek church, the earliest records—from the late second to early third century—show a particular eucharistic prayer used. The prayer was addressed to God as Creator and Father of Jesus, who is prayed to through Jesus, in remembrance of Jesus' saving action for us in crucifixion, death, and resurrection, which the community participates in through the memorial meal of the Eucharist. The prayer remembers Jesus' deeds, and invokes the Spirit on the offering and on those who would receive it, "for the strengthening of faith in truth; that we may praise and glorify you through your child Jesus."[21]

This structure, known as Antiochene, perhaps because it originated in Antioch, spread through the Greek church and all others influenced by Constantinople. The eucharistic prayer has a clear trinitarian format, one concerned with Creator, Redeemer, and Sanctifier.[22] In the Latin tradition, the eucharistic prayer is addressed to God, Father and Creator, through Jesus Christ. God the Father is supplicated to transform the bread and wine into the body and blood of Jesus. The Latin theology understands "the words of Christ in the following institution narrative" to effect the consecration.[23] There is no explicit mention of a work of the Holy Spirit.

Both this theology and this form prevailed in the West in the Middle Ages. The Reformers took this prevailing theology one step further, and reduced the eucharistic narrative to prayer to God the Father and recitation of the words of Jesus as consecratory before the communion.[24] Luther's communion order in the *Formula Missae* and the *Deutsche Messe* called for the distribution of the bread after the consecration of the bread, and distribution of the cup after those words of Jesus.[25] Zwingli's Zurich Liturgy prefaces the words of institution with a prayer to the "Lord, God Almighty, who by thy Spirit has brought us together into thy one body."[26] Although this was far from an explicit prayer to the Spirit that recognized the Spirit's activity in our redemption, it is an implicit recognition in the eucharistic prayer of the role of the Spirit in Baptism and in our eucharistic life in the community of God's people.

Reformer Martin Bucer's *Straussburg Liturgy* is replete with references to God the Father and to the work of Jesus. The prayers for true reception and transformation are addressed to the heavenly Father. The only reference to the Spirit is in a somewhat ambiguous dismissal: "Depart! The Spirit of the Lord go with you unto eternal life! Amen."[27] Calvin's *Form of Church Prayers* retains the same theology and structure; the only reference to the Holy Spirit is in the doxology at the end of a prayer of thanksgiving after communion.[28] The 1552 *Book of Common Prayer* in England used material from the Sarum Missal, via the 1549 *Book of Common Prayer*, for the Preface and prayers before the consecration. But in 1552 Cranmer followed the Continental Reform in placing the communion immediately after the words of institution. The Trinity is invoked only in the Gloria, following communion, and in the final blessing.[29]

Note that in each of these Reform liturgies there is an extensive and explicit attempt to connect the sacramental communion with God with a reformation and transformation of behavior. However, any moral change is not connected with the Trinity as such or even with any member of the Trinity; it is more likely to be linked with God's grace of forgiveness through Jesus Christ and our partaking in the benefits of Christ's passion.[30] With a few exceptions, such as William Laud's revision of the Eucharistic Prayer in the early seventeenth century, it was not until the liturgical revival of the late nineteenth and twentieth centuries that the three persons of the Trinity reappear in the Eucharistic Prayer explicitly as active participants in the Eucharist and in our lives as sharers at the Holy Table.

In the Episcopal church's 1976 *Book of Common Prayer* an effort was made to restore a trinitarian structure to the Eucharistic Prayer. This is particularly clear with the insistence on the *epiclesis*, the invocation of the Holy Spirit to transform the elements into "the holy food of new and unending life" and to sanctify the people who receive these gifts.[31] The United Church of Christ's *Book of Worship*, Service of Word and Sacrament I, addresses all three persons of the Trinity in the Preface, connecting each one with the economy of salvation, as does the Eucharistic Prayer.[32] The same pattern is followed in Service of Word and Sacrament II, and both postcommunion prayers are also explicitly trinitarian, with a connection to the communicants' moral behavior in the world.[33]

The revised Roman Missal contains four Eucharistic Prayers for ordinary use. The first is a translation of the Roman canon. The second contains an invocation of the Holy Spirit over the gifts before the words of consecration and after, over the communicants. The third contains a trinitarian reference at the beginning of the canon and one invocation of the

Spirit over the gifts and another over the people after the consecration of the elements. The fourth prayer is an adaptation of Saint Basil's liturgy, similar to that in the Episcopal liturgy, with the invocation of the Spirit over the gifts and one over the people after the words of consecration.[34]

The Trinity in Invocation, Doxology, and Blessing

Perhaps the most familiar and frequent references to the Trinity are the invocations at the beginning of liturgies: "In the name of the Father and of the Son and of the Holy Spirit. Amen" or the "Blessed be the kingdom of the Father and of the Son and of the Holy Spirit, now and forever and from all ages to all ages" recited at the beginning of the Eastern Orthodox Church's Divine Liturgy.[35] This latter greeting is now also used in the Episcopal Church's ordinary eucharistic liturgies.

Some contemporary liturgies that want to use a trinitarian form contain the blessing from 2 Corinthians 13:14: "The grace of our Lord Jesus Christ, and the love of God, and the communion of the Holy Spirit be with all of you." The Orthodox use this greeting to the faithful who remain after the dismissal of the catecumens. It is the only familiar short formula in the liturgy that articulates particular work among humanity for each of the three persons and implies behavior expected within the Christian community.

Blessings, although in recent years more expansive in their language and imagery, have for most of Christian history in East and West been of the order of "the blessing of God the Father, the Son, and the Holy Spirit, be with you now and evermore," or in come circles, the Aaronic benediction from Numbers 6:24–26.

The trinitarian doxologies used at the end of the prayers and collects have generally expressed praise of Jesus Christ the Lord, who with God the Father (or God, with some modifying adjective) will live and reign eternally, in the communion of the Holy Spirit. At least sometimes, in the praise of the Trinity, the communion or union of the Trinity is linked with the Holy Spirit.

Some contemporary greetings and blessings are now more aware of the connection between the Trinity and Christian life and behavior. However, a review of many of the recommended wordings suggests that (1) often they are just differently worded versions of the traditional trinitarian blessings, or (2) people have given up on the use of trinitarian formulas and use language about the one God or divine life/energy.[36]

TRINITY AND ETHICS IN OUR LITURGIES

This brief survey suggests that in our liturgical art, and in the liturgies we pray, there is a complex but frequently not very substantial connection between the Trinity and human life and behavior in the world. The Trinity has, in fact, most frequently been but the background to our worship as it relates to our behavior in the world and the transformed life that we believe God empowers us to live through the liturgy.

It is important to acknowledge this reality, as well as to see clearly how we have prayed over the centuries. We cannot immediately change what generations of practice have shaped, but we can know what we have done, work with this tradition where possible, and reclaim and reimagine for our liturgy a more biblically faithful connection between the Trinity and our ethics.

Two great movements of trinitarian life, both of which shape Christian ethics, are alive, even if not particularly well articulated, in our worship. Elizabeth Johnson wrote about trinitarian life as God's life and as icon for our lives: "At its most basic, the symbol of the Trinity evokes a livingness in God, a dynamic coming and going with the world that points to an inner divine circling around in unimaginable relation."[37] Her statement encompasses what theologians term the economic Trinity and the immanent Trinity, making clear that the Trinity in mission itself reveals to us what is knowable of God's life. Because we are created in God's image, we can thus expect that God's relationship with the world will point us toward the essential qualities of our own ethical life as Christians in the world.

Catherine LaCugna describes the doctrine of the Trinity as a practical doctrine that offers "a wisdom, a discernment, a guide for seeing 'the two hands of God' (Irenaeus) at work in our salvation . . . a way of contemplating the mystery of God and ourselves, a heuristic framework."[38] She notes that the life of the Trinity is made known to us through the life of Jesus, and the reign of God which Jesus preached and manifested. Thus Christian orthopraxis (right actions, right practice) is living to serve the reign of God as made known through Jesus.

This reign of God is the (economy) household that God establishes in the world through Jesus, and our ethics grow from living in this household of God. LaCugna understands the church in Acts as the community in which the Spirit of Jesus dwelt, those devoted to the apostles' teaching and to communion, to breaking of bread and prayer. A particular way of living is crucial to this trinitarian economy: God calls us to live in a relationship of radical equality within the community of all who accept inclusion in this family, and who strive to live in love, communion, and harmony with one another.

LaCugna affirms the political (life in the *polis*) quality of trinitarian ethics: The radical equality of the trinitarian life of God in sharing mission to creation is a model for our society and our communion with one another. For human beings, mutual love, involving respect and equality, is "supreme" because "for God mutual love among persons is supreme." She regards God's covenant with Israel, Jesus' life and work on earth, and the community created by the Spirit as "icons" of this personal trinitarian life of God.[39]

We know this divine life most clearly through Jesus Christ, in the mission of each person of the Trinity to us as made known in the story of our creation, reconciliation, and growth in the life of the Spirit. Through this divine self-revealing, we learn that God's own life is a life of communion and mutual self-giving and empowerment. To live a Christian life is to embody, as best human beings can, the communion of the persons of the Trinity and our participation in this life. Such a moral life encompasses our relationship with God, our interpersonal life, and our social relationships.

Some theologians, such as Jürgen Moltmann[40] and Leonardo Boff,[41] have pushed the boundaries of a trinitarian ethic in social and political life. Mar Osthathios, of the Orthodox Syrian Church in India, wrote about the trinitarian imperative for a classless society in which the abolition of class and economic boundaries are necessary goals if a society is to be authentic. He identifies specific ways in which the church and state need to be changed if such a society is to be achieved. Acknowledging that "the ideal of the classless society is not obtainable in history," he insists that this ideal is a model we can try to "appropriate as closely as possible."[42]

What Is and What Might Be

As we have seen, neither liturgical visual art nor the words or shape of our liturgical services express much about the relationship between the trinitarian life that we share and our ethical lives as baptized Christians. Today's challenge is, within the context of our past, to imagine new and more creative liturgical connections.

Visual liturgical art has been somewhat more expressive than liturgy. The biblical images—either the three angels and Abraham and Sarah, or the events of Jesus' life—have pictured a divine mission and the triune God intimately involved with humanity. Each person of the Trinity has a specific role, and a response to this triune God is being asked of the human beings involved. This response to God will change each human being's relationship to God and, by extension, to one another. This art is intended to connect the contemporary community with the faith community in past ages, and to provoke us to explore our own responses to God's presence in our lives.

Some of the images of the Trinity on the walls of churches from the medieval period and later were intended to be objects of devotion, which invited those looking at the images to enter into the life of the Trinity and to pray to this Trinity. Such imagery implies that the trinitarian God is accessible to us through prayer to Jesus and through the Holy Spirit, who comes from God the Father to us.

Today we are much more dubious, if not disbelieving, about the value of such imagery. Gail Ramshaw, no radical protester on these matters, observes that one summer she saw in a German church "next to a portrait of Luther, a picture of the Trinity, with God wearing a papal crown, Jesus on the cross below, and the dove flying about." Her reaction: "Really, now!"[43]

Not so fast! As problematic as images like these are in many regards, they offer the worshiper an accessible God, who reaches out to draw viewers into the divine activity and life and invites us to respond. Both the patriarchal hierarchy of this particular image and its sexism are offensive. But unless we are genuine iconoclasts, with little use for the continuing expression of the incarnation, we affirm the possibility of the acceptability of some inadequate but helpful imaging of God's trinitarian life to us. What images can we offer to express God's involvement with us, and the life that grows from this response to the Trinity?

One possibility is to picture biblical events that explicitly involve the Trinity. In these images, whether stained glass, wall paintings, or pictures in the church, we speak of the Trinity and of God's involvement in our human history. Images of the nativity of Jesus, the baptism, the crucifixion, and perhaps of other events of Jesus' life, such as the resurrection and ascension, communicate God's trinitarian relationship with us. The economic Trinity is involved in our lives in order to reconcile us to God and to model the way in which we are called to live with one another within the reign of God.

In liturgical art, as in any other art, propaganda and simplistically telling a story do not communicate effectively. Images show and invite us into a way of being and living. Perhaps the best traditional image for such an expression of a trinitarian life is the Orthodox image of the Old Testament Trinity—the three angels with Abraham, Sarah, and their household, or the three angels as painted by Rublev. The popularity of the Rublev image of the Trinity today—in the West as well as the East—may well be due to the subtlety of its invitation and its resonance with daily life in its sharing at the meal and the eucharistic sharing. The strong, gracious, androgynous angels, seated around the triangular table with the vessel containing bread before them, gaze serenely at each other, their wings touching and their hands gesturing toward each other. The circle is incomplete, not to exclude but to include us: the triangularity of the table and the platforms on which the angels sit all extend out to us. The Trinitarian communion is a mutual love of equals, which extends out to include and invite all those who would come to join them at the table.

Such an image of the Trinity embodies the fundamental trinitarian values of mutual love, respect, and equality in internal relationship and in mission to creation. The core values it shows include mutual love, respect, relationships of equality with one another, and sharing, by prayer and sacraments, in the life the Trinity offers us. Thus we see communion (*koinonia*), with its activity of mutual love and respect for one another, as the root of the Christian ethical life, embodied by those who accept the invitation to enter and share at the table of life which the Trinity opens to us.

What other representations of the Trinity might speak to our time? Liturgical art today faces a new audience, people who are not willing to accept three white males as appropriate anthropomorphisms for the Trinity. Some traditional imagery can and should be modified. We need new images that are accessible to various people and cultures and also speak faithfully of God's life with us and the way of life God calls us to lead. With fabrics and other, newer materials, gifted artists can experiment with new forms and interpretations of biblical stories and Christian appropriation of that biblical faith.

Contemporary artists find it difficult at times to envision or create an image of the Trinity that our society might understand or by which it might be moved. Perhaps the starting point in creating new images is to go back and listen to the story the scriptural writers speak to us and hear the many interpretations and imaginings of this story through the ages. Another source for contemporary images is the joyful searching and angry cries of our contemporary sisters and brothers who seek the Trinity, who is present in and around them.

In *She Who Is*, Elizabeth Johnson presents several images for our consideration as we imagine the Trinity in new ways.[44] Johnson includes artist Meinrad Craighead's "Hagia Sophia," whose heavy female body and deep colors provide counterpoint to the facing "Holy Trinity" of Lucas Cranach. Craighead's journey to the immanent divine is inward, to nature, to the "faceless source which is the place of origination." Dina Cormick also portrays a creative divine power in "Creative God Most Beautiful," but her black creative woman God dances across an unfolding flowered circle of light, from which all the richness of creation flies, jumps, crawls, or creeps. Neither of these pieces of art is explicitly trinitarian, but they offer hints and insights at the kind of re-visioning into which our trinitarian faith is invited.

In his *Divine Comedy*, Dante imagined the Empyrean of Paradise as a great unfolding white rose in which the saints and angels move about. In its center is the true light, in which is the Trinity and the unity of all in this Trinity. Dante represented the Trinity through three differently-colored spheres within the true light that occupy the same space and mirror one another.[45] Although illustrators have been tempted to depict the Trinity in the center as three men,[46] Dante himself was careful not to anthropomorphize the image of the Trinity.

A use of color and movement such as Dante's, along with the inclusion of all the goodness of creation within the Trinity, might suggest some contemporary expressions of the Trinity, its interconnectedness with creation, and the peace and love of the community of the blessed in communion with the Trinity. The combination of light and flower, an organic interconnection combined with freedom and individuality, might take some interesting contemporary course. The imagery conveys the combination of self-realization and centeredness in the divine life which is an element of classical Christian theology and is congruent with contemporary concerns for individuality and freedom.

Transforming the Words of the Liturgy

I confess to some surprise at how impoverished our traditional liturgical texts in the Western churches are in terms of connecting the Trinity with our Christian life. Recent changes are clearly moving us in a positive and biblically authentic direction with regard to expressing in our worship the relationship between Trinity and ethical transformation. But we have hundreds of years of inadequacy in our worship. Liturgical and sacramental churches can track their inadequacies more clearly; churches centered on the Liturgy of the Word can probably assume the same issues, with even more varied individual expressions. For the most part, our words have focused on either a unitary godhead as object of worship, or the binitarianism of a Jesus piety which prays to God the Father. Now we are moving into a renewed liturgical day, but we all have much to do.

Leaders of worship, when presiding or preaching, will be transforming and renewing a long worship history. We ourselves will have to assimilate, reflect upon, and transform new and recovered liturgies that articulate more clearly and overtly the role of the Trinity in living the Christian life. When, for instance, we pray for the healing and sanctifying of our world to God the Creator and Father of Jesus, through Jesus our Brother and Savior, in the Holy Spirit who makes us holy, we are uttering a trinitarian truth that the words of our liturgies have usually not articulated. Our Christian communities will want and need much reflection, prayerful reinforcement, and frequent preaching and teaching about the Trinity and the Trinity's relationship to Christian life to incorporate and accept these liturgical images.

We do not want worship to become a time of heavy-handed enforcement of the details of a trinitarian ethic. But we do want our prayers, our hymns, and our sermons to reflect the way of life which, through Jesus, we know as the life of God's reign on earth. God our Creator made a covenant with Israel that roots and illumines our way of life; Jesus, sent by God his Father, lived and worked among us, and died and rose to show us the fullness possible in God's reign; the Holy Spirit, through Baptism, Eucharist, prayer, and Christian community, dwells in us and transforms us to live as Jesus showed us.

The Trinity in mission to us, the economic Trinity, reflects to us the perfect mutual love and interrelationship that are the essence of the Trinity's immanent life and the ideal of communion into which we are invited. Liturgical language hints at the unending communion of God's life and its implications for our earthly life. The role of each person of the Trinity in mission to us shows us something of God's life as it calls us to act.

Bread of Tomorrow, a contemporary collection of prayers for worship, has several examples.[47] A Lenten prayer composed by Peruvian campesinos uses the imagery of Israel's wandering in the desert to express their own situation as "strangers in our own land, without bread, a roof, a future." God is their promised land; Christ, the way; and Spirit is present with them in exile, offering them hope, and encouraging them "toward that joyous home-coming."[48]

A responsive prayer for Pentecost in *Bread of Tomorrow* uses the imagery of dance, thereby implying the interconnectedness of each person of the Trinity with the other. God the Creator invites us to dance, and we, moving with creation's music, "rejoice to be part of the making of earth." Following Jesus, we reach out to one another, moving into freedom and sharing hope. In the Spirit we embrace the world in joy, dancing "for salvation and justice" as we "rejoice to be part of the moving of love."[49] Each person of the Trinity, who, it is implied, is eternally dancing in communion, extends to humans an invitation to dance. The form of that invitation is shaped by the mission of each person in creation, and that particular person's dance with us has its own specific moral direction.

A blessing that encompasses trinitarian and ethical dimensions is also suggested in *Bread of Tomorrow*. After an introductory invocation, God is three times asked to bless us with a particular gift: "strength to seek justice, . . . wisdom to care for the earth, . . . love to bring forth new life." The trinitarian invocation is in the name of God, who creates the world, Jesus who is "our new covenant," and the "Holy Spirit, who opens eyes and hearts."[50] Such a form, modeled on classical lines, makes a clear connection between the blessing, which asks God's grace as the worshipers are sent into the world, and the ethical task before them as God's people sent into the world.

I referred earlier in this chapter to eucharistic prayers. In the General Liturgical Resources section I have included an example of a eucharistic prayer that illustrates some of the issues about Trinity and ethics about which I have written, and I have included a few sample prayers that might be offered in the service. These give additional examples of the kind of expressions easily possible in public worship. The suggestions I offer are moderate, traditional, and orthodox and so should serve in any service of worship. They suggest the many more wonderful developments that are possible for a sensitive and theologically aware leader of worship.

CONCLUSION

Trinitarian faith is an icon, model, and symbol of divine life in which we grow and shape our own lives. As such it provides the rooting and grounding of our liturgy of life, a consistent theme of corporate worship, and a core reality of our faith. To give this faith its full role in our worship, hymns, movement, visual art, sermons, set liturgies, and free prayer should all work together to express the connection between trinitarian life and our Christian life in the world. I have pointed to a few dimensions of such worship in our past and present developments. May these help us as our worship leads us closer to the Holy One in Three, in whose life we find true life.

Epilogue and Introduction to the Liturgical Resources

"O God, thy sea is so great and my boat is so small." Those words with which chapter 2 began are appropriate once more. We have sailed the boundless waters of reflection on the mystery of God, passing through treacherous waters of naming the unnameable and challenging age-old traditions. We have sought to keep our sights on the North Star of faithfulness to the gospel of Jesus Christ in all its fullness, knowing the destination of our voyage lies on some distant horizon. Though some call the journey foolhardy, we have been constrained by our love of God and of Christ's church to traverse these perilous seas. We have been well aware that we could provide no final answers, and that the test of these musings is in the life and worship of the church, as in its diverse ways it worships the triune God.

The worship resources that follow are not intended to offer final answers to the search for adequate trinitarian language, much less timeless words and formulas. Yet, since our concerns in the preceding chapters have centered on the words of worship, it is only fair to demonstrate how these ideas might be embodied in actual services of Christian worship. Churches may use these liturgies, prayers, and blessings in full or adapted form, or as inspirations for their own search for language that is faithful and just.

The section that follows immediately, "General Liturgical Resources," includes resources using trinitarian images we have developed for various worship contexts, along with two prayers by Patricia Wilson-Kastner. These are followed by a eucharistic liturgy by Patricia Wilson-Kastner only weeks before her death. When students and faculty touched by her presence at Garrett-Evangelical Theological Seminary gathered to remember and give thanks to God for her life, this beautiful and faith-filled liturgy gave voice to our praise and remembrance. In the same way, it provides a fitting end to this book, as a tribute to her and a fulfillment of the book's purpose. For the only fitting end to reflection on the boundless mystery of the triune God is praise, as it culminates in the eucharistic prayer, the church's Great Thanksgiving to the God who is Source of Life, Word of Truth, and Spirit of Love.[1]

General Liturgical Resources

CALL TO WORSHIP

We come to offer ourselves to God our Source, in worship as in daily life.
We seek the presence of Jesus, who beckons us each to ministry.
We open ourselves to the wind of the Spirit,
who blows through our lives to change us,
that we may do justice, love kindness, and live humbly with the Holy One.
Let us worship the Living God,
who gives us life, who calls us to ministry, and who empowers us for
    holy living. Amen.
(RD)

INVOCATIONS

1. *Based on John 3:16–21, Lent 4, B.*

    Loving God, we praise you that you sent Jesus not to condemn but to
        save us.
    As we worship today, touch our hearts and our imaginations,
    that we may abide in you and live in care toward the world you love in
        Jesus Christ.
    Glory be to you, God, Fountain of Love, Word of Truth, Spirit of
        Power. Amen.
    (RD)

2.   God of struggle and blessing,
    we thank you that you are so willing to meet us in love here and now,

as you met our mothers and fathers in faith on their journeys,
as you entered our human life in Jesus.
Help us open our hearts to you in this time of worship,
that we may grow in love toward you and all people
through the gentle wind of your Spirit. Amen.
(RD)

3.   Living God, we thank you that wherever we may go,
and however our lives may change,
you are as sure as the northern star and as constant as the evergreen.
Inconstant as we are, shape our lives through the gospel of Jesus Christ,
that our light may shine, a steady beacon of your love.
Infuse our lives with your Spirit,
that we may live and grow, ever green as seasons change,
taking part in your work of bringing justice and harmony to this world
    you love,
Living God, Risen Christ, Life-Giving Spirit. Amen.
(RD)

SUNG DOXOLOGIES

Advent

Praise Spirit-God, who comes with fire.
Praise Jesus Christ, our heart's desire.
Praise Love who comes to seek us all,
one God on whom our spirits call.
    God comes! God comes!
    Lift heart and voice.
    The Savior comes; let earth rejoice.

TUNE: VENI EMMANUEL, LM WITH REFRAIN. (WITHOUT THE CHORUS, AN-
OTHER LM TUNE MAY BE USED.)

Christmastide

Praise the eternal Holy One, and tell the Spirit's worth.
to Christ sing praise, God-with-us all our days.
O sing the Savior's birth, O sing the Savior's birth,
O sing, O sing the Savior's birth.

TUNE: ANTIOCH, CM WITH REPEAT.

Epiphany

Praise Love who made all time and space.
Praise Love who came in truth and grace.
Praise Love on humankind outpoured,
that all may love forevermore.

TUNE: OLD HUNDREDTH, LM.

Lent

Praise the Source who gives us life.
Praise to Christ, who shares our strife.
Praise the Spirit, who sustains,
bearing us through grief and pain.
To the holy Trinity glory, praise, and honor be.

TUNE: REDHEAD, 77.77.77.

Eastertide

Praise Jesus Christ, who rose from death!
Praise to the Source of life and breath!
Alleluia! Alleluia!
Praise to the Spirit, holy dove,
Giver of life, of peace, of love.
Alleluia! Christ is risen!
Alleluia! Christ is risen! Alleluia!

TUNE: LASST UNS ERFREUEN, 88.44.88 WITH REFRAIN.

Pentecost

Praise to the One who has destined us all to salvation.
Praise to Christ Jesus, who sends us in love to all nations.
Worship afresh One who is poured on all flesh,
Spirit of love and vocation!

TUNE: LOBE DEN HERREN, 14 14.478.

Trinity

Praise God the Father and the Son
and Holy Spirit, always one,

the God whose holy name we call,
one God and Mother of us all.

TUNE: OLD HUNDREDTH, LM.

All doxologies © 1999 Ruth Duck.

COLLECTS

1. Based on Isaiah 35:1–10, Advent 3, A.

Holy One, you lead through times of dryness and loss
to seasons of overflowing joy.
Water our parched lives through the stream of your Spirit,
that new life may spring forth.
Come to us in Christ, the living Water, that we may never thirst again.
All glory be to you, Giver of life and joy, through Jesus Christ in the
    Holy Spirit. Amen.
(RD)

2. Based on Matthew 14:13–21, Proper 13, A (July 31–August 6).

God of quiet places and busy streets,
you invite us to come apart and commune with you in times of grief
    and joy.
On the mountain of prayer, fill us with your healing and your peace,
that we may be renewed to love and serve you,
through Jesus Christ, who on earth sought your presence
and who lives forever in communion with you and the Holy Spirit.
    Amen.
(RD)

3. Philippians 2:1–13, Proper 21, A (September 25–October 1).

Living, exalted Christ, who lived as a servant and died on a cross,
help us to discover what it means to have your mind among us
even when we are not of full accord in our thinking.
Encourage us, that we may share in the Spirit,
showing compassion and sympathy to one another
and concern for those who are hurt.
So may we shine like stars in the world, and know the joy of your
    resurrection. Amen.
(RD)

4. Example of a Sunday Collect. For 1st Advent, Year C.

Gracious God, your creative love sustains the world from its beginning to its end. May we listen with open ears and hearts to Jesus' words of judgment, calling us to repentance and renewal. Through the life-giving power of the Holy Spirit, may we respond to your call and grow strong in your love, awaiting the fullness of your reign on earth. Amen.
(PW-K)

PRAYERS OF CONFESSION

1. Based on Matthew 26:14–16, Passion/Palm Sunday, A.

Eternal God, your love is constant, but you cannot depend on us.
Sometimes we are faithful to you, acting in love and courage, praising you with joy,
yet sometimes we confuse your purpose with our desires,
and sometimes, like Judas, we betray you, greedy for the world's rewards.
Through your Spirit of holiness,
free us to resist silvery lures that lead us away from you,
that we may be steadfast disciples of Jesus Christ, in whose name we pray. Amen.
(RD)

2. Based on Genesis 17:1–7, 15–16, Lent 2, B.

Prayer of Confession:

Faithful God of Sarah and Abraham,
you guide your people from generation to generation,
yet we confess that we laugh at your promises
and we ignore the stirrings of your Spirit.
When you act, bringing new life, we smile with surprise.
We do not expect you to move in our daily lives and work.
Patient God, accept us in our unbelief,
and continue to fulfill your promise in us,
through Jesus the Christ, in whom we find true life. Amen.

Words of assurance:

This is the good news: God accepts us as we are

and continues to offer us the new life of the promise.
Laugh the laughter of those whom God forgives and sets free to life.
By the grace of Jesus Christ, you are forgiven.
(RD)

3.   Holy One, you fill the earth with the light of your presence,
but we are not always aware.
Open our hearts, that we may know you in the face of friend or
    stranger,
and trust you in times of trouble or danger.
We pray in the name of Christ, who is within us, between us, and
    around us,
through the moving of your Spirit. Amen.
(RD)

PRAYERS OF THANKSGIVING

1. Based on Julian of Norwich.[1]

Christ our Mother, God our Father, Spirit of love and grace,
we come before you knowing that we do not fulfill your intention
    for us,
yet we thank you for your endless love and your kindness to us in our
    failure and despair.
We praise you for creating us so that our souls are subtly knit and
    united to you
and we cannot cut ourselves off from your love.
Guide our growth in knowledge of you and ourselves,
that you may rejoice in our return to you. Amen.
(RD)

2.   We thank you, Holy One, for the eternal song of praise
to Jesus Christ that you have put in our hearts.
We praise you for the sisters and brothers in ministry
who surround us now, and for the great cloud of witnesses,
past and present, who encourage us in the journey of faith.
Unite our lives in a glorious harmony that brings honor to you,
through the grace of Christ and the power of the Holy Spirit. Amen.
(RD)

MISCELLANEOUS PRAYERS

1. A Prayer for Epiphany

Majestic God, womb of all life, we thank you that you created the
worlds in love
and that in love you have come to us in Jesus Christ.
As you have bridged heaven and earth to come to us,
strengthen us to cross distances that divide us from people who share
our lives.
As you have bridged time and eternity to dwell with us,
inspire the peoples of earth to cross distances
between nation and nation, class and class, privilege and poverty,
to live in common love and concern.
Send your Spirit to kindle the hearts of all who have been baptized into
Christ,
that our acts of justice and care may show your love once revealed in
Jesus of Nazareth,
in whose name we pray. Amen.
(RD)

2. Unison Prayer of Commitment

Creative God, we thank you that you invite us to be partners in your
new creation.
You plant in us your hope, your dream of the world as it should be.
Through your Spirit at work among us,
turn our prayers for the healing of the earth
into deeds that express your will.
We pray in the name of Jesus Christ, who came to manifest the way of
life you intend. Amen.
(RD)

3. Prayer before Preaching

Holy Radiance, I want to be a transparent window through which your
light may shine.
Let my self recede so that you may be made known
and the good news of Jesus Christ may be proclaimed.
Through your Holy Spirit, use my words beyond my intentions and
beyond my inadequacy;
for you have asked us to live not by power nor by might, but by your
Spirit.

We want to be touched and changed by you,
for we are the people you have called to yourself through Jesus Christ,
in whose name we pray.
Amen.
(RD)

4. *A Prayer for Ministries of the Church (Based on Romans 12:4–8 and Ephesians 4:11–16).*

Gracious giver of all good and perfect gifts,
we thank you for your living Spirit at work in the body of Christ,
inspiring all with gifts for ministry.
Give wisdom to our leaders, as they guide our life together.
Give the spirit of understanding to those who teach and those who learn.
Anoint the pastors and prophets and healers among us
with the full measure of your Spirit.
May those with the gift to be generous find joy in their giving.
In all things, may your saints be equipped for the ministry,
building up the body of Christ our Head, in the unity of the Holy
    Spirit,
that your name may be praised, eternal, Triune God. Amen.
(RD)

5. *Prayer for Inner Peace and Transformation*

Loving heart of the universe, sunlight of the soul,
warm our restless lives with your peace.
Like still pools that mirror the sky,
and fall trees turning from green to flaming colors,
may we reflect your beauty.
Less wearied by our efforts, more aware of your call, may we find life
    in you,
still point and center of our fast-paced, overloaded lives.
Loving heart of the universe, love in us and through us and among us.
O tranquil, radiant Sunlight, bring our lives to flower in their season,
through the life-giving Spirit breathed on us by Christ,
whom we meet in broken bread and fragmented life. Amen.
(RD)

6.   O Source and Fountain of life,
in whom we live and move and have our being,
we thank you for your creative presence in all your creation,

and even among us, as we seek new paths into the future.
O Word Incarnate, who lived and moved among us,
teacher and disturber of the peace, we thank you for your liberating
 presence among us,
as we seek to be signs of divine love and justice on earth.
Spirit-Wind and breath of new life, prime mover of our life together,
we thank you for your surprising presence among us,
nudging us to new insight and new ways to live in community together.
Holy God, Source, Word, and Wind of new life,
to you be all praise and glory in all creation. Amen.
(RD)

7. *For Any Sunday*

O gracious Trinity, Source of all life, Word of truth, and Spirit of
love, we praise you for your life of perfect communion of three in
one. We pray that you will turn our injustice into justice, our hatred
into love, and our oppression into mutual respect and care for one
another. May our lives on earth imitate your life. As by your grace
we share in your life and love, may we grow in communion with one
another. We thank you for your goodness to us, Holy One, through
Jesus, in the power of the Spirit. Amen.
(PW-K)

BENEDICTIONS

1.   Through the creative power of God,
the Word spoken in Jesus,
and the love the Spirit pours into our hearts,
may you be strengthened and filled to do the ministry to which you are
 called.
(RD)

2. *Based on 2 Peter 3:8–18, Advent 2, B.*

Through the promised fire of the Holy Spirit,
and the word of God which preserves heaven and earth,
may you grow in the grace and knowledge of Jesus Christ,
to whom be glory both now and to the day of eternity. Amen.
(RD)

3. *Based on Julian of Norwich*[2]

> The high power of God our Father keep you,
> the deep wisdom of Christ our Mother surround you,
> and the great love of the Holy Spirit fill you with grace,
> one God and one endless love.
> (RD)

AN ORDER FOR CHRISTIAN BAPTISM

The baptismal ritual begins as the presider and a representative of the congregation stand by the baptismal font.

Opening Address

Presider: Sisters and brothers, we come to the waters of baptism,
a sacrament and visible sign of divine love at work in
human lives.
In baptism, the Eternal One who created us
claims us for holy living, freeing us from the power
of sin and death.
In baptism, we are joined to Jesus Christ and one
another in living and dying:
"As many of you as were baptized into Christ
have clothed yourselves with Christ.
There is no longer Jew or Greek,
there is no longer slave or free,
there is no longer male or female,
for all of you are one in Christ Jesus."
In baptism, the Spirit of God anoints us for ministry
in the world
and makes us signs of divine love for the whole
creation.

Presentation

The church leader invites baptismal candidates and their parents and sponsors to come forward.

Church Leader: I present [name] to receive the sacrament of Baptism.
Presider: (*To persons who are baptized by confession of faith*):

[Name], do you desire to be baptized into Jesus Christ?

Candidate: I do.

OR

(*To parents or sponsors of those who cannot confess the faith for themselves*):
Do you desire that [name] be baptized into Jesus Christ?

Parents or sponsors: I do.

Profession of Faith and Pledges of Commitment

The following questions are addressed by the presider and the church leader to the candidates, parents, and sponsors who can speak for themselves:

Presider: Do you turn from the powers of evil
and receive the freedom of new life in Christ?

Candidates,
parents, sponsors: I do.

Leader: Do you confess your faith in God, Source of life,
Word of love, Spirit of power?

Candidates,
parents, sponsors: I do.

Presider: Do you commit yourselves, by the grace of God,
to be faithful disciples of Jesus Christ,
turning to the way our Savior lived and taught,
a way of love and justice toward all?

Candidates,
parents, sponsors: I do.

Leader: Do you promise, by the grace of God,
to share in the life of the church of Jesus Christ,
in its worship and its witness and work of love and
justice,
and to be responsive to the gifts and calling of the
Holy Spirit?

Candidates,
parents, sponsors: I do.

To parents and sponsors of children who are unable to speak for themselves:

Presider: Do you promise, by the grace of God,
to nurture [this child/these children] in the Christian
faith,
through the love you show,
through the life you lead,
through the witness of your faith,
and through your participation with [him/her/them]
in the life of the church?
Parents, sponsors: I do.

Leader: And now at this time the congregation may stand
and promise their love and support of these candidates and their families. I ask you,
Do you, members of the church of Jesus Christ,
promise to support those who are about to be baptized
to turn away from evil and to turn toward God
by welcoming them in love to the community of faith,
and sharing with them in the ongoing journey of
growth in faith, love, and justice?
Congregation: By the grace of God, we promise.

Congregational Profession of Faith

Leader: Let us profess the faith of the church of Jesus Christ.
We believe in God, Creator of all the worlds,
parent of Jesus Christ, source of the Spirit,
in whom we live and move and have our being.
We believe in Jesus Christ, God's Word made flesh,
child of Mary,
who lived on earth, challenging the mighty,
loving the shamed, befriending all people,
and dying on a cross,
rising in three days to share forever in divine life.

We believe in the Holy Spirit, breath of life,
who leads all people to the truth
and bestows gifts for the upbuilding of the church and
the world.
We believe in one God, Source, Word, and Spirit,
in whose name we live and trust,
together with the church of all times and places.

Prayer over the Water

Presider: We give you thanks, Holy One, fountain of life,
that you are faithful to people of all times and places
and that you invite all people to join in covenant with you.
At earth's beginning, when you created earth, sky, and
water, your Spirit brooded over creation,
hovering over the sea like a mighty bird.
When waters flooded the earth, you set a rainbow in the sky
and made covenant with Noah to bring not destruction,
but new life.
When your covenant people were oppressed in Egypt
you led them through the Red Sea and across Jordan's River
to a new land of freedom and dignity,
and gave them a law to lead them toward love and justice.
Many years passed, and then, by the streams of Jordan,
your child Jesus came to be baptized by John.
You declared, "This is my beloved Son; hear him,"
and the Holy Spirit descended like a dove,
empowering Jesus to face temptation and to minister with
love.
And now, as your covenant people, the church of Jesus
Christ,
we gather at the font of baptism, seeking the water of life.

*As the following words are spoken, the presider may hold hands downward
in a gesture of invoking the Spirit upon the water.*

Pour out your Spirit on this water, on all of us gathered here,
and on your whole church,

that we may be faithful disciples of Christ
and always drink of the living water Christ offers.
All glory be to you,
Fountain of Life, Living Water, Spirit of New Life,
now and forever one God. Amen.

The Ritual of Baptism

The presider says words such as the following, while visibly administering water three times to each candidate.

1. [Name], you are baptized in the name of the Father and of the Son and of the Holy Spirit, one God, Mother of us all.[3]

2. [Name], you are baptized in the name of God the Source, Word, and Spirit.

3. [Name], I baptize you in the name of God, Source of love,
   in the name of Jesus Christ, love incarnate,
   and in the name of the Holy Spirit, love's power.[4]

4. [Name], I baptize you in the name of God the Father and Mother,
   and of Jesus Christ, God incarnate,
   and of the Spirit, God ever-present.

The presider and church leader lay hands on the candidate's head and invoke the Holy Spirit; family members or sponsors may also join in laying on hands, while the church leader says these or similar words:

May the Holy Spirit fill you with grace,
that you may be a faithful disciple of Jesus Christ.

Congregation: Amen.

Anointing

The presider anoints each person who has been baptized with oil in the sign of the cross, saying these or similar words:

[Name], you are sealed with the Holy Spirit
in the name of Christ, the anointed One.

Gift of the Paschal Candle (Optional)

The church leader presents each baptizand with a lighted baptismal candle, saying these or similar words:

This candle is a reminder of your union with Jesus Christ in life and in death. Light it each year, remember you are baptized, and give thanks to God.

Welcome

Acts of welcome by the congregation follow. The congregation may process to the font to give signs of peace and welcome to the baptismal party, or the presider may walk with the newly baptized persons in the midst of the congregation. Or, church leaders (other than the one leading the liturgy to this point) may express words of welcome and present items such as a baptismal certificate. Or, the congregation may say together words such as the following:

We welcome you to the life of this church,
rejoicing in your new birth in water and the Spirit
and in the grace of Jesus Christ already at work in your life.
We will join with you in seeking God's word in the scriptures
and seeking God's presence in the life of the world,
growing together in faithful discipleship and love for all people.

Blessing and Dismissal
of the Baptismal Party

Presider: The grace of God, the love of Christ, and the communion of the Holy Spirit be with you all.
Leader: Go to love and serve God.

Members of the baptismal party return to their seats.

Holy Communion

It is appropriate to celebrate Communion as an act of welcome and belonging as the closing act of the order for Baptism, especially when the newly baptized have professed faith for themselves. (The practice of the Orthodox churches of communing infants with a spoon containing a bit of bread in wine continues the ancient church's practice of communing people immediately after they have been baptized.)

EUCHARISTIC PRAYERS

A Eucharistic Prayer
Celebrating the Risen Christ

This order was designed for use in Eastertide, but it would also serve in other seasons, since we always celebrate the Eucharist in the presence of the risen Christ.

Taking the Bread and Cup

Bring the elements forward from the midst of the people,
as a sign of the divine presence in the midst of human life.

Blessing the Bread and Cup

Leader: The Source of all life is with us.
All: The Life-giving Spirit is with us.
Leader: The risen Christ is with us.
All: We offer our hearts in praise to the living God.
Leader: Let us give thanks.
All: We thank God with joy.
Leader: Living, eternal God, you are worthy of our thanks and praise.
Your breath gives us life; your word brings new life out of death.
You call us from separation and sin to a joyful life of communion with you and all your creatures.
With all people and all creation, we sing your praise:
All: Holy, holy, holy,
God of resurrection power.
Heaven and earth are full of your glory.
Hosanna in the highest!
Blessed is Christ who comes in your name, O God.
Hosanna in the highest!
Leader: Holy are you, source of all, and blessed is Jesus the Christ,
in whom you share our life and death.
At the table of communion Jesus welcomed the sinful and the
righteous,
the powerful and the poor, proclaiming your love for all.
When death was at hand, once again Jesus gathered the disciples

and gave you thanks and praise, blessing gifts of bread and
  wine.[5]
After you raised him from death,
Christ was made known in the breaking of bread.
And even now we come to meet Christ in the breaking of bread,
praising you that by your great mercy
we have been born anew to a living hope
through the resurrection of Christ from the dead.
We offer ourselves to you,
boldly proclaiming what we believe:

All: Christ has died.
Christ is risen.
Christ will come again.

Leader: Holy One, draw us into the eternal communion
you share with Jesus Christ and with the Spirit, who moves
  among us.
Through your Spirit, reveal to us the presence of Christ
as we partake these earthly gifts of bread and wine,
as we share in the life of your church,
as we offer our hearts to you,
that we may take part in the pouring out of your love into the world.

All: All praise to you, Living One,
through Christ who is present among us
and the Spirit who gives us new life. Amen.

Breaking the Bread

*Before distribution of elements, the bread is broken, and the following
words are said:*

Leader: Through the bread that we break we recognize Christ's presence.
Through the cup of thanksgiving we share in Christ's life and death.

Giving the Bread and Cup

Prayer after Receiving

Holy, triune God, we thank you for your presence in all of life
and in this meal of thanksgiving

through which we remember your life, death, and new life
among us in Jesus the Christ.
Through your Spirit present in this feast and in all the world,
kindle in us divine love and compassion,
that in all things we may give you glory. Amen.
(RD)

A Eucharistic Prayer
Based on Luke 5:1–11 (The Call to Discipleship)

One: God be with you.

All: And also with you.

One: Let us lift up our hearts.

All: We lift them to God.

One: Let us offer our praise.

All: It is right to give God thanks and praise.

One: We give you thanks, Holy One, source and goal of life,
that you have created us in your own image and called us by name.
You called to us in the garden,
setting before us the ways of life and death.
You called us out of Egypt,
leading us to a new life of freedom and love.
You speak to us through your prophets,
pursuing us when we go astray,
challenging us to live in peace and justice.
In the unity of your Spirit,
we praise you together with the whole family of your faithful
people everywhere.

All: Holy, holy, holy God of power and love,
the earth is full of your glory.
Blessed is Jesus Christ, who comes in your name.
Hosanna in the highest.

One: Praise be to you, Holy One,
for you have come to us in Jesus Christ to reveal the sacred
purpose of our lives.
We bless you, for in Christ you have cast into deep waters
to reach us with your love
and to gather us into new life in community.

We thank you that Jesus did not turn back in the face of danger,
but remained faithful until death,
continuing to show forth your reign of love.
When the hour had come, Jesus gathered the apostles
and passed a cup among them,
still speaking of your reign.
Then he took a loaf of bread, gave thanks to you,
broke it, and gave it to the disciples,
saying, "This is my body, given for you."
After supper he did the same with the cup,
saying, "This is the new covenant in my blood."
Remembering the love of Christ,
we hand over our lives to you in trust,
accepting your call to proclaim and live the mystery of faith:

All: Living, Christ sanctifies our life.
Dying, Christ sanctifies our death.
Rising, Christ clothes us with power from on high.

One: We give you thanks, bountiful God, for the gift of your Holy Spirit,
the power from on high who anoints us with gifts to live out your
call.
Pour out your Spirit on your waiting church,
that we may discern the presence of Christ
in the bread and cup, in one another, and in the world you love.
Stir up the gifts of your Spirit within us.
Give us courage to cast our nets in deep waters,
to love and respect each other,
and to do justice, walking humbly with you.

All: Be present with us as we share this meal,
and throughout all our lives,
that we may know and praise you as the Holy One,
who with the Christ and the Holy Spirit lives forever. Amen.
(RD)

A Eucharistic Prayer:
Longing for God's Reign

One: God is with us.
All: In God we live and move and have our being.

One: Let us open our hearts.

All: We open our hearts to God and to one another.

One: Let us offer thanks to God, the giver of all good gifts.

All: It is right to offer thanks and praise.

One: Holy God, our loving Father and Mother,
we thank you for your constant care for all your children.
We thank you for people of faith in every generation
who have prayed without ceasing for the coming of your reign.
We thank you especially for Jesus Christ,
whom you have sent from your heart to assure us
that you labor with us for justice on earth.
In unity with all who yearn for your will to be done on earth,
we praise your name:

All: Holy, holy, holy God of love and justice,
your compassion enfolds the whole earth.
Blessed is Jesus Christ, who comes in your name.
Hosanna in the highest: God, come to save us.

One: We remember that even when human justice had failed,
Jesus took bread and cup, gave you thanks,
and shared a meal with disciples,
asking them to remember him in all their eating and drinking.

All: Recalling Christ's suffering and death,
rejoicing in Christ's resurrection,
we fervently await the day when your reign comes.

One: Holy One, we thank you for the presence of your life-giving Word
and Spirit to sustain us in hope.
Sanctify us and your whole church through your Spirit,
that, partaking this meal of thanksgiving,
we may be nurtured to labor with patience
for the coming of your justice,
living each day in love toward friend and stranger.

All: May all hearts turn to you in praise and faith,
O God our Mother and Father,
in Christ our hope of justice,
and the Spirit our comfort and strength. Amen.
(RD)

A Eucharistic Prayer:
Peace and Justice

One: We give you thanks, Abundant God,
for sounding the heartbeat of creation,
and for breathing life into our dust and ashes.
We bless you for the abundance of the earth
and for the promise that one day
all will share at one table
and none will be turned away hungry or thirsty.
We praise you, Lover of all people,
that you labor to restore the earth,
bring new life amid destruction.
Together with all people and all created things, we sing:

All: Holy, holy, holy God of love and power,
heaven and earth are full of your glory.
Hosanna in the highest!
Blest is the One who comes in your name, O God.
Hosanna in the highest!

One: Holy are you, God, and blessed is Christ who has come in your name,
living and dying in love and courage,
sanctifying the life of this world.
We praise you that you have raised Christ to live among us forever,
and that you send your Spirit to create and renew your church.
Thankful for all you do for us,
we offer ourselves in praise and thanksgiving.
Pour out your Holy Spirit on us,
that we may recognize the risen Christ in our midst,
in the gifts of bread and cup,
and in the world you cherish.
All praise be yours, God of the ages,
through Jesus Christ in the Holy Spirit, now and forever.

All: Amen.
(RD)

The words of institution would follow.

A Eucharistic Prayer
for Earth Day

Invitation: Let us join in blessing God for the good gifts of creation as we gather around Christ's Table.

Presider: We praise you, Holy Mystery, for your vast creation:
for the rose and the lotus, the crane and the wolf,
the dolphin who leaps in the ocean,
and all creatures of the deep.
We thank you that you have made humankind in your image
and entrusted the earth to our care.
We bless you that though we fail your trust,
you continue to love us with a steadfast love.
And so, with all your creatures on earth
and the faithful who live in your presence,
we praise you, holy God:

All: Holy, holy, holy God of creative power.
All your creatures sing your praise;
the earth is full of your glory.

Presider: Living God, your holiness saturates the life around us,
making all the world a sacred place.
We praise you for the dreamers
who acknowledge the holy and see the sacred in life.
We thank you for all who have gifted us with spirit and vision,
compassion and joy.
We thank you for all who have blessed us with the gift of their lives, coming in your name.

All: Blessed are the ones who come in your name, holy God.
Blessed is Jesus Christ. Hosanna in the highest!

Presider: Holy God, we bless you for Jesus Christ,
who comes in your name to heal and reconcile the whole creation,
bringing hope out of destruction and new life out of death.
We thank you that Jesus Christ invites us to the Table of love,
now as on the night before he was betrayed,
when he took bread, gave thanks to you,
and said, "This is my body, which is given for you."

We remember also that he took the cup, gave thanks to you,
and said, "This cup that is poured out for you
is the new covenant in my blood."
Remembering Jesus' death in love for your whole creation,
we offer our praise and thanksgiving
and our commitment to care for the earth.
Send forth your Spirit, O God,
and renew the face of the earth.
As through your Spirit these earthly creatures of grain and grape
show forth the gift of your grace.
So through your Spirit may your people
be signs of your love that fills the earth.

All: To you, creative God,
and to Jesus Christ, the living one,
with the life-giving Spirit,
be glory now and forever. Amen.

Great Thanksgiving for Trinity Sunday

Leader: God is with us.
All: The Spirit is with us.
Leader: Let us open our hearts.
All: We open them to God and one another.
Leader: Let us give thanks.
All: We thank God with joy.
Leader: It is good to give you thanks, Holy Source of Life, Lover of the
Universe, our Father and Mother.
Your hands set the stars in the sky,
you formed the waters by your word,
and your breath gives us life.
You call us from our sin and fear
and offer us rebirth through water and the Spirit,
that we may be your daughters and sons.
And so, with all your people and all creation,
we sing to you:
All: Holy, holy, holy, God of power and might.
Heaven and earth are full of your glory.
Hosanna in the highest.

Blest is the one who comes in your name, O God.

Hosanna in the highest.

Leader: We see and touch your Word and Wisdom in Jesus the Christ,

who danced with you at creation,

who communed with the outcast,

who died among sinners,

and who lives among us still,

seeking us when we are lost,

and inviting all people to the Table of grace.

Even on the night before he died in love for you and all people,

Jesus shared a meal with the disciples.

He took bread, gave thanks to you,

broke the bread and gave it to them, saying,

"Take, eat. This is my body."

After supper, he took the cup,

gave thanks to you, and shared the cup, saying,

"Drink this, all of you. This is the new covenant in my blood."

Remembering your boundless love for us in Jesus Christ,

we offer our grateful praise,

and proclaim the mystery of faith:

All: Christ has died. Christ is risen. Christ will come again.

Leader: Pour out your Spirit on your church

and on these gifts of bread and wine,

to guide us in all truth, that we may share in your life,

growing in the image of Christ,

and pouring out your love toward the whole creation.

All: All praise to you, Eternal One, Source and Goal of life,

with Jesus Christ, your Word and Wisdom,

and the Holy Spirit, breath and flame,

one God forever and ever.

Amen.

(RD)

A Eucharistic Prayer:
Wisdom Has Set Her Table

Leader: Wisdom has built her house.

Congregation: Sophia has set her table.

Leader:	She invites us to come and eat her bread.
Congregation:	And to live in the way of insight.
Leader:	Let us give thanks to God, Holy Wisdom.
Congregation:	It is good, it is wise, so to do.
Leader:	It is indeed a good and joyful thing, only wise God,
	to praise you, for with you is life.
	In wisdom you separated the sea from the dry land,
	rejoicing in the world, delighting in the human race.
	In wisdom, you call to us when we are foolish,
	asking us to learn from you how to turn from death to life.
	And so, with your whole creation we sing your praise:
All:	Holy, holy, holy, only wise God, the earth is your delight.
	Blessed are the wise ones who follow your way.
	Hosanna, Holy Wisdom.
Leader:	Holy are you, God,
	source of our life in Jesus your Word,
	who was with you at the beginning
	before you created the world,
	and who became flesh, full of grace and truth.
	Jesus set a table for the foolish, the hungry, and the poor,
	and for all who would live in the way of life.
	Even at the hour of death, Jesus called his disciples to dine,
	thanking you for gifts of bread and wine
	and sharing in Wisdom's feast.
	Dying in shame on the cross,
	Christ became your wisdom and your power,
	making foolish the wisdom of this world.
	And so we remember Christ-Sophia
	in our eating and drinking,
	and in Christ we choose the way of discipleship,
	the path of wisdom and of life.
All:	Glory be to the Word made flesh!
	Glory be to Christ, our Sophia!
Leader:	Holy One, bestow your Wisdom on us,
	for she is the Spirit, the breath of your power,
	who reflects eternal light and renews all things.
	Through the gift of the Spirit at this Table of love,

pass into our souls and make us your friends who live
wisely in your ways.

All: Glory be to you, Holy Wisdom, Christ-Sophia, Breath of
Power, for you are the way and the life! Amen.
(RD)

Brief Eucharistic Prayers

*In denominations such as the United Church of Christ and the Baptist
churches, the eucharistic prayer (often termed the "Prayer of Consecration") is sometimes spoken only by the presider and is often quite brief. The
following two prayers are appropriate for such contexts, yet their eucharistic theology is fuller than that of some brief prayers. In each case,
an institution narrative would follow, telling the story of the Last Supper
and other times when Jesus gathered people to eat, drink, praise God, and
love one another.*

1.   We thank you, Source of Life, for creating the worlds with care,
      and for coming to us in Jesus Christ.
      We thank you for the gift of your grace
      displayed in the life, death, and resurrection of Christ,
      and in the pouring out of your Spirit on the church.
      Send your Spirit on us now,
      that this sacrament of love may encourage us anew
      to die to sin and to come alive to your way and will.
      Through your Spirit moving on this earth,
      unite all people and all creation
      in a communion of justice and peace.
      To you be glory forever, Holy God our Source,
      with Jesus, the Word of your grace,
      and the Holy Spirit, the outpouring of your love. Amen.
      (RD)

2. *To be used with readings from John's Gospel.*

      God of life, God of power, we thank you for creating the world and
         calling it good.
      We praise you for seeking us in love from the beginning of time until now.
      Most of all, we thank you that you loved the world so much
      as to give Jesus the Christ, your beloved child, to save us and set us free.
      We remember that before he was lifted up on the cross,

Jesus washed the feet of those who shared his ministry, shared a meal
    with them,
and told them to love one another that all might be one in you.
We gather once more at the table of Jesus, the Living Bread.
Breathe your Spirit upon us to guide us into your truth,
that we may abide in you and live always in love.
All glory and power and honor be unto you,
Heart of Love, Word of Life, Spirit of peace, one God, forever and
    ever. Amen.
(RD)

SERVICE OF HEALING

*Inspired by Jesus' compassionate ministry of healing, many congregations
today are extending their ministry of healing beyond individual pastoral
care and private prayer to liturgical services of healing. Healing is a work
of the triune God, as this service assumes. Careful choices about music and
the visual environment help to set the tone for a gentle, compassionate service of healing.*

Opening Music

Call to Worship (Based freely on Ps. 103:1–5)

Leader: Let us raise our voices to praise the living God,
           who satisfies us with good as long as we live,
           so that our youth is renewed like the eagle's.
People: Let us praise Jesus Christ, who heals our diseases
           and saves our lives from despair.
Leader: Let us praise the Spirit, who anoints us with grace and power.
All: Let all creation bless the God of healing love! Amen.

Hymn

Call to Awareness

Leader: As we draw near to the fountain of grace,
           let us lay down burdens of hurt and guilt
           that we may receive with open hands
           the gifts God intends for us.

Unison Prayer of Awareness

All: We lay down our need before you,
holy God of compassion and grace,
trusting in your great love for us and for all creation.
We bear wounds, and we ourselves have wounded others.
We open ourselves to the work of your Spirit among us
to free us from all that is not of you
and to recreate us in your image.
Praise and thanksgiving, honor and blessing be to you,
divine Fount of healing and love,
through your Word of grace made flesh,
and your Spirit of holiness and power. Amen.

Assurance of God's Love

Leader: Hear the good news:
Nothing in all creation,
neither what we do nor what has been done to us,
can separate us from love of God made known in Jesus Christ
and poured out on the church through the Spirit.
Thanks be to God!

The congregation may respond with a song of thanksgiving and by the sharing of signs of reconciliation and peace.

Scripture Reading(s)

Texts that tell the story of the healing ministry of Jesus are particularly recommended.

Witness to God's Healing Power

The witness to God's healing power may come through a sermon, a testimony by one person, or through a time when the community is invited to share testimonies with thanksgiving for what God has done in their lives.

Hymn

Thanksgiving over Oil

Leader: Holy Source of life and healing,
we give you thanks for the gift of oil,

sign of your Spirit's power within and among us.
We thank you for Jesus, your anointed one,
who healed the sick, raised the dead,
brought good news to the poor,
and proclaimed the year of your favor.
Anoint us now by your grace,
that we may receive the healing and peace you intend for us,
and so be renewed to be your people in the world:
through Jesus Christ we pray.
People: Amen.

Intercessions

There may be a time of free prayer, during which the congregation lifts their concerns to God, or a responsive time of intercession such as the following.

Leader: We pray to you, O God, for all who need your healing.
People: God, hear our prayer.
Leader: For all among us who are sick,
People: God, hear our prayer.
Leader: For all who are troubled in mind,
People: God, hear our prayer.
Leader: For all who are cut off from community,
People: God, hear our prayer.
Leader: For all who struggle with shattered relationships.
People: God, hear our prayer.
Leader: For our broken, hurting, conflicted world,
People: God, hear our prayer.
Leader: For all who heal by their words and actions,
People: God, hear our prayer.
All: Healing God, we trust ourselves, our friends, our families, and our world to your keeping. We open ourselves to your healing power. Make us instruments of your peace, through the power of your spirit and the grace of Jesus Christ. Amen.

Invitation

The invitation, which should be tailored to each service of healing, summarizes the meaning of the rituals, provides specific directions to facilitate participation, and encourages people to participate in the way they feel most comfortable. The following sample invitation can be adapted according to a congregation's theology, needs, and practices:

> At this time, anointing, laying on of hands, and prayer is available, for healing of body, mind, or spirit, through the love of God. All who wish may advance to one of the four stations at the front and center of the sanctuary. Please let the team know if you have particular prayer requests, or if you prefer only one ritual: prayer, anointing, or laying on of hands. Please feel free to participate only in ways that are comfortable to you at this time.

Anointing and Laying On of Hands

The team members listen to each person's request in turn. One member anoints each with words such as the following:

> I anoint you in the name of the triune God, Holy Creator, Healing
>   Word, Reviving Breath.
> *OR*
> I anoint you in the name of God, weaver of life's fabric, mender of
>   frayed strands, shaper of new creation.
> *OR*
> I anoint you in the name of Love poured out in the world's creation,
>   spoken in the Word's incarnation,
>   whispered in the Spirit's breath.
> *OR*
> I anoint you in the name of the Father, and of the Son, and of the Holy
>   Spirit, one God, Mother of us all.[6]
> *OR*
> You are anointed in the name of God the Fountain of Life,
>   and of Christ the Living Water,
>   and of the Spirit, Wellspring of New Life.

Another team member lays on hands and offers a brief prayer appropriate to any needs that have been expressed. When all who wish have come for prayer, anointing, and the laying on of hands, the service continues in thanksgiving, through celebration of the Eucharist, or through a brief prayer of thanksgiving.

Celebration of the Eucharist

The gifts of bread and cup are brought forward from among the congregation. The community gives thanks to God, with words such as the following:

One: God is present among us in mystery and power.
All: God is truly with us.
One: Let us give thanks to the Holy One.
All: Let us praise the God of healing and of hope.
One: We give you thanks, wondrous God, for the mystery of creation,
for the miracle of life,
and for seeds of renewal you plant deep within all living things.
We praise you that you continue to create and recreate forever,
mending what is broken, and making all things new.
With saints who have gone before us,
with sisters and brothers who now surround us,
and with all creation, we join the eternal chorus of praise to you:
All: Holy, holy, holy God,
the whole creation is full of your love.
Blessed is Christ, who comes in your name
to heal and to save.
One: Holy God of mystery, love, and power,
we bless you for your child Jesus Christ,
who has come among us to restore all things to your purpose
and to teach your song of love to all people.
Jesus healed the sick, fed the hungry,
and offered to all, whether honored or despised by the world,
a destiny as your daughters and sons.
Jesus shared our pain and sorrow,
and knew our fear when his life was threatened,
yet united in love to you, and empowered by your Spirit,
he continued to heal and preach good news.
On the night before he died, Jesus shared a meal with disciples.
He took bread, gave thanks to you,
broke the bread, and gave it to them, saying,
"This is my body, which is broken for you."
He also took a cup, gave you thanks,
and shared it with them, saying,

"This cup is the new covenant in my blood."
After you raised Jesus from the dead,
once again he broke bread with disciples
and asked them to care for human need
as a shepherd tends the sheep.
Remembering Jesus,
we offer you our love, our praise, and our thanksgiving
in joy and suffering, in sickness and health,
in union with Christ in life and death.

All: Living, Christ led the way to true life.
Dying, Christ showed the way to life beyond death.
Rising, Christ offers us new life.

One: Anoint us with your Spirit, Holy God,
that these gifts of bread and cup may be signs of your healing love.
By your Spirit empower us for a ministry of healing and care
to the world you love so dearly,
and inspire us to live in harmony with all your creatures.
Holy, Living God, with our whole hearts we praise you
and with our lives we give you glory,
through Jesus Christ the Healer,
and the Spirit who labors to bring forth new creation.

All: Amen.

The bread is broken, and the bread and cup are shared, as joyful songs of thanksgiving and praise are sung. The service concludes with a benediction and joyful music. If the Eucharist is not celebrated, the following prayer of thanksgiving may be offered, followed by a closing hymn and benediction.

Prayer of Thanksgiving

Leader: We give you thanks, wondrous God,
for the mystery of creation, for the miracle of life,
and for seeds of renewal you plant deep within all living things.
We praise you that you continue to create and recreate forever,
mending what is broken, and making all things new.
Holy God of mystery, love, and power,
we bless you for your child Jesus Christ,

who has come among us to restore all things to your purpose,
to heal the sick and feed the hungry,
and to offer all people a destiny as your daughters and sons.
Remembering Jesus,
we offer you our love, our praise, and our thanksgiving
in joy and suffering, in sickness and health,
in union with Christ in life and death.
By your Spirit anoint us for a ministry of care,
that we who have known your healing touch
may share your love with those in need of your grace.
Holy, Living God, with our whole hearts we praise you
and with our lives we give you glory,
through Jesus Christ the Healer,
and the Spirit who labors to bring forth new creation.
Amen.
(RD)

A Sunday Eucharistic Liturgy

The service that follows could be used for a Sunday worship service with a congregation. Two specific issues of the order are to be noted as relevant to issues of language about the Trinity in worship. This order omits both the Nicene (or any other) Creed and the Lord's Prayer. I have suggested that they not always be used in the Eucharist, in part because of the flow of the liturgy but also because these particular prayers have been the focus for so much debate about sexism and God-language. The Creed is necessary in Baptism and perhaps in certain particular Eucharists, but is not necessary every Sunday as an ordinary part of the service. The Lord's Prayer seems to have been introduced sometime around the year 400 as a preparatory prayer for the congregation before receiving communion. If they are to be used, I would suggest using the ELLC (English Language Liturgical Consultation) version, a translation that is more accurate and is ecumenically accepted. A constructive alternative to the Lord's Prayer is the excellent theological and liturgical paraphrase of the Lord's Prayer by Jim Cotter in A New Zealand Prayer Book.[7] *(PW-K)*

LITURGY OF THE WORD

Gathering with (a Hymn) Greeting and Prayer

Presider: The grace of Jesus Christ our Savior, and the love of God, and the communion of the Holy Spirit, be with you all.

People: And also with you.
Presider: Let us pray.

Collect of the Day or Prayer to the Trinity

Presider: O gracious and all holy God, with your infinite love, you create the entire cosmos, make us in your image, and make a covenant with Israel. Through your saving love, you have become human as Jesus of Nazareth, dwelling among us to reconcile us with you and with one another. In your redeeming love, you are the Holy Spirit among us and within us, drawing us into unending life with you and the whole reconciled creation. We praise you for inviting us to share in the joyful communion of your unending love. To you we give thanks, O life-giving Trinity.

People: Amen.

Readings

Normally these will be from the common lectionary or from the lectionary appointed for use or encouraged in the particular denomination in which the service is celebrated. From time to time a reading from a nonbiblical source may be substituted for one of the first two readings. At the Eucharist, a reading from the Gospel will always be the final reading.

First Reading. From the Hebrew Bible.
Psalm or canticle, sung or recited.
Second Reading. From the New Testament.
Hymn or canticle, sung or recited.
Gospel.

Sermon/Homily

[Creed]

Prayers of the People

This is an opportunity for the congregation to pray for the world and for all its living things, the church universal, for all who seek and serve God, for peace and justice on the earth, especially for our own country with its hopes and its needs, for our own community, for the sick and suffering, those in any need or trouble, and for the departed. Here is one simple form. Congregational participation is to be encouraged.

Introduction
by the
Leader: Let us pray, in the power of the Holy Spirit, whom God gives us through Jesus Christ. You are invited to add to each petition your own concerns. After the words "Hear us, Holy God," everyone is invited to respond, "We pray to you, O God."

Leader: Let us pray for the universe God has created and is creating, and for all living beings.
(Petitions from the congregation are added silently or out loud.)

Leader: Hear us, Holy God.
All: We pray to you, O God.
Leader: Let us pray for God's church throughout the world, for its mission and its ministry, and for all who seek and serve God in the world.
(Petitions from the congregation are added silently or out loud.)

Leader: Hear us, Holy God.
All: We pray to you, O God.
Leader: Let us pray for justice and peace throughout the world.
(Petitions from the congregation are added silently or out loud.)

Leader: Hear us, Holy God.
All: We pray to you, O God.
Leader: Let us pray for the United States of America, for our leaders, [names of leaders], and for all of our people.
(Petitions from the congregation are added silently or out loud.)

Leader: Hear us, Holy God.
All: We pray to you, O God.
Leader: Let us pray for our own community, in thanksgiving for its joys and celebrations, its needs and its aspirations.
(Petitions from the congregation are added silently or out loud.)

Leader: Hear us, Holy God.

All: We pray to you, O God.

Leader: Let us pray for the forgiveness of our sins and for God's gift of repentance and renewal of our lives.

         (Petitions from the congregation are added silently or out loud.)

Leader: Hear us, Holy God.

All: We pray to you, O God.

Leader: Let us pray for our own community, for the sick and suffering, those in any need or trouble, and all others commended to our prayer.

         (Petitions from the congregation are added silently or out loud.)

Leader: Hear us, Holy God.

All: We pray to you, O God.

Leader: Let us pray for all those who have died, that your will for them may be fulfilled, and we may rejoice with them in your eternal life.

         (Petitions from the congregation are added silently or out loud.)

Leader: Hear us, Holy God.

All: We pray to you, O God.

Presider: Let us pray.

         Hear the prayers of your people, O God; pour into our hearts your life and truth, and may your reign spread throughout the whole world.

All: Amen.

Confession

[If the petition for forgiveness of sins is not used, a separate Confession is provided.]

Leader: Let us confess our sins to God and before one another.

         Silence is observed for confession to God.

All: O God of justice and mercy, you have made us in your image, and call us to return to you and repent when we have fallen short of the goodness you have entrusted to us. Forgive us for all of our sins: those intended and those actually carried out, those known to us and those unknown, for harm done and good works undone.

Presider: May our Creator God of the Covenant, Jesus Christ our Redeemer and Brother, and the Spirit of Holiness and all Truth, forgive us [you], reform us [you], and renew us [you] in God's own life.

All: Amen.

Peace

Presider: May the peace of the holy and life-giving God be among us.
People: May we be instruments of God's peace.

A sign of peace is exchanged among the worshipers.

LITURGY OF COMMUNION

Offertory

An appropriate hymn or anthem may be sung as the elements for the Eucharist and the people's offerings of money and other gifts are brought to the altar. The altar/table is prepared for the communion.

Great Thanksgiving

Presider: God is here.
All: God's Spirit is with us.
Presider: Lift up your hearts.
All: We lift them up unto our God.
Presider: Let us give thanks to our holy God.
All: It is right to give God thanks and praise.
Presider: With joy and hope, we give you thanks and praise, O gracious and life-giving God. In love you created the galaxies, the richness of time and space, and the manifold beauty of the cosmos. You breathed your spirit upon us, to form the earth, the moon, the sun, and the stars, O creator God, with all the creatures who dwell here. You made us in your image, to love one another and

to care for the earth and its creatures. [You draw all creation to yourself through Jesus Christ, your living and incarnate Word. Your Holy Spirit dwells in us, to teach and illumine us with your light, and to walk in your ways of life and peace.] We praise you, who are the font of life, grace, and truth. You are all holy, and with the communion of the saints, with angels, archangels, cherubim and seraphim, all the hosts of heaven, in one voice with all creation we sing (say):

All: Holy, holy, holy, God of power and might,

         [Holy, holy, holy, God of infinite love,

OR

      Holy, holy, holy, God of gracious power]

      heaven and earth are full of your glory,

         Hosanna in the highest.

      Blessed in the one who comes in the name of our God.

         Hosanna in the highest.

Presider: You speak your Word and you make this earth to be our home. You call us into covenant communion with you and with one another, to share the fullness of your life. Our ancestors in the faith, Abraham and Sarah, Hagar and Ishmael, Isaac and Rebecca, Jacob, Rachel, and Leah, Moses, Miriam, and Aaron, Joshua, Deborah, Ruth and Naomi, David, Solomon, prophets, kings and queens, the poor and the humble, followed your way of truth, sinned and were forgiven, and cried to you that your reign would come on earth and in heaven.

Jesus Christ, the Word made flesh, was born of Mary, in Bethlehem, to dwell among us and to show us divine glory visible on earth. He grew among us in grace and truth, was baptized as one of us, and called together a community of disciples. Jesus preached, taught, and healed us. He was faithful to you even unto death.

At supper on the night he was betrayed and arrested, he took bread, gave thanks to you, broke it, and gave it to his disciples, saying: Take, eat, this is my body which is given for you; do this to remember me.

After supper he took the cup, gave you thanks, and gave it to them, saying: Drink this, all of you. This is my blood of the new covenant, which is shed for you and for many, for the forgiveness of sins. As often as you drink it, do this to remember me.

Therefore, O Most Holy One, we offer you these gifts of bread and wine. Accept this sacrifice of praise and thanksgiving. In this banquet we celebrate our redemption:

All: Glory to you, O Jesus Christ,
who died for the world's reconciliation,
who rises from death to give us life,
who will come again to complete God's reign among us.

Leader: May the Holy Spirit come upon these gifts of bread and wine. May they be to us who receive them the body and blood of Jesus, God's gift of everlasting life and joy.

May this same Spirit dwell in us in grace and power, that we who eat at this table may be renewed in love and justice to serve God's reign on earth, and throughout all creation.

Blessing, honor, glory, and power be unto you, gracious and holy God, now and throughout all ages.

People: Amen.

Lord's Prayer

Invitation and Communion

Leader: The gifts of God for the people of God.
Congregation: Amen.

Distribution of the Gifts

A simple formula works best, whether clergy and assistants are distributing communion, or the people are serving each other the communion. The communicant may respond "Amen."

The body of Christ, the bread of heaven.
The blood of Christ, the cup of salvation.
OR
The body of Christ, given for you.
The blood of Christ, shed for you.
OR
The bread of life.
The cup of blessing.

A hymn may be sung during communion or immediately after. When the remaining elements of communion are either reverently consumed or placed in the customary place of reservation, all the people join in a prayer of thanksgiving for communion.

Post-Communion Prayer

Presider: Let us pray.

All: All holy and ever-gracious God, we who have partaken of your holy gifts of bread and wine thank you for your gracious gift of life in Jesus Christ, through the power of the Holy Spirit. By this Spirit poured forth into our hearts, may our hearts and minds be illumined, and may we be empowered through your love to live unendingly in communion with you, and faithfully to love and serve one another in your world. Amen.

Blessing

Presider: May the Holy God, One in Three, living in full and perfect communion and mutual self-giving, fill us with grace and peace, so that we may share this divine love with one another, and together dance its hope and joy in all creation.

Congregation: So be it!

OR

Presider: May the blessing of God, the gracious Source of all life, and Jesus, God's Word, Love made flesh for us, and the Holy Spirit, God's power for justice and peace, be with you all.

Congregation: So be it!

Dismissal

Leader: Let us go forth in God's peace.

Congregation: Thanks be to God.

OR

Leader: Let us go, to pray and work for God's reign on earth.

Congregation: Thanks be to God.

OR

Leader: Let us go forth into the world in God's name.

Congregation: Thanks be to God.

(PW-K)

APPENDIX: A SAMPLING OF TRINITARIAN HYMNS FROM SELECTED U.S. HYMNALS, 1982–1995

ABBREVIATIONS

BAP   *The Baptist Hymnal*, Southern Baptist Convention (Nashville: Convention Press, 1991)

CH   *Chalice Hymnal*, Christian Church, Disciples of Christ (St. Louis: Chalice Press, 1995)

H   *The Hymnal 1982*, Episcopal Church (New York: Church Hymnal Corp., 1982)

HWB   *Hymnal: A Worship Book*, Church of the Brethren, General Conference Mennonite Church, and the Mennonite Church of North America (Elgin, Ill.: Brethren Press; Newton, Kans.: Faith and Life Press; Scottdale, Pa.: Mennonite Publishing House, 1992)

NCH   *New Century Hymnal*, United Church of Christ (Cleveland: United Church Board for Homeland Ministries, 1995)

PH   *The Presbyterian Hymnal*, Presbyterian Church (U.S.A.) (Louisville, Ky.: Westminster / John Knox Press, 1990)

RL   *Rejoice in the Lord*, Reformed Church in America (Grand Rapids: Wm. B. Eerdmans Publishing Co., 1985)

UMH   *The United Methodist Hymnal*, United Methodist Church (Nashville: United Methodist Publishing House, 1989)

TRINITARIAN HYMNS

TYPE 1: Hymns with trinitarian doxologies as last stanzas. (Some of these address one person of the Trinity, then end with praise naming all three persons.)

"Alleluia, Hearts to Heaven," Christopher Wordsworth, 1872
Hymnal: NCH 243 (alt.)

"All Praise to Thee [Be Yours], My God, This Night," Thomas Ken,
1692
Hymnals: H 43, RL 77, UMH 682, BAP 449, PH 542, HWB
658, NCH 100 (with new doxology by Carl Daw, 1992)

"Behold the Lamb of God," Matthew Bridges, 1848
Hymnal: RL 291

"Christ Is Made the Sure Foundation," Latin, seventh century, trans.
J. M. Neale, 1851
Hymnals: H 518, RL 392, BAP 356, UMH 559, PH 416, 417,
CH 275

"Come, O Creator Spirit, Come," medieval Latin, trans. Robert S.
Bridges, 1899
Hymnals: H 502 (503 alt. trans), RL 377, NCH 268

"Lord of All Good," Albert Bayly, 1950
Hymnals: RL 430, PH 375

"May the Grace of Christ Our Savior," John Newton, 1779
Hymnal: HWB 423

"Now Thank We All Our God," Martin Rinkart, 1663, trans. Kather-
ine Winkworth, 1858
Hymnals: H 396, 397, RL 61, UMH 102, BAP 638, PH 555,
HWB 85, 86, CH 715, NCH 419

"O Gladsome Light," ancient Greek hymn, trans. Robert S. Bridges,
1899
Hymnals: H 36, RL 623, UMH 686, PH 549

"Of the Father's Love Begotten," Prudentius (348–413), trans. John
Mason Neale, 1851 and Henry W. Baker, 1859
Hymnals: H 82, RL 190, 191, UMH 184, BAP 251, PH 309,
HWB 104, CH 104, NCH 118 (alt.)

"Rejoice Ye [You] Pure in Heart," Edward H. Plumptre, 1865
Hymnals: UMH 160, 161, BAP 39, PH 145, 146 (CH 15 and
NCH 55, 71 have substitute doxology by Ruth Duck)

"She Is the Spirit," John Bell, 1988
Hymnal: CH 255

"Sing, My Tongue, the Glorious Battle," Fortunatus (530–609) trans. varied
> Hymnals: H 165, 166, RL 289, 290, UMH 296, HWB 256, NCH 220

"Sing to Him in Whom Creation," Michael Hewlett, 1975
> Hymnal: RL 383

"The Baptist Shouts on Jordan's Shore," Matthew Bridges, 1848
> Hymnal: RL 291

"They'll Know We Are Christians," Peter Scholtes, 1966
> Hymnal: CH 494

TYPE 2: Three- or four-stanza structure, with one stanza addressed to each person of the Trinity; there may be a fourth stanza at the beginning or end which is a trinitarian doxology.

"All Glory Be to God on High," Nikolaus Decius, c. 1522, trans. F. Bland Tucker, 1977
> Hymnals: H 421, RL 620, PH 133, HWB 122

"Ancient of Days," William C. Doane, 1886, 1892
> Hymnals: H 363, RL 621

"Come, God, Creator, Be Our Shield," Marion Meyer, 1990
> Hymnal: NCH 69

"Come, Great God of All the Ages," Mary Jackson Cathey, 1987
> Hymnal: PH 132

"Come, Thou Almighty King," anonymous, c. 1757
> Hymnals: H 365, RL 618, UMH 61, BAP 247, PH 139, HWB 41, CH 27, NCH 275

"Creating God, Your Fingers Trace," Jeffrey Rowthorn, 1979
> Hymnals: H 394, 395, UMH 109, PH 134, HWB 168, 325, CH 335, NCH 462

"Creator God, Creating Still," Jane Parker Huber, 1977
> Hymnals: BAP 51, CH 62, NCH 278

"Eternal Father, Strong to Save," William Whiting, 1860
> Hymnals: H 608, RL 525, BAP 69, PH 562, CH 85

"Father, I Adore You," Terrye Coelho (1952–)
    Hymnal: BAP 256

"God, Our Father, We Adore Thee," George W. Frazer (1830–1896),
    stanzas 1, 2, 4, and Alfred S. Loizeaux (1877–1962), stanza 3
    Hymnal: BAP 248

"God the Spirit, Guide, and Guardian," Carl Daw, 1987
    Hymnals: UMH 648, PH 523, HWB 632, CH 450, NCH 355

"Holy Father, Great Creator," Alexander Viets Griswold (1766–
    1843), alt.
    Hymnal: H 368

"Maker [Father], in Whom We Live," Charles Wesley, 1747
    Hymnal: UMH 88

"Mothering God," Jean Janzen, 1991, from Julian of Norwich
    Hymnals: HWB 482, CH 83, NCH 467

"O God, Almighty Father," anonymous, trans. Irvin Udulutsch
    (1920–)
    Hymnal: BAP 258

"O God in Heaven," Elena G. Maquiso, 1961, trans. D. T. Niles, 1964
    Hymnals: UMH 119, NCH 279

"O Mighty God," Erik Routley, 1982
    Hymnal: RL 466

"Praise and Thanksgiving Be to God," J. Francis Yardley, 1982
    Hymnal: UMH 604

"Praise to God, Praise to God, for the Greenness of the Trees,"
    Nobuaki Hanaoka, 1980
    Hymnal: NCH 5

"Source and Sovereign, Rock and Cloud," Thomas Troeger, 1987
    Hymnals: UMH 113, CH 12

"Sovereign Lord of All Creation," Stewart Cross (1928–1989)
    Hymnal: PH 136

"We Believe in One True God," Tobias Clausnitzer, 1668, trans.
    Katherine Winkworth, 1863
    Hymnals: RL 609 (stanzas 1, 2, 4), UMH 85, BAP 85, PH 137

"Thou Whose Almighty Word," John Marriott (1780–1825)
Hymnal: H 371

"Womb of Life and Source of Being," Ruth Duck, 1986
Hymnals: CH 14, NCH 274

TYPE 3: Hymns addressed to the whole Trinity.

"God Is One, Unique and Holy," Brian Wren, 1983
Hymnal: PH 135

"Eternal Light, Shine in My Heart," Alcuin (c. 735–804), para.
Christopher Idle, 1977
Hymnals: PH 340, HWB 518

"Father, Most Holy, Merciful, and Loving," tenth-century Latin
hymn, trans. A. E. Alston, 1904
Hymnal: RL 617

"Holy God, We Praise Thy Name," attr. Ignaz Franz, 1770, trans.
Clarence Walworth, 1853
Hymnals: H 366 (stanzas 1–4), RL 619, UMH 79, PH 460,
HWB 121, NCH 276

"Holy, Holy, Holy," Reginald Heber, 1826
Hymnals: H 362, RL 611, UMH 64, BAP 2, PH 138, HWB
120, CH 4, NCH 277

"How Wondrous Great, Our Creator," Isaac Watts, c. 1707–9
Hymnals: H 369, HWB 126

"O Holy Radiance," Greek, second to fourth century, trans. *New Century Hymnal,* 1994
Hymnal: NCH 739

"O Trinity, Your Face We See," Douglas Eschbach, 1988
Hymnal: NCH 280

"O Wisdom, Breathed from God," in part a translation of the O antiphons, Latin, sixth to seventh centuries, trans. *New Century Hymnal,* 1994
Hymnal: NCH 740

"The Royal Banners Forward Go [Fly]," Fortunatus, c. 574, various
   translations
   Hymnals: H 162, RL 286, 287, NCH 221

TYPE 4: Service music.

"Dios Padre, Dios Hijo," Pablo Fernandez Badillo, twentieth century
   Hymnal: CH 45

"Glory Be to God and to the Christ," Elaine Clemens Berkenstock,
   1991
   Hymnal: CH 37

"Glory Be to the Father," lesser doxology, third to fourth century
   Hymnals: RL 561, 562, 563, UMH 70, 71, BAP 252, PH 567
   (var.), 577, 578, 579, HWB 127, CH 35, 36, NCH 759 (alt.)

"Glory to God in the Highest," ancient Latin text (Gloria in Excelsis)
   Hymnals: H S201ff., S272ff., PH 566, 575, NCH 757 (alt.)

"Grace to You and Peace," Rom. 1:7 (Alice Parker, 1962)
   Hymnal: HWB 24

"Holy, Holy, Holy Is the Lord," traditional
   Hymnal: BAP 666

"May the Grace of Christ Our Savior," Tom Fettke (1941–)
   Hymnal: BAP 661

"O Gracious Light," ancient Greek hymn
   Hymnal: H S27, S59, S60, S61

"Praise God, from Whom All Blessings Flow," Thomas Ken, 1674,
   adapt. by Gilbert H. Vieira, 1978 (LASST UNS ERFREDUEN
   tune)
   Hymnals: UMH 94, CH 50

"Praise God, from Whom All Blessings Flow," Thomas Ken, 1674
   (OLD HUNDREDTH tune)
   Hymnals: RL 556, UMH 95, BAP 253, PH 591 (alt.), 592,
   593 (alt.), HWB 118, 119, CH 46, 47, 48, NCH 776–782
   (varied texts)

"Praise God, the Source of Life and Birth," Ruth Duck, 1986
   Hymnal: HWB 95

"Somos Uno en Cristo," Latin American (twentieth century), trans.
    by Frank Colon, 1994
    Hymnal: CH 493

"We Praise Thee," ancient Latin text (Te Deum Laudamus)
    Hymnal: H S205ff., S282ff.

TYPE 5: Economic trinitarian hymns.

"A Woman and a Coin," Jaroslav Vajda, 1990
    Hymnal: CH 74

"A Mighty Fortress," Martin Luther, c. 1529, trans. Frederick H.
    Hedge, 1853
    Hymnals: H 687, 688, RL 179, UMH 110, BAP 8, PH 260,
    HWB 165, 329, CH 65, NCH 439, 440

"Baptized in Your Name Most Holy," Johann J. Rambach, 1723,
    trans. Katherine Winkworth, 1863
    Hymnals: RL 529, NCH 324

"Blessed Assurance," Fanny J. Crosby, 1973
    Hymnals: RL 453, UMH 369, BAP 334, PH 341, HWB 332,
    CH 543, NCH 473

"Child of Blessing, Child of Promise," Ronald S. Cole-Turner, 1981
    Hymnals: UMH 611, PH 498, HWB 620, NCH 325

"En Santa Hermandad," William Loperena, 1989
    Hymnal: NCH 392

"God of Eve and God of Mary," Fred Kaan, 1989
    Hymnal: HWB 492

"Hoy Celebramos con Gozo al Dios," Mortimer Arias, 1981, trans.
    Roberto Escamilla and Elise Esslinger
    Hymnal: NCH 246

"I Bind unto Myself Today," attr. St. Patrick (c. 430, para. Cecil
    Frances Alexander, 1889)
    Hymnals: H 370, RL 478, HWB 441

"Love Divine, All Loves Excelling," Charles Wesley, 1747
    Hymnals: H 657, RL 464, BAP 208, UMH 384, PH 376,
    HWB 592, CH 517, NCH 43

"May the Sending One," Brian Wren, 1989, 1993
     Hymnal: NCH 79

"Now the Silence," Jaroslav Vajda, 1968
     Hymnals: H 333, UMH 619, HWB 462, CH 415

"O God, Great Womb of Wondrous Love," Harris Loewen, 1983
     Hymnal: HWB 155

"O Holy Spirit, Root of Life," Jean Janzen, 1991, from Hildegard of Bingen
     Hymnals: HWB 123, CH 251, NCH 57

"O Splendor of God's Glory Bright," Ambrose of Milan, fourth century, trans. Robert S. Bridges, 1899
     Hymnals: H 5, RL 76, UMH 679, PH 474, HWB 646, NCH 87

"Sing of a God in Majestic Divinity," Herbert O'Driscoll, 1980
     Hymnal: CH 331

"There's a Spirit in the Air," Brian Wren, 1969
     Hymnals: RL 380, UMH 192, BAP 393, PH 433, CH 257, NCH 294

"This Is the Day," stanza 1, Leslie Garrett, 1967; stanzas 2 and 3, anonymous
     Hymnal: NCH 84 (stanzas 2 and 3, which do not appear in the other hymnals, make this hymn trinitarian in NCH)

"We Limit Not the Truth of God," George Rawson, alt.
     Hymnals: H 629, NCH 316

"We, Your People, God, Confessing," based on a church document, 1993
     Hymnal: CH 356

Other hymns referenced in this book

"Glorious Is Your Name, O Jesus," Robert J. Fryson, 1982
     Hymnals: CH 118, NCH 53

"God of Many Names," Brian Wren, 1985
     Hymnals: UMH 106, CH 13

NOTES

PREFACE

1. Patricia Wilson-Kastner, *Faith, Feminism, and the Christ* (Philadelphia: Fortress Press, 1983).
2. Patricia Wilson-Kastner, *Imagery for Preaching* (Minneapolis: Fortress Press, 1989).
3. Ruth C. Duck, *Gender and the Name of God: The Trinitarian Baptismal Formula* (New York: Pilgrim Press, 1991).
4. David Cunningham, *These Three Are One: The Practice of Trinitarian Theology* (Malden, Mass.: Basil Blackwell Publisher, 1998).

INTRODUCTION

1. Although we will discuss later the problematic of habitually referring to the first person of the trinity as "God" (as well as the problematic of "person" language), here we simply point to common understandings of the sacrament which assume participation of each persona of the Trinity.
2. James Forbes, *The Holy Spirit and Preaching* (Nashville: Abingdon Press, 1989).
3. Ted Peters, *God as Trinity: Relationality and Temporality in Divine Life* (Louisville, Ky.: Westminster/John Knox Press, 1993).
4. Geoffrey Wainwright, "Trinitarian Worship," in *Speaking the Christian God* (Grand Rapids: Wm. B. Eerdmans Publishing Co., 1992), 209–21, and Gail Ramshaw, *God beyond Gender: Feminist Christian God-Language* (Minneapolis: Fortress Press, 1995), 76.
5. Leonardo Boff, *Trinity and Society* (Maryknoll, N.Y.: Orbis Books, 1988), 100.
6. Ibid., 111.
7. United Church of Christ statement of faith.
8. In this volume, we usually speak of "masculine" and "feminine" language (rather than "male" and "female" language) to indicate the socially constructed nature of gendered language, rather than to reinforce gender stereotypes.
9. Refer to Ruth C. Duck, *Gender and the Name of God: The Trinitarian Baptismal Formula* (New York: Pilgrim Press, 1991), chapters 2 and 3 (31–57 and 59–83), for a more detailed cultural and biblical exploration of "Father" as a name for God.

CHAPTER 1: WHERE DO WE START?

1. For some feminists, even the word "God" is problematic. Gail Ramshaw entitled a helpful discussion of the issue "God as a Common Noun" in her volume *God beyond Gender: Feminist Christian God-Language* (Minneapolis: Fortress Press, 1995), 8–22. Although some would prefer "Goddess," and Rosemary Radford Ruether has proposed "God/dess," I concur with Ramshaw that "god" is a common noun that can designate a male deity, but does not have to, and can usefully be reclaimed for feminist discourse and feminist liturgical prayer.
2. Ruth Duck, "Inclusive Language," in *Dictionary of Feminist Theologies*, ed. Letty M. Russell and J. Shannon Clarkson (Louisville, Ky.: Westminster John Knox Press, 1996), 152.
3. The divine, I believe, is encountered in other traditions. Here, my concern is with the Christian tradition and the trinitarian God.
4. Starhawk, *The Spiral Dance* (San Francisco: Harper & Row, 1979), 10–12; Morning Glory and Otter G'Zell, "Who on Earth Is the Goddess?" 25–33, and Dennis D. Carpenter, "Emergent Nature Spirituality . . . ," 35–72, in *Magical Religion and Modern Witchcraft*, ed. James R. Lewis (Albany: State University of New York Press, 1996). Feminists who prefer the name "Goddess" for the divine often refer to themselves as "thealogians," since in Greek *ho theos* (the root of "theologian") is a masculine grammatical term; *hē thea* is the corresponding feminine term, i.e., goddess.
5. Naomi Goldenberg, *The Changing of the Gods* (Boston: Beacon Press, 1979), 89.
6. John B. Cobb, Jr., "The Revitalization of the Trinity," 1–22; Marjorie H. Suchocki, "Spirit in and through the World," 184–89, in *Trinity in Process: A Relational Theology of God*, ed. Joseph A. Bracken and Marjorie Hewitt Suchocki (New York: Continuum, 1997).
7. Richard Grigg, *When God Becomes Goddess* (New York: Continuum, 1995), 13.
8. Ibid., 55; Grigg perceives that for Carter Heyward, among others, God may in a sense be transcendent as the power underlying all relation (138). Refer also to Rosemary Radford Ruether, *Gaia and God* (San Francisco: Harper & Row, 1992), 1–2; idem, *Womanguides: Readings toward a Feminist Theology* (Boston: Beacon Press, 1985). ix–xii; Isabel Carter Heyward, *The Redemption of God* (Washington, D.C.: University Press of America, 1982), especially 1–23.
9. Grigg, *When God Becomes Goddess*, 56–61.
10. Catherine Mowry LaCugna, "God in Communion with Us," in *Freeing Theology*, ed. Catherine Mowry LaCugna (San Francisco: HarperCollins, 1993), identifies this group of theologians who argue that "Father, Son, and Holy Spirit are the revealed names of God" (10). She identifies five other approaches

that respond to the exclusive use of masculine language about the deity: "the incomprehensible and unnameable God; feminine as well as masculine images; Jesus, the Iconoclast; the Holy Spirit as feminine; Creator, Redeemer and Sustainer" (102–5).

11. William Oddie, *What Will Happen to God?* (London: SPCK, 1984), 11–15.

12. Ibid., 97–127.

13. Alvin F. Kimel, ed., *Speaking the Christian God: The Holy Trinity and the Language of Feminism* (Grand Rapids: Wm. B. Eerdmans Publishing Co., 1992), x.

14. Donald D. Hook and Alvin F. Kimel, "Forum: Is God a He?" *Worship* 68, no. 2 (March 1994), 149.

15. Ibid., 156.

16. Athanasius of Alexandria, "De Decretis," in *Athanasius Werke* (Berlin: Walter de Gruyter, 1935), vol. 2, part 1, 18:4. Athanasius was, of course, formed by the interpretive tradition rooted in the work of Philo of Alexandria. Its classic exposition is in Harry Austryn Wolfson, *Philo* (Cambridge, Mass.: Harvard University Press, 1947) vol. 1, 115–37.

17. John Thompson's *Modern Trinitarian Perspectives* (Oxford: Oxford University Press, 1994) 114–17, treats seriously a feminist critique of the doctrine of the Trinity from the perspective of its patriarchal structure and language, looks at mediating positions, and identifies some of the strengths and weaknesses of the feminist critique, including the Athanasian argument applied in a feminist perspective. His moderate and open approach would be more helpful if he took more seriously the variety of feminist critiques and their different theological rootings.

18. For example, Catherine Mowry LaCugna, *God for Us* (San Francisco: Harper-Collins, 1991); Elizabeth A. Johnson, *She Who Is: The Mystery of God in Feminist Theological Discourse* (New York: Crossroad, 1993); Anne E. Carr, *Transforming Grace* (San Francisco: Harper & Row, 1988); Rebecca S. Chopp, *The Power to Speak: Feminism, Language, God* (New York: Crossroad, 1991); Pamela Dickey Young, *Feminist Theology/Christian Theology* (Minneapolis: Fortress Press, 1990); Marjorie Hewitt Suchocki, *God Christ Church: A Practical Guide to Process Theology* (New York: Crossroad, 1982).

19. Ruth C. Duck, *Gender and the Name of God: The Trinitarian Baptismal Formula* (New York: Pilgrim Press, 1991), idem, *Finding Words for Worship: A Guide for Leaders* (Louisville, Ky.: Westminster John Knox Press, 1995); Gail Ramshaw, *Christ in Sacred Speech: The Meaning of Liturgical Language* (Minneapolis: Fortress Press, 1986), idem, *God beyond Gender: Feminist Christian God-Language* (Minneapolis: Fortress Press, 1995).

20. Two categories of models about God, defined by Charles Hartshorne and William L. Reese, express in philosophical language an interrelationship between God and the world. Theism asserts God's existence and allows for a revelation of God's nature and reality to the world, as well as a relationship of

some likeness and love that God freely chooses to bestow. Panentheism allows for a much broader vision of an intrinsic relationship of the world with God, and can also express a relationship between God and the world that is in some sense part of God's nature. (Charles Hartshorne and William L. Reese, eds., *Philosophers Speak of God* [Chicago: University of Chicago Press, 1953], xii–xv, 1–25.)

21. Sallie McFague, *Metaphorical Theology* (Philadelphia: Fortress Press, 1982), 125.
22. Ian Ramsey, *Models for Divine Activity* (London: SCM Press, 1972), 40–55.
23. John Habgood, "Models," in *The Westminster Dictionary of Christian Theology*, ed. Alan Richardson and John Bowden (Philadelphia: Westminster Press, 1983), 375–76.
24. McFague, *Metaphorical Theology*, 145–92.
25. Paul Tillich, *Systematic Theology* 1 (Chicago: University of Chicago Press, 1967), 131, 238–41, uses symbol in a way for our purposes comparable to analogy.
26. Basil of Caesarea, *Epistula*, 38, 2.
27. Augustine of Hippo, *De Trinitate*, IX, 4–8.
28. J. Gwyn Griffiths, *Triads and Trinity* (Cardiff: University of Wales Press, 1996), 174–83.
29. David Tracy, *The Analogical Imagination* (New York: Crossroad, 1982), 405–45.
30. Johnson, *She Who Is*, 1–18.
31. LaCugna, "God in Communion with Us," 83–114.
32. Johnson, *She Who Is*, 205.
33. In addition to LaCugna's *God for Us,* and Johnson's *She Who Is*, refer to Leonardo Boff, *Trinity and Society* (Maryknoll, N.Y.: Orbis Books, 1988), and Jürgen Moltmann, *The Trinity and the Kingdom* (San Francisco: Harper & Row, 1981).
34. Harry Austrin Wolfson, *The Philosophy of the Church Fathers* (Cambridge, Mass.: Harvard University Press, 1970), 305–63.
35. *Supplemental Liturgical Texts: Prayer Book Studies 30* (New York: Church Hymnal Corporation, 1989), C-20; refer to C8–C14 for introductory comments.
36. Carmelites of Indianapolis, *The New Companion to the Breviary with Seasonal Supplement* (Indianapolis: Carmelite Monastery, 1988), 1 and *passim.*
37. *Book of Worship United Church of Christ* (New York: Office for Church Life and Leadership, 1986), 39.
38. Paul Avis, *Anglicanism and the Christian Church* (Minneapolis: Fortress Press, 1989), 9–11; James Shaughnessy, ed., *The Roots of Ritual* (Grand Rapids: Wm. B. Eerdmans Publishing Co., 1973), contains a number of useful basic studies in this area, particularly Christopher Crocker, "Ritual and the Development of Social Structure: Liminality and Inversion," 47–86; Jonathan

Smith, "The Influence of Symbols upon Social Change: A Place on Which to Stand," 121–44; Aidan Kavanagh, "The Role of Ritual in Personal Development," 145–60.

39. Paul Johnson, *The Quest for God: A Personal Pilgrimage* (London: Phoenix, 1996), 47–49.

40. For instance, Cheslyn Jones, Geoffrey Wainwright, Edward Yarnold, and Paul Bradshaw, eds., *The Study of Liturgy*, rev. ed. (London: SPCK, 1992).

41. Hippolytus, 13–24, Roman liturgy, 27–91, in *Liturgies of the Western Church*, ed. Bard Thompson (Cleveland: Collins/Fontana, 1961).

42. Colin Richmond, "The English Gentry and Religion, c. 1500," in *Religious Belief and Ecclesiastical Careers in Late Medieval England*, ed. Christopher Harper-Bill (Suffolk: Boydell Press, 1991), 140–43. Another example is the way the Collects in the Eucharist are translated into English, so that the opening address to "Deus" almost systematically becomes "Father" in contemporary English-language Roman Catholic liturgies.

CHAPTER 2: PRAISING A MYSTERY

1. Brian Wren, *Praising a Mystery* (Carol Stream, Ill.: Hope Publishing Co., 1986), second [unnumbered] page of the introduction.

2. Catherine Mowry LaCugna, *God for Us: The Trinity and Christian Life* (San Francisco: HarperCollins, 1991), 1.

3. Ibid., 274.

4. The Latin *persona* and the Greek *prosopon* originally referred to the mask an actor wore or a person's self-presentation, rather than an individuated human self-consciousness (J. N. D. Kelly, *Early Christian Doctrines*, 5th ed. [New York: Harper & Row, 1978], 115).

5. Karl Rahner, *The Trinity*, trans. Joseph Donceel (New York: Herder & Herder, 1970), 75–76.

6. This term was suggested by LaCugna's metaphor of human participation as "partner[s] in the divine dance," *God for Us*, 274.

7. Athanasius, in *Nicene and Post-Nicene Fathers*, ed. Philip Schaff and Henry Wace, vol. 4. (Peabody, Mass.: Hendrickson, 1994), 162. Later councils also affirmed that the Spirit was not a creature but one with the godhead (Bernard Lohse, *A Short History of Christian Doctrine* [Philadelphia: Fortress Press, 1966], 61–66).

8. There has been much controversy since Western churches added "and the Son" (in Latin, *filioque*) to a phrase in the Nicene Creed which affirmed that the Spirit proceeds "from the Father," saying that the Spirit proceeds "from the Father and the Son." Scripture passages such as John 20:22, in which Jesus breathes the Holy Spirit on the disciples, support the idea that the Spirit comes from the Son as well as the Father. Yet in John 14:16–17a, Jesus says, "I will ask the Father, and he will give you another Helper, to be with you forever.

This is the Spirit of truth." Here I support the Eastern position, simply stating that the Spirit proceeds from the Father. The *filioque* seems to image the divine self-giving as moving only in one direction, through Father to Son, then through Father and Son to Spirit, which is an inadequate picture of perichoretic mutuality in the life of God. (Refer to Elizabeth A. Johnson, *She Who Is* [New York: Crossroad, 1993], 194–97, for an elaboration of this idea.) The Eastern notion that the Father is Source of Son and Spirit also emphasizes the relationality of the Trinity more than the Western notion of a godhead behind all three persons of the Trinity, which emphasizes the category of substance (LaCugna, *God for Us*, 101). Indeed, overdependence on "Father" as a name for God tends to emphasize the intratrinitarian relationship between Father and Son to the neglect of the relationship between the Source and Spirit.

9. James Cone, *God of the Oppressed* (New York: Seabury Press, 1975), 115.
10. Kelly, *Early Christian Doctrines*, 113.
11. LaCugna, *God for Us*, 99.
12. Ibid., 103.
13. Ibid., 270–78.
14. For example, Geoffrey Wainwright says in his book *Doxology* (New York: Oxford University Press, 1990), 353, that in speaking of the Trinity "forfeiture of sexual language is to risk falling into an impersonal neuter."
15. Gerard S. Sloyan, "The Mystery of Christ's Death and Resurrection as Revelatory of the Inner Life of the Triune God" (paper presented at the Liturgical Theology study group of the North American Academy of Liturgy, January 1996, 10 pages), 10.
16. Refer to Alvin F. Kimel, Jr., "The God Who Likes His Name," in *Speaking the Christian God*, ed. Alvin F. Kimel (Grand Rapids: Wm. B. Eerdmans Publishing Co., 1992), 188–208.
17. Johanna W. H. van Wijk-Bos, a Hebrew Bible scholar, argues from the verb forms that "I WILL BE WHAT I WILL BE" is a better translation, and that this wording also indicates that "the discussion about speaking of God is never closed" (in *Reimagining God* [Louisville, Ky.: Westminster John Knox Press, 1995], 98).
18. For more background on this name of God, refer to Ruth C. Duck, *What to Do about Lord* (Cleveland: United Church Board for Homeland Ministries, 1996).
19. Gail Ramshaw, *God beyond Gender: Feminist Christian God-Language* (Minneapolis: Fortress Press, 1995), 54–57.
20. Van Wijk-Bos, *Reimagining God*, 50–65.
21. Ibid., 69.
22. Joachim Jeremias, *The Prayers of Jesus* (Philadelphia: Fortress Press, 1967), 12. Refer to Ruth C. Duck, *Gender and the Name of God* (New York: Pilgrim Press, 1991), 59–69, for reflection and biblical study on Jesus' use of "Father" as a name for God.

23. For example, refer to Elizabeth Achtemeier, "Exchanging God for 'No Gods'," in Kimel, ed. *Speaking the Christian God*, 4. She says, "By insisting on female language for God, the feminists simply continue to emphasize the nonbiblical view that God does indeed have sexuality," yet Achtemeier approves masculine language for God.

24. Ibid., 4–5.

25. Translation by van Wijk-Bos, *Reimagining God*, 60.

26. G. W. H. Lampe, ed., *A Patristic Greek Lexicon* (Oxford: Clarendon Press, 1961), 1077–78.

27. John of Damascus, *Exposition of the Orthodox Faith,* trans. S. D. F. Salmond, in *A Select Library of Nicene and Post-Nicene Fathers of the Christian Church*, Series II, eds. Philip Schaff and Henry Wace (Grand Rapids: Wm. B. Eerdmans Publishing Co., [1955]), vol. IX, 11.

28. LaCugna, *God for Us*, 274.

29. Elizabeth A. Johnson, in *She Who Is*, 220–21, provides an exceptionally lucid discussion of the use of *perichoreuō* as a metaphor for *perichoresis*.

30. Brian Wren, *Bring Many Names* (Carol Stream, Ill.: Hope Publishing Co., 1989), number 22.

31. Wren, *Faith Looking Forward* (Carol Stream, Ill.: Hope Publishing Company, 1983), number 1.

32. Rahner, *Trinity*, 61; the underlining is Rahner's.

33. Leonardo Boff, *Trinity and Society* (Maryknoll, N.Y.: Orbis Books, 1988), 164, 172.

34. Johnson, *She Who Is*, 179.

35. Although "Son of man" is a New Testament name for Jesus and is found in English translations of the hymn "Fairest Lord Jesus," its liturgical use is rare. Under influence of debates about orthodoxy, the name "Son" in liturgy has come to refer to the uncreated Son of the Father, and not to speak of Jesus' humanity.

36. Johnson, *She Who Is*, 122.

37. Ramshaw, *God beyond Gender,* 110.

38. Refer to Mary Daly, *Beyond God the Father* (Boston: Beacon Press, 1973), 33.

39. Geoffrey Wainwright, "Trinitarian Worship," in *Speaking the Christian God*, 220. Critics of inclusive language, such as J. A. DiNoia, "Knowing and Naming the Triune God," in *Speaking the Christian God*, 170, have been quick to make the charge of modalism when functional terms (terms describing God's actions) have been substituted for relational terms such as "Father." Yet praise and thanksgiving for what God has done, is doing, and will do is an important part of Christian worship; refer to John E. Burkhart, *Worship: A Searching Examination of the Liturgical Experience* (Philadelphia: Westminster Press, 1982), 17. Further dialogue about naming based on what God does, as well as about the doctrine of appropriations, would be helpful.

40. LaCugna, *God for Us*, 100–101. Contrary to the impression this passage might

create, LaCugna uses nongendered language for the Trinity and does not oppose alternative language to complement traditional language. In this passage
she is critiquing the thought of Augustine, while using some of his language.

41. Thanks to Constance Collora Groh for this insight.

42. In this list, the author of the hymn is named only the first time the hymn appears. Refer to the Appendix, "A Sampling of Trinitarian Hymns," for infor-
mation on sources where the full texts of these hymns appear.

CHAPTER 3: THE TRINITY IN SUNDAY WORSHIP

1. Michael Downey, "Praying the Creed," in *The New Dictionary of Sacramental Worship*, ed. Peter Fink (Collegeville, Minn.: Liturgical Press, 1990), 303.

2. Alan Richardson, "Creed, Creeds," in *The New Dictionary of Liturgy and
Worship*, ed. J. G. Davies (Philadelphia: Westminster Press, 1986), 199.

3. Allen H. Marheine, *You Belong: A Handbook for Church Members* (New
York: United Church Press, 1980), 19.

4. Downey, "Praying the Creed."

5. Episcopal Church, U.S., *The Book of Common Prayer* (New York: Church
Hymnal Corp., 1979), 864, in the section entitled "Historical Documents of
the Church"; "Holy Ghost" was changed here to "Holy Spirit."

6. Richardson, "Creed," 199.

7. Marilyn Stulken, "Singing the Trinity," *Liturgy* 13, no. 1 (winter 1996): 29.
This article is part of a special issue, *Trinity Sunday and Beyond*, with articles
about the liturgy and the Trinity.

8. W. Jardine Grisbrooke, "Doxology," in Davies, *The New Dictionary of
Liturgy and Worship*, 214.

9. Ibid.

10. English translation of *Gloria in Excelsis* prepared by the English Language
Liturgical Consultation (ELLC), and published in *Praying Together* (Norwich, England: Canterbury Press, 1988), 6.

11. *Patrologiæ Græcæ Tomus XXXII, S. Basilius Cæsariensis Episcopus* (J. P.
Migne, 1857), 72.

12. Basil of Caesarea, *The Treatise de Spiritu Sancto*, in *Nicene and Post-Nicene
Fathers*, ed. Philip Schaff and Henry Wace, vol. 8 (Peabody, Mass.: Hendrickson Publishers, 1994), 3; see pages 1–11 and 36–38 for the fuller discussion.

13. Writing in Greek, Basil used the term *hypostasis* (a "standing out" or distinct
subsistence), which has a different connotation than the Latin *persona* (mask
or self-presentation). Refer also to R. P. C. Hanson, *The Search for the Christian Doctrine of God: The Arian Controversy 318–381* (Edinburgh: T. & T.
Clark, 1988), chapter 22, especially 772–79.

14. Garrett-Evangelical Theological Seminary student Kristin Stoneking suggested this alternative because of her legitimate concern that the words
"through Christ" might seem to imply that only through Jesus Christ can per-

sons participate in the life of God. Sharing her universalist perspective, I also favor the language of "in Jesus Christ through the Holy Spirit."

15. Refer to Ruth Duck and Maren Tirabassi, eds., *Touch Holiness: Resources for Worship* (New York: Pilgrim Press, 1990), 236–37, for several seasonal doxologies; many of these were developed at First Church — Congregational (United Church of Christ) in Cambridge, Massachusetts. See also pp. 140–142 of the present volume.

16. Carmelite Monastery, *The New Companion to the Breviary with Seasonal Supplement* (Indianapolis: Carmelite Monastery, 1988), 1 and throughout the book. It is interesting to note that this doxology is very similar to my suggested short trinitarian formula. We developed the wording separately, but perhaps members of this group were, like myself, influenced by Karl Rahner's writings.

17. United Church of Christ Office for Church Life and Leadership, *Book of Worship United Church of Christ* (New York: Office for Church Life and Leadership, 1986), 39–40.

18. Neil Weatherhogg, in *The Presbyterian Hymnal* (Louisville, Ky.: Westminster/John Knox Press, 1990), number 591.

19. Original by Ruth Duck, for this volume.

20. *Baptism, Eucharist and Ministry: Faith and Order Paper No. 111* (Geneva: World Council of Churches, 1982), 2. Succeeding citations from *Baptism, Eucharist and Ministry* are indicated by page numbers within the text.

21. Eduard Schweizer, *The Good News according to Matthew* (Richmond, Va.: John Knox Press, 1975), 530.

22. Ruth Duck, *Gender and the Name of God: The Trinitarian Baptismal Formula* (New York: Pilgrim Press, 1991), 185.

23. Based on the doxology cited above from the Carmelite Monastery, *New Companion*, 1.

24. Duck, *Gender*, 163–66.

25. United Methodist Church, *The United Methodist Book of Worship* (Nashville: United Methodist Publishing House, 1992), 91.

26. Ibid.

27. Ibid., and Carlton R. Young, ed., *The United Methodist Hymnal* (Nashville: United Methodist Publishing House, 1989), 37.

28. For a thorough discussion of issues related to confirmation and its relation to baptism, refer to Robert L. Browning and Roy A. Reed, *Models of Confirmation and Baptismal Affirmation: Liturgical and Educational Designs* (Birmingham, Ala.: Religious Education Press, 1995).

29. Albert Curry Winn, "The Role of the Holy Spirit in Communion," *Reformed Liturgy and Music* 29, no. 4 (1995): 229–31.

30. John Calvin, *Institutes of the Christian Religion*, ed. John T. McNeill, trans. Ford Lewis Battles (Philadelphia: Westminster Press, 1960), book 4, chapter 17, par. 10, 1370, and par. 31, 1403. (Winn quotes par. 10, but here I am paraphrasing par. 31.)

31. *Book of Worship United Church of Christ*, 69–71.
32. Janet Morley, *All Desires Known: Prayers Uniting Faith and Feminism* (Wilton, Conn.: Morehouse-Barlow, 1988), 38.
33. Ibid., 36.
34. Ibid.
35. Ibid., 37.
36. Hoyt Hickman, ed., *Holy Communion: A Service Book for Use by the Minister* (Nashville: Abingdon Press, 1988), 50.
37. Timothy J. Crouch, *The Book of Offices and Services after the Usage of the Order of St. Luke* (Cleveland, Ohio: Order of St. Luke Publishing Office, 1988), 76. The prayer is written and copyrighted by Crouch; it appears in adapted form in the *United Methodist Book of Worship*, 620, and the *Book of Worship: United Church of Christ*; 303, italics mine.
38. David James Randolph, *The Power That Heals: Love, Healing, and the Trinity* (Nashville: Abingdon Press, 1994), 111.
39. Consultation on Common Texts, *The Revised Common Lectionary* (Washington, D.C.: Consultation on Common Texts, 1992), 12.
40. Ibid., 18.
41. See also Ann Patrick Ware, "The Easter Vigil: A Theological and Liturgical Critique," in *Women at Worship*, ed. Marjorie Procter-Smith and Janet R. Walton (Louisville, Ky.: Westminster John Knox Press, 1993), 83–106.
42. Catherine LaCugna, "Trinity and Liturgy," in Fink, *The New Dictionary of Sacramental Worship*, 1296.
43. Ibid.
44. Ibid., 1297.
45. Ibid.

CHAPTER 4: THE TRINITY AND PREACHING

1. The meaning of the terms "sermon" and "homily" is still unsettled in common usage. "Homily," from the Greek word for discourse, is most often used in the context of the Roman Catholic eucharistic liturgy, to refer to brief, usually moral, applications of the scriptural readings. "Sermon" is more commonly used among Protestants to refer to a longer, more developed oral discourse, either in the eucharistic liturgy or in a preaching service, which is often a liturgy of the Word.
2. Patricia Wilson-Kastner, *Imagery for Preaching* (Minneapolis: Fortress Press, 1989), 95–96; Ruth Duck, *Finding Words for Worship* (Louisville, Ky.: Westminster John Knox Press, 1995), 45–48.
3. Christine Smith, *Preaching as Weeping, Confession, and Resistance* (Louisville, Ky.: Westminster/John Knox Press, 1992), 1–2.
4. Wilson-Kastner, *Imagery for Preaching*, 17–31, 47–61.
5. H. J. Carpenter, *Popular Christianity and the Early Theologians* (Philadelphia: Fortress Press, 1966), 16–19.

6. Tertullian, *Against Praxeas,* chapter 3, *The Ante-Nicene Fathers,* Vol. 3, ed. Alexander Roberts and James Donaldson (Grand Rapids: Wm. B. Eerdmans Publishing Co., 1973), 599.

7. J. N. D. Kelly, *Early Christian Doctrines* (New York: Harper & Row, 1960) is still the most comprehensive brief survey of the development of early doctrine about the Trinity.

8. Rudolph Otto, *The Idea of the Holy* (London: Oxford University Press, 1950, 1968), 5–40.

9. *Prayer Book and Hymnal* (New York: Church Hymnal Corporation, 1986), Reginald Heber, number 362.

10. George Forell, ed., *The Christian Year*, vol. 2 (New York: Thomas Nelson Publishers, 1965), 13–26: "Trinity Sunday."

11. Chapter 7 of this book, "Living the Trinitarian Life: Ethics and Worship," explores a trinitarian relational theology in the context of our life in the world as disciples.

12. Catherine Mowry LaCugna, "Making the Most of Trinity Sunday," *Worship,* 60, no. 3 (May 1986): 210.

13. Ibid.

14. The Episcopal Church [USA], *The Book of Common Prayer*, (New York: Church Hymnal Corporation, 1979), 228.

15. National Conference of Catholic Bishops, *The Sacramentary* (Collegeville, Minn.: Liturgical Press, 1985), 392.

16. The Anglican Church in Aotearoa, New Zealand, and Polynesia, *A New Zealand Prayer Book / He Karakia Mihinare o Aotearoa* (San Francisco: Harper & Row, 1989, 1997), 545.

17. Ibid., 464.

18. Susan Cady, Marian Ronan, and Hal Taussig, *Sophia: The Future of Feminist Spirituality* (San Francisco: Harper & Row, 1986), is an early and still useful study of Sophia in spirituality and liturgy, especially 21–26, 43–47. See also chapter 6 in this book.

19. LaCugna, "Making the Most of Trinity Sunday," 210–24: Gerard S. Sloyan, "A People Delights in the Triune Name: Preaching the Readings," *Liturgy: Trinity Sunday and Beyond, Journal of the Liturgical Conference*, 13, no. 1: 4–9.

20. Sloyan, "A People Delights," 9.

CHAPTER 5: TRINITARIAN LANGUAGE IN HYMNS

1. Pliny the Younger, Letter 10, trans. Henry Bettenson, *Documents of the Christian Church* (New York: Oxford University Press, 1947, 1982 ed.), 4. See also Eusebius, *Church History,* 3:33, in *Nicene and Post-Nicene Fathers*, ed. Philip Schaff and Henry Wace (Peabody, Mass.: Hendrickson Publishers, 1994), 1:165, who cites Pliny as saying that the Christians "arose early in the morning and sang hymns to Christ as a God."

2. Kathleen McVey, "Ephraem the Syrian," in *Encyclopedia of Early Christianity*, ed. Everett Ferguson, 2nd ed., vol. 1 (A–K) (New York and London: Garland Publishing, 1997), 376–77.
3. In *Ephraem the Syrian: Hymns*, Classics of Western Spirituality series, trans. and ed. Kathleen McVey (New York: Paulist Press, 1989), 83.
4. Millar Patrick, *The Story of the Church's Song* (Richmond: John Knox Press, 1962, a revision by James Rawlings Sydnor of Patrick's 1927 ed.), 32.
5. Erik Routley, *A Panorama of Christian Hymnody* (Chicago: G.I.A., 1979), 56.
6. Socrates, *Ecclesiastical History*, in Schaff and Wace, *Nicene and Post-Nicene Fathers*, 2:144.
7. Everett Ferguson, "Hymns," in *Encyclopedia of Early Christianity*, vol. 1 (A–K), 550.
8. Translated from the Greek by Egon Wellesz, *A History of Byzantine Music and Hymnography* (Oxford: Clarendon Press, 1961), 154–55.
9. Patrick, *Story of the Church's Song*, 35.
10. Harry Eskew and Hugh T. McElrath, *Sing with Understanding* (Nashville: Church Street Press, 1995), 95.
11. Ibid., 86.
12. Augustine, *The Confessions and Letters of Augustin* in Schaff and Wace, *Nicene and Post-Nicene Fathers*, 1:134.
13. Louis J. Swift, "Ambrose," in *Encyclopedia of Early Christianity*, vol. 1 (A–K), 42.
14. From *Ambroise de Milan: Hymnes*, trans. Jacques Fontaine et al., (Paris: Les Editions du Cerf, 1992), 239.
15. Ibid., 238–39.
16. Bernhard Lohse, *A Short History of Christian Doctrine* (Philadelphia: Fortress Press, 1966), 65.
17. Louis F. Benson, *The Hymnody of the Christian Church* (New York: George H. Doran Co., 1927), 70–71.
18. Ibid., 65, 71.
19. Ibid., 73.
20. For examples, refer to *The Hymnal 1982 Companion*, Raymond F. Glover, general editor (New York: Church Hymnal Corp. 1990), 29–30, 147, 270, and Marilyn K. Stulken, *Hymnal Companion to the Lutheran Book of Worship* (Philadelphia: Fortress Press, 1981), 11, 167.
21. John Julian, ed., *A Dictionary of Hymnology* (New York: Charles Scribner's Sons, 1892), 309.
22. Refer to *Luther's Works*, vol. 53: *Liturgy and Hymns*, ed. Ulrich S. Leupold (Philadelphia: Fortress Press, 1965), 191–309.
23. Ibid., 309.
24. Trans. Charles Garside, *The Origins of Calvin's Theology of Music: 1536–1543* (Philadelphia: American Philosophical Society, 1979), 33; for original, see "Epistre au Lecteur," introduction to *La Forme des Prières*, in *Ioannis Calvini*